P9-ARF-018

THE FAITHFUL MOHAWKS

Joseph Brant (Thayendanegea), Paramount Chief of the Iroquois
(From an engraving by A. Dick after the painting by George Romney)

THE
FAITHFUL MOHAWKS

by

JOHN WOLFE LYDEKKER
M.A., F.R.Hist.S.

Associate Member of the New York Historical Society
Archivist to the Society for the Propagation
of the Gospel

With a Foreword by

THE RIGHT HONOURABLE
LORD TWEEDSMUIR
G.C.M.G., C.H.

IRA J. FRIEDMAN, INC.
Port Washington, Long Island, N.Y.

BY THE SAME AUTHOR

The Life and Letters of Charles Inglis:
His Ministry in America and Consecration
as First Colonial Bishop, from 1759 to 1787.

LONDON:

SOCIETY FOR PROMOTING

CHRISTIAN KNOWLEDGE

THE FAITHFUL MOHAWKS

First Published in 1938
Reissued in 1968 by Ira J. Friedman, Inc.
Library of Congress Catalog Card No: 68-18362
Manufactured in the United States of America

EMPIRE STATE HISTORICAL PUBLICATIONS SERIES No. 50

CONTENTS

page

FOREWORD   ix

BY THE RIGHT HONOURABLE LORD TWEEDSMUIR, G.C.M.G., C.H.

PREFACE   xi

INTRODUCTION   xv

Chapter I. PRELUDE (1664–1704)   1

    II. THE FIRST DECADE (1704–1713)   16

    III. THE NEXT THIRTY-THREE YEARS (1714–1746)   42

    IV. THE CONFLICT FOR CANADA (i) (1747–1755)   61

    V. THE CONFLICT FOR CANADA (ii) (1756–1760)   82

    VI. THE YEARS BETWEEN (1761–1774)   107

    VII. THE REVOLUTIONARY WAR (1775–1782)   139

    VIII. "THE FAITHFUL MOHAWKS" (1783–1807)   169

Appendix A. Deed from the Five Nations to King William III of their Beaver Hunting Grounds (1701) (showing *totem* signatures)   190

    B. Pedigree of "King" Hendrick and Joseph Brant   *Between* 194 *and* 195

BIBLIOGRAPHY   195

INDEX   197

ILLUSTRATIONS

I. Joseph Brant (Thayendanegea)   *Frontispiece*

Facing page

II. "King" Hendrick (Thoyanoguen)   26

III. Facsimile of the *Sachems'* letter to the S.P.G.
(1710)   30

IV. Communion Plate presented by Queen Anne
to the Mohawks' Chapel, Fort Hunter   31

V. Plans of Fort Hunter (drawn by Colonel John
Redknap, October 1711)   32

VI. The Old Church of St Peter, Albany (1715–
1820)   52

VII. The Rev. Henry Barclay, D.D.   54

VIII. The Rev. John Ogilvie, D.D.   64

IX. "King" Hendrick and Sir William Johnson
(Statue in the State Park, Lake George)   77

X. "The Death of Wolfe"   97

XI. Colonel Guy Johnson's Map of the Indian
Boundaries after the Treaty at Fort Stanwix
(1768)   116

XII. Sir William Johnson, Bart.   134

XIII. The Rev. John Stuart, D.D.   148

XIV. Statue of Joseph Brant (Thayendanegea) at
Brantford   171

XV. Frontispiece and Title-page of the Mohawk
Prayer Book (1787 edition)   181

MAP

Part of Canada and the British Colonies of North
America showing Indian Territories   *At end*

FOREWORD

I WELCOME MR LYDEKKER'S WORK as the first-fruits of what I hope will be a continuing harvest, researches among the archives of the Society for the Propagation of the Gospel. The Society was founded by Royal Charter in 1701, and three years later sent out its first missionary to America to work among the Indians. Its archives are therefore important material for the history of the American colonies from that date to the Revolution. They give us, too, a special point of view. The Society's evangelists, like Doty and Stuart, were educated men of high character whose evidence cannot be disregarded.

In history and literature the Iroquois of the Long House are by far the most famous of Indian peoples. Though they never numbered more than three thousand fighting men, they controlled for long the precarious balance of the frontier, and their alliance with the English settlers as against the French was a decisive factor in America's history. Of the five Iroquois nations the Mohawks were the most vigorous stock. They produced not only warriors but statesmen. Their chief figures, like Hendrick and Joseph Brant, fortunately visited England and have their place in the chronicle of English life. You will find Hendrick in the pages of Steele and Addison, and on the canvas of Verelst, while Brant was visited by Boswell, painted by Romney, and given the rank of captain in the British Army. The consequence was that "Mohawk" became as familiar a name in English letters as "Huron" in French.

The Iroquois have not found unprejudiced chroniclers, for the latter stages of their history were shadowed by the American Revolution. But it would appear that the mist is lifting. A recent American scholar has done much to clear the character of Walter Butler, and Sir William Johnson is no longer the monster of the old revolutionary histories. The

Society's records shed considerable light upon Johnson, who appears to have taken a real interest in its work, and to have been one of the earliest advocates of colonial bishoprics.

The Mohawks were always true to their salt and loyal to Britain, down to Joseph Brant's son John, who led his tribe in the war of 1812. What is left of the nation is now settled on Canadian soil. The old church at Brantford to-day bears, by the authority of the late King Edward VII, the same name as that given to the first church by Queen Anne—"His Majesty's Chapel of the Mohawks".

Tweedsmuir

OTTAWA

3 February 1938

PREFACE

THE survey of our relations with the Mohawk Indians during the eighteenth century is the principal theme of this volume, which has been largely compiled from the *Documents Relating to the Colonial History of the State of New York* collected by J. R. Brodhead, and original MS. letters and documents in the Archives of the Society for the Propagation of the Gospel.

In writing this book it has been my endeavour to illustrate the importance of the political (apart from the evangelistic) aspect of the Society's labours in establishing and cementing the English alliance with the Mohawks, which became an essential factor in our colonial expansion in North America. For this reason the earlier chapters are divided into convenient periods corresponding to the progress of the Society's work among the tribe.

My grateful acknowledgments are due to F. C. Nicholson, Esq., M.A., Librarian of the University of Edinburgh, and to that University for the very courteous loan of the first eight volumes of the *Documents Relating to the Colonial History of the State of New York*; to the Rev. Canon Gould, M.D., D.C.L., D.D., General Secretary of the Church of England Missionary Society in Canada, for a photograph of the Communion Plate presented by Queen Anne to the Mohawks' Chapel, Fort Hunter, New York; to the Rev. H. W. Snell, B.A., Principal of the Mohawk Institute, Brantford, Ontario, for a photograph of the statue of Joseph Brant (Thayendanegea); to George P. Hoff, Esq., of Albany, New York, for a photograph of a painting of the Old Church of St Peter, Albany; to the Rischgitz International Art Supply Agency, London, for their courtesy in lending me their photograph of the picture "The Death of Wolfe"; to the D. Appleton-Century Co. Inc. of New York and London, for permission to reproduce the illustration of "King" Hendrick and Sir William Johnson (taken from the bronze statue in the State Park, Lake George) which appears in the biography *Sir William Johnson* by A. C. Buell; and to Miss Blanche Thompson, B.A., Assistant Archivist to the S.P.G., for her valuable assistance in indexing.

J. W. L.

WESTMINSTER ·
February 1938

ABBREVIATIONS
USED IN FOOTNOTES AND INDEX

Conn. = Connecticut.

L.I. = Long Island.

Mass. = Massachusetts.

N.E. = New England.

N.H. = New Hampshire.

N.J. = New Jersey.

N.S. = Nova Scotia.

N.Y. = New York.

Pa. = Pennsylvania.

S.C. = South Carolina.

Sm. = Schoolmaster.

Va. = Virginia.

Dict. Nat. Biog. = *Dictionary of National Biography.*

New York Docs. = *Documents Relating to the Colonial History of the State of New York.*

P.R.O. = Public Record Office.

S.P.G. = Society for the Propagation of the Gospel.

'A', 'B' and 'C' MSS. = the corresponding classification of documents in the S.P.G. Archives.

INTRODUCTION

THE successful administration of native races in all parts of the world is one of the most prominent achievements of the British nation. The great territorial acquisitions which now form the units of the Empire are not only a proof of the hardihood and vision of bygone adventurers and colonizers, but are also an eloquent testimony to the wise and far-sighted statesmanship which has been extended to the indigenous peoples under our sovereignty.

Upwards of three centuries have passed since the commencement of our earliest attempts at native administration which began among the great Iroquois confederacy of North American Indians, but in this instance the term "administration" must be narrowly construed. The Iroquois looked upon themselves as the powerful allies of the English—which indeed they were—with whom they were prepared to unite against the insidious encroachments of the French.

In the history of their own country the Iroquois were outstanding as the predominant confederation of the North American continent, and with the coming of the white man they became a vital factor in the schemes for American colonization. From the establishment of the first Dutch settlement at Manhattan at the beginning of the seventeenth century to the close of the War of Independence nearly 200 years later, the Iroquois exercised the most profound influence upon the destinies of the colonies. Of this great Indian confederation the warlike Mohawk tribe had long been regarded as the "elder brother" in the symbolical chain of the "Five Nations" league. It has been rightly said of the Mohawks that: "No nation of the widely spread red race of America has displayed so high and heroic a love of liberty, united with the true art of government, personal energy and stamina of character."[1]

[1] H. R. Schoolcraft, *Notes on the Iroquois*, p. iii.

CHAPTER I

PRELUDE

(1664–1704)

THE MOHAWK TRIBE of Indians of North America claim the distinction of being the progenitors of Hiawatha,[1] the legendary "maker of rivers" whose far-reaching influence is said to have induced the Mohawks, Oneidas, Onondagas, Cayugas, and Senecas to form themselves into the defensive league of the Iroquois. These tribes were originally a nation of one stock of eight clans which gradually separated into the five sections known as the "Five Nations". They inhabited a territory which extended from the Genesee to the Mohawk Rivers and included the area between Lakes Huron and Erie.

The five tribes forming the Iroquois confederacy (which emerges into historic form towards the end of the sixteenth century) possessed a common medium in the Iroquoian stock language, of which each tribe spoke its own dialect. These dialects were sufficiently akin to be mutually understood for the purposes of deliberation, and by means of this *lingua franca* a general council of fifty chiefs or *sachems* was evolved which administered the affairs of the league. The tribes were, however, distinct as regards their own individual government, and they possessed separate territories and jurisdiction. In questions of peace or war each tribe was free to act on its own initiative, and the other members of the confederation were not bound to co-operate unless they had given their assent at a general council of the league. For military purposes the supreme command was vested in two war-chiefs of equal authority who were chosen by the general council.

Although the Iroquois never numbered more than 3000 fighting men, their natural hardihood and efficient military

[1] Hiawatha is supposed to have flourished *circa* 1450.

organization made them superior to all the other tribes of North America.

Among their tribal customs the Iroquois observed the *totem* differentiation of their various families and clans, each clan having a name derived from an animal. The *totem* mark was in fact a species of heraldry, somewhat analogous to the hereditary tribal shield marks still in use among the Masai of East Africa. In the Iroquois villages rude representations of the *totems* were usually hung over the doors of the "long houses"—so called from the elongated shape of the buildings —in which several families of close relationship lived. The signs of the Tortoise, Bear and Wolf, adopted by the leading Mohawk clans, were for many years the most conspicuous *totems* among the Five Nations.

In the latter half of the sixteenth century the Iroquois drove from the neighbourhood of the St Lawrence a medley of tribes allied with the Hurons, and in the first half of the seventeenth century they forced back the Conestogas to their south and the war-like Algonquin tribes to their east. Having entered into friendly relations with the Dutch colony of New Netherland,[1] the Iroquois obtained a great advantage over the other tribes by equipping themselves with fire-arms which they bartered from the Hollanders.

But in its dealings with the European colonies the league of the Iroquois seldom acted as a corporate whole, and many instances occurred of one or more members of the confederacy making a separate alliance with their French and English neighbours.

In 1644 the Mohawk tribe made a treaty with the Dutch and remained their allies until the conquest of New Netherland by England in 1664. Thereafter the Mohawks confirmed the treaty with the English which had formerly bound them to the Dutch. In this alliance the Mohawks were joined by the Senecas, but the other three tribes of the confederacy refused to participate. The following year (1665) saw an

[1] The colony received its charter in 1623, and thus replaced the New Netherland Company formed in 1614.

important change in the French administration of Canada
with the appointment of a new Governor, the Marquis de
Tracy, who at once began to fortify the French-Canadian
frontier by building block-houses between Lake Champlain
and the St Lawrence. The French had previously made an
alliance with the Hurons, and their military preparations now
threatened the territory of the Five Nations of the Iroquois.
As a result, the Oneidas and Onondagas, and a section of the
Cayugas and Senecas, made a treaty with the French, in
which the King of France was declared to be the sovereign of
the four signatory nations. The Mohawks, however, refused
to participate and remained loyal to their English alliance.

The history of the Five Nations for the next half-century
is bound up with the interminable rivalry between France
and England which had its counterpart in the fight for colonial
expansion in both the eastern and western hemispheres until
the culminating victories of Clive and Wolfe. In North
America the combat between these two great European
Powers centred largely upon an alliance with the Iroquois
whose superiority in warfare over the other indigenous tribes
made them a dominant factor in the struggle.

In 1666 a French attack on the Mohawks resulted in an
embassy from that tribe to Quebec, albeit against the urgent
representations of Nicolls, the English Governor of New
York. The Mohawk *sachems* asked the French to send missionaries to their country, and a way was thus opened for
insidious campaign and political intrigue by the French
Jesuits.

The appointment of Count Frontenac in 1673 as Governor
of Canada presaged further propaganda among the Iroquois.
A fort was built at Cataraqui[1] (near the present site of Kingston, Ontario) and in 1677 the French established permanent
missions among the Oneidas, and later the Cayugas. The
recall of Frontenac in 1682 had a detrimental effect on the
French activities among the Five Nations. The Iroquois had
recently begun hostilities with two of the Algonquin tribes

[1] Generally known as Fort Frontenac.

(who were allies of the French) and had also attacked a French outpost. De la Barre, Frontenac's successor, proved incapable of dealing with the situation, and was soon superseded by the Marquis de Denonville. The new Governor adopted a policy of endeavouring to control the Iroquois by force, and of neutralizing the English activities among the tribes. Having treacherously kidnapped fifty Iroquois chiefs through the medium of a Jesuit missionary, de Denonville attacked the Iroquois country (1687). As a result of these high-handed proceedings the Iroquois turned to the English for protection, and this gave the English Government the opportunity of acknowledging the Five Nations as subjects of the English Crown. A conference with the Iroquois *sachems* was held at Albany at which Colonel Thomas Dongan, the Governor of New York, told them they were under the protection of the King of England, and that thenceforward the place of the French missionaries would be taken by English clergy. Moreover, as an earnest of his friendly intentions, Dongan offered to build a fort on Lake Ontario for the Iroquois' defence and to supply arms and ammunition to the Senecas.

In the spring of 1688 Dongan was recalled, and was succeeded by Sir Edmund Andros, a protégé of James II.[1] The change of governorship came at an inopportune time, for within a few months King James was forced to abdicate. This circumstance gave France an unlooked-for opportunity of consolidating her American Empire by seizing New York, since England being in the throes of the Orangist Revolution was no longer a friendly Power. A plan for invading the New York Province by way of Lake Champlain was set on foot, but before the scheme could be put into execution the Mohawks suddenly avenged de Denonville's former treachery, by attacking and destroying the village of La Chine, massacring the inhabitants and devastating Montreal.

---

[1] Andros had been Governor of New York from 1674 to 1681 and was succeeded by Dongan. On Andros' reappointment in 1688 the New York and New England Provinces were united into a single province called New England.

In the summer of 1689 Count Frontenac was reappointed to Canada. In the meantime important developments had occurred in New York. As soon as the news of King James' abdication reached America the citizens of Boston rose against the Jacobite Governor Andros and imprisoned him.[1] Colonel Francis Nicholson, the Governor's deputy at New York, was unable to stem the popular clamour led by a fanatical German brewer named Leisler, who proclaimed William of Orange king and appointed himself Governor. Nicholson showed a lamentable incapacity and lack of initiative by following the advice of his council and taking ship to England (June 1689). For the next two years Leisler ruled New York, having appropriated to himself a belated commission from the Sovereigns, William and Mary, addressed to Nicholson "or to such as for the time being take care for preserving the peace & laws of the Colony".[2] But although Leisler had a considerable following among the irresponsible section of New Yorkers, a strong party of the more sober-minded citizens was soon formed against him, and in May 1690 the leaders of the anti-Leislerites memorialized William and Mary against the tyranny and arbitrary proceedings of the self-styled Governor.

As a result of this action by the memorialists the people of New York who were not in Leisler's interest resolved to take matters into their own hands, and for some days the city was subjected to serious rioting. The mob assaulted Leisler in the streets and an alderman named Teunis de Kay endeavoured to release those of his fellow-citizens who had been imprisoned by the Governor's orders, by leading an armed attack on the militia guarding the fort.[3] Leisler, however,

[1] Andros had made Boston his administrative headquarters.
[2] I.e. the New York Council, in the absence of the Deputy Governor.
[3] *Vide* the depositions of Gerrit Leydecker (a burgher living on Broadway) and others (cf. J. R. Brodhead, *Documents Relating to the Colonial History of New York*, Vol. III, pp. 741, 742, 746). (References to this work are hereafter quoted as *New York Docs.*) Nearly a century later Gerrit's grandson, the Rev. Gerrit (Gerard) Lydekker, was the leader of the loyalist Anglo-Dutch community of New York

managed to overawe the rioters and imprisoned a number of the ringleaders.

Meanwhile Frontenac had been making great efforts to win over the Iroquois, and early in 1690 a council of the Five Nations met at Onondaga (the headquarters of the league) to consider the future policy of their league towards the French and English. As a result of this conference, the Mohawks, Onondagas and Senecas agreed to side with the English and refused to negotiate with Frontenac. In spite of this drawback Frontenac decided on a second invasion of New England, and the terrible massacre of Schenectady followed. A retaliatory expedition organized by the Massachusetts, Connecticut and New York provinces proved abortive, the only success being the attack by Captain John Schuyler[1] (brother of Major Peter Schuyler, the Mayor of Albany) on Prairie de la Madelaine, a settlement near Montreal. In each of these campaigns both French and English employed Indian auxiliaries.

In the following October (1690) a new Governor, Colonel William Sloughter, sailed for New York with a fleet of four ships carrying troops under the command of Colonel Richard Ingoldsby. On his arrival at the capital Sloughter arrested Leisler, who was tried for high treason and executed (16 May 1691). Three months later Sloughter fell ill and died. The pacification of the Province following Leisler's execution and the re-establishment of a settled government under Sloughter's successor, Colonel Benjamin Fletcher, gave greater opportunity for a more constructive policy with the Indians. A scheme for organizing a militia along the Canadian frontier was drawn up and the Home Government was asked to authorize an annual subsidy of £1000 to be granted to our

during the Revolutionary War. He emigrated to England after the peace of 1783 (cf. P.R.O. Audit Office Papers, and family papers in the possession of the author).

[1] The Schuylers were sons of Philip Pieterse Schuyler who emigrated from Holland in 1650. Captain John Schuyler (1668–1747) was the grandfather of the Revolutionary General, Philip John Schuyler (1733–1804).

Indian allies and to sanction the erection of forts at Albany and Schenectady. In these important matters Fletcher relied on the advice of Captain John Schuyler, the most able and experienced Indian diplomatist in the Colony.

Meanwhile Frontenac was preparing another plan of invasion, while the French Jesuits were exerting all their influence to alienate the Mohawks from the English alliance. That their efforts were largely successful is shown by a letter written some years later by Robert Livingston, Secretary for Indian Affairs in New York:

> It is almost incredible what Artifices the French (who are sensible of the Mischiefs they have suffer'd from those Indians) use by their Priests' Insinuations and False Witness, to gett ye Indians of the 5 Nations over to their Side; they have raised a Great Faction in their Castles, yea, to that Degree that Diverse of the Sachems or great Men, that were true to the English (whom they could not bring over) were Poyson'd, insomuch that they were forced to fly from their Castles, & many of our Indians were reduced to goe to Canada to be Instructed in the Popish Religion by the Jesuits....[1]

Frontenac launched his expedition in January 1693: his intention was to capture New York, but beyond seizing three Mohawk villages nothing was accomplished. A counter expedition was immediately organized by Peter Schuyler, the Mayor of Albany, who overtook and severely defeated Frontenac's Indian levies. A few months later Fletcher held a conference with the Mohawk chiefs at Albany, but this did not prevent the other four tribes of the confederacy from sending an embassy to Frontenac at Quebec.

As a result of his intrigues Frontenac succeeded in winning over the Cayugas and Senecas, and their neutrality enabled him to rebuild Fort Frontenac which had been destroyed seven years before.

Having reoccupied Fort Frontenac, the French Governor determined to make a supreme effort to establish the ascen-

[1] Livingston's Memorial to the S.P.G. Appendix to Journal A, No. 19.

dancy of France over the Five Nations of the Iroquois. With a force of 1700 regular troops and militia and 500 Hurons, he raided the Seneca and Oneida territories (July 1696). But his expedition again proved fruitless, the Iroquois leaving their villages and dispersing through the forests, and within a few weeks the French force was obliged to retire owing to lack of provisions. This was the last expedition undertaken by Frontenac, and a year later (September 1697) hostilities were formally terminated by the Peace of Ryswick.

In November 1698 Count Frontenac died. His successor, de Callières (formerly Governor of Montreal), realized the need for an alliance with the Iroquois, since any renewal of the war might well expose Canada to an English invasion. In fact, the English Government had no such intention and moreover determined to make its Indian allies respect the Peace. To this end, Lord Bellamont (who had succeeded Fletcher in 1697[1]) was instructed to co-operate with de Callières in the English Government's pacific intentions. The French Governor, however, refused his co-operation and prevailed on the Iroquois to sign a treaty of alliance with France. As a counterstroke to this, two English Commissioners were sent to Onondaga to hold a conference with the confederate tribes, two of whom, the Cayugas and Senecas, abstained from attending. As a result of this conference the Iroquois agreed to send representatives to a further conference at Albany. Encouraged by this partial success, Bellamont pronounced that the Iroquois were to be regarded as subjects of the English Crown, and sent his deputy, Colonel John Nanfan, to Quebec to demand the return of some Mohawk prisoners and to warn de Callières against any future trespass of what was now declared to be English territory.

Bellamont next turned his attention to the activities of the French missionaries among the Iroquois. Like his predecessor, Dongan, he realized the grave political significance of

---

[1] Fletcher had been recalled in 1695 and there had thus been a two years' interregnum.

the insidious propaganda of the Jesuits, and decided that not
only must the French missionaries be excluded from the Five
Nations but that English missionaries must be established
among them. In a dispatch to the Commissioners for Trade
and Plantations he pressed for two missionaries to be sent to
the Five Nations.[1]

Bellamont's proposals were approved by the Commissioners and the following letter was sent by them to Dr
Tenison, Archbishop of Canterbury, for his co-operation in
the scheme:

Whitehall.
October the 25. 1700.

My Lord

The Earl of Bellamont having severall times represented to us
the great want of some Ministers of the Church of England to
instruct the Five Nations of Indians on the Frontiers of New York
and prevent their being practis'd upon by French Priests and
Jesuits who are conversant amongst them, and very industrious
in perswading them by pretences of Religion to espouse the French
Interest: We have thereupon represented to their Excellencies the
Lords Justices our humble Opinion, that, if a Fund can be found
for the Maintenance of such Ministers they may be of very good
Use and Service as well for the Propagation of the Reformed
Religion as for Improving the Interest of England.

We have also lately received from his Lordship some further
Advice upon the same Subject, of which we send your Grace the
inclos'd Extract, desiring your Grace would be pleas'd to consider of the most speedy & effectual Means for the Promoting of
so good a Work.

We are

My Lord

Your Grace's most humble Servts.

STAMFORD[2]	WILLIAM BLATHWAYT[3]
JNO. POLLEXFEN[4]	ABR. HILL[5]
GEO. STEPNEY[6]	MAT. PRIOR[7]

We have recommended the same thing to the Lord Bishop of
London.[8]

[For Notes 1–8 vide p. 10.]

The enclosure mentioned in the letter was as follows:

Extract of what was said by the Sachems of the Praying Indians of Canada, (vizt. such as have been converted to some sort of Profession of Christianity) to the Commissioners for the Indian Affairs in Albany.

June 28. 1700.

We are now come to Trade and not to speak of Religion; only this much I must say, all the while I was here before I went to Canada I never heard any thing talk'd of Religion, or the least Mention made of converting us to the Christian Faith, and we shall be glad to hear if at last you are so piously inclined to take some Pains to instruct your Indians in the Christian Religion, I will not say but it may induce some to return to their Native Country.

I wish it had been done sooner that you had Ministers to instruct your Indians in the Christian Faith; I doubt whether any of us ever had deserted our Native Country. But I must say I am solely beholden to the French of Canada for the Light I have received to know there was a Saviour born for Mankind; and now we are taught God is everywhere, and we can be instructed at Canada, Dowaganhae, or the uttermost Parts of the Earth as well as here.[1]

[1] S.P.G. Appendix to Journal A, No. 5a. Cf. also *New York Docs*. Vol. IV, pp. 693, 769.

---

[1] *New York Docs*. Vol. IV, p. 717. The Commissioners for Trade and Plantations were the forerunners of the Secretaries of State for the Colonies, the first of whom, Lord Hillsborough, was appointed some seventy years later in 1768.

[2] Stamford, Thomas Grey, Earl of (1654–1720), only son of Lord Grey of Groby, the Regicide. Tried for alleged participation in the Rye House Plot and acquitted. Appointed Commissioner for Trade 1695; President 1699. Dismissed 1702 and reinstated 1707–11.

[3] William Blathwayt (1649?–1717). Appointed Secretary-at-War 1683. Clerk of the Privy Council 1686. Commissioner for Trade 1696–1706.

[4] John Pollexfen, economic writer and brother of Sir Henry Pollexfen (1632–91), who successfully defended the Seven Bishops in 1688. Commissioner for Trade 1695–1705.

[5] Abraham Hill (1635–1721). First Treasurer of the Royal Society. Appointed Commissioner for Trade 1689.

[6] George Stepney (1663–1707). Poet and envoy. Commissioner for Trade 1697–1707.

[7] Matthew Prior (1664–1721). Poet and diplomatist. Appointed Secretary of State for Ireland 1698 and Commissioner for Trade 1700.

[8] S.P.G. Appendix to Journal A, No. 5. (The Bishop of London was approached as being the diocesan of the Church overseas, this jurisdiction dating from an Order in Council of 1634.)

As a result of the conference with the Iroquois at which the foregoing statement was made, Robert Livingston, the Secretary for Indian Affairs at Albany, also wrote to the Commissioners for Trade suggesting, *inter alia*, that missionaries should be stationed among the Five Nations, and that the Crown should acquire their territory and then reinstate them as its tenants.[1] Livingston's suggestion was adopted and in July 1701 the principal *sachems* of the Iroquois conveyed an area of 800 square miles of their hunting grounds to King William III.[2]

A few months later Lord Bellamont died. He was succeeded by Lord Cornbury, who owed his appointment to his near relationship with the Royal Family.[3]

The new Governor was not a successful administrator but he at least showed creditable initiative in his Indian policy. On his arrival at New York in May 1702, he received a deputation from the Iroquois, who expressed satisfaction at having as their ruler a near relative of the Queen, and quaintly testified their loyalty to the new monarch.[4]

Lord Cornbury showed a keen appreciation of the necessity for counteracting French propaganda among the Iroquois and in his dispatches to the home authorities he corroborated

[1] *New York Docs.* Vol. IV, pp. 870 *et seq.*

[2] The deed of conveyance is published in the *New York Docs.* Vol. IV, pp. 908-11, with facsimiles of the *sachems' totem* signatures, which will be found reproduced in Appendix A of this book.

[3] Edward Hyde, Lord Cornbury, was the grandson of the first Earl of Clarendon and first cousin of the Princess (afterwards Queen) Anne.

[4] *New York Docs.* Vol. IV, pp. 980 and 986. Cf. also a letter from the Rev. John Talbot (the first S.P.G. missionary in New Jersey): "...Even the Indians themselves have promised obedience to the Faith, as appears by a Conference that my Lord Cornbury...has had with them at Albany. 5 of their Sachems or Kings told him they were glad to hear that the sun shined in England again since K[ing] Wm's death: they did admire [i.e. wonder] at first that we should have a Squaw Sachem vizt. a woman King, but they hoped she would be a good Mother & send them some to teach them Religion & establish Traffick [i.e. trade] amongst them...and so they send our Queen a Present, 10 Beaver skins to make her fine, & one fur muff to keep her warm...."

'A' MSS. Vol. 2, No. 56.

Bellamont's former proposals for the establishment of English missionaries among the Five Nations. These suggestions were furthered by the newly formed Society for the Propagation of the Gospel in Foreign Parts which had been founded by a Royal Charter of King William III in June 1701. Archbishop Tenison, the first President of the Society (who had been asked for his assistance by the Commissioners for Trade in 1700),[1] brought the matter to the notice of the members, and proposals for work among the Iroquois were accordingly included in the general scheme for the Society's activities in America.[2] Encouraged by the Society's willingness to co-operate, the Commissioners for Trade memorialized the Queen[3] and the following Order-in-Council was promulgated:

Att the Court of St James the 3rd day of Aprill 1703.

Present

The Queen's Most Excellent Majesty in Council.

Upon reading this day at the Board a Representation from the Lords Commissioners of Trade & Plantations dated the 2nd of this month relating to her Maty's Province of New York in America setting forth among other things that as to the Nations of Indians bordering upon New York, lest the Intrigues of the French of Canada, & the Influence of their Priests who frequently converse & sometimes inhabit with these Indians should debauch them from her Maty's Allegiance, their Lordships are humbly of opinion that besides the usual method of engaging the said Indians by Presents, another means to prevent the Influence of the French Missionaries upon them & thereby more effectually to secure their Fidelity, would be that two Protestant Ministers be appointed with a competent Allowance to dwell amongst them in order to instruct them in the true Religion and confirm them in their Duty to her Maty; It is ordered by her Maty. in Council that it be as it is hereby referred to his Grace the Lord Archbishop of Canterbury, to take such care therein as may most effectually answer this Service.

(sgd) EDWARD SOUTHWELL[4]

[1] *Vide* p. 9 *supra*.
[2] S.P.G. Journal, Vol. I, p. 104.
[3] *New York Docs.* Vol. IV, p. 1035.
[4] S.P.G. Journal, Vol. I, p. 104.

On receipt of the Order-in-Council Archbishop Tenison sent a copy to the Society, and at a meeting held on 16 April it was agreed to endeavour to find two clergymen who would be willing to go out as missionaries to the Five Nations in accordance with the resolutions of the Privy Council.[1]

In the following September Robert Livingston (then in England) presented a Memorial to the Society with reference to the proposal of sending missionaries to the Iroquois.[2] At the same meeting the Rev. Thoroughgood Moore (who had offered his services in the preceding February) was formally accepted by the Society as their missionary to the Indians,[3] and on 15 October it was agreed that the Rev. Charles Smith should be permitted to accompany him.[4] In February 1704 Chamberlayne,[5] the Secretary of the Society, wrote to the Commissioners for Trade and Plantations in the following terms:

To the Right Hon.ble the Lords Commissrs. for Trade and Plantations.

May it please Your Lordships,

Having attempted several times to wait upon your Hon.ble Board without meeting a favourable opportunity, I am bold to take this method of acquainting your Lordships, by order of the Society for promoting the Gospell in foreign parts, what measures have been taken by that body towards sending Missionaries among the Indians of the Five Nations bordering on New Yorke and in consequence of the representation made by your Lord.pps to the Queen upon that head; your Lord.pps must be pleased to know then, that the Society (not without a great deal of pains and time spent to that purpose) have found out two Reverend Divines, M.r Smith[6] and M.r Moor, whom they think well qualified for that

---

[1] S.P.G. Journal, Vol. 1, p. 105.
[2] *Ibid.* p. 117.   [3] *Ibid.*   [4] *Ibid.* p. 120.
[5] John Chamberlayne, F.R.S. (1666–1723), son of Edward Chamberlayne, LL.D., F.R.S., and great-grandson of Sir Thomas Chamberlayne, Ambassador to the Netherlands *temp.* Elizabeth. He was appointed Gentleman Waiter to Prince George of Denmark, and Gentleman of the Privy Chamber to Queen Anne and George I, and was Secretary to Queen Anne's Bounty Commission.
[6] Rev. Charles Smith. Later, he declined to go as a missionary (*vide* S.P.G. Journal, Vol. 1, p. 139), and Mr Moore went alone.

Errand; that they have agreed to allow the said Gentlemen 100£ per annum each, over an above which they will have 20£ a piece to buy them utensils for the little Caban [i.e. cabin] they are supposed to have among the Indians and 10 or 15£ for books ettc. Now, My Lords, I am to tell you that the Society having done so much (and indeed 'tis too much considering their small and intirely precarious stock) they would gladly know what assistance they may expect in an affaire that does at least as much concerne the State as the Church (vid: Lord Cornbury's letters etc) either at home by your Lord^{pps} kind representation of the matter to Her Majesty, or abroad from the Govern^t of New Yorke; especially, My Lords, seeing that there remains so much to be done still; for Mr Livingston Secretary of the Indian affaires of the above-mentioned Govern^t acquaints us that four more Missionaries are still wanting, that is to say three more for the Five Nations and one for the River Indians, tho' I am told, My Lords, that these last are no longer formidable to us, they having been almost consumed in former wars; but this is submitted to your Lord^{pps} The said Gent: says moreover that each of our Missionaries must have distinct houses, which for fear of insults [i.e. attacks] of drunken Indians ettc. must be Pallisaded; that the cost of such houses will be 60£ or 80£ each; that they can not subsist without two servants to attend each Minister; That there must be presents for the Indians and several other items which swell the account considerably, and which are hardly to be compast by any but a Royal purse, at least not by ours, which has exerted its utmost efforts.

I must beg your Lord^{pps} pardon for taking up so much of your time, but the weightiness of the matter as well as the faithful discharge of my duty must apologize for my being so full and particular.

I humbly submit it to your Lord^{pps} great wisdome and remain

My Lords ettc

JOHN CHAMBERLAYNE.[1]

Westminster.
1 Feb^r 1703/4.

An answer to this letter was received from Sir William Popple, Secretary to the Lords of Trade, stating that the Queen allowed £20 passage money to all ministers going to

---

[1] *New York Docs.* Vol. IV, p. 1077.

the "Plantations", and that the Lords of Trade would re-commend the Rev. Messrs Smith and Moore to the Governor, Lord Cornbury.[1]

As a result of this correspondence, Mr Moore sailed for America in May. Having narrowly escaped capture by a French privateer at the mouth of the Hudson River, he landed at New York early in August to begin the Society's great work of evangelization among the Indians.[2]

[1] *New York Docs.* Vol. IV, p. 1078.   [2] 'A' MSS. Vol. 2, No. 25.

CHAPTER II
THE FIRST DECADE
(1704–1713)

A FEW weeks after Mr Moore's arrival Lord Cornbury and Colonel Francis Nicholson (the former Lieutenant-Governor of New York who had become Governor of Virginia in 1698) convened a conference of the Anglican clergy at New York. At this period the majority of the clergy in the province were missionaries of the Society for the Propagation of the Gospel which had sent out several men to the American colonies during the previous eighteen months.[1] This conference drew up a report of the work of the Church in Pennsylvania, East and West Jersey, New York, Rhode Island and Boston, and expressed its satisfaction that the Society had now undertaken a mission to the Indians in the person of "our good Brother Mr Thorogood Moore".

In the following November Mr Moore took up his residence at Albany, a town situated on the west bank of the Hudson, below the mouth of the Mohawk River, some 145 miles north-west of New York.

At this period Albany could only boast some 250 houses, but as early as 1686 it had achieved the dignity of a city by a charter from Governor Dongan who appointed Peter

[1] The clergy who attended the convention were as follows: Rev. Evan Evans, D.D., Bp. of London's Commissary at Philadelphia; Rev. John Talbot, M.A., S.P.G. missionary in New Jersey; Rev. Thoroughgood Moore; Rev. John Sharpe, S.P.G. missionary in New Jersey; Rev. John Bartow, S.P.G. missionary at West Chester, N.Y.; Rev. Thomas Pritchard, S.P.G. missionary at Rye, N.Y.; Rev. Henry Nicholls, B.A., S.P.G. missionary at Chester, Pa.; Rev. William Urquhart, S.P.G. missionary at Jamaica, L.I.; Rev. R. Owen; Rev. Daniel Bondet (a French Huguenot) who became an S.P.G. missionary at New Rochelle, N.Y. Cf. 'A' MSS. Vol. 2, No. 22.

Schuyler as its first mayor. The city ranked high in strategic importance from its position at the head of navigation on the Hudson River and at the gateway of the Iroquois territory. It possessed a stockaded fort mounted with twenty-three cannon and a garrison of two companies of troops.[1]

The clerical ministrations of the city were conducted by the Rev. John Lydius, a minister of the Dutch Reformed Church, who had succeeded his compatriot the Rev. Godfrey Dellius. From time to time these gentlemen had given some instruction to the Iroquois, and the S.P.G. had recently sent Mr Lydius a consignment of books in recognition of his missionary services.[2]

For some years past Albany had been the headquarters of the Commissioners for Indian Affairs—a body of local residents who were entrusted by the Governor with the administration of the Iroquois. By the terms of their appointment the commissioners were empowered "to treat, confer and consult with the Five Nations" and were required to give a formal account of their proceedings to the Governor and his Council at New York.[3] The original commissioners were only two in number, the Rev. Godfrey Dellius and Dirck Wessels, Mayor of Albany, who had been appointed by Governor Fletcher in 1696. In course of time the numbers of the Commissioners were increased, but the majority of them were still recruited from the Dutch burghers of Albany. Their administration was never very satisfactory and some fifty years later their successors were stigmatized by Governor Clinton as being "traders with the Indians" who had "more regard to their private profit than to the public good".[4] Eventually they were deprived of their office and were superseded by the greatest native administrator of his time, the celebrated Sir William Johnson. Nevertheless, the Indian

[1] *New York Docs.* Vol. IV, p. 968.
[2] S.P.G. Journal, Vol. I, p. 143.
[3] *New York Docs.* Vol. IV, p. 177.
[4] Cf. Clinton's dispatch to the Lords of Trade, 17 August 1748 (*ibid.* Vol. VI, p. 439).

Commissioners of Albany have a definite place in history as constituting the embryo of our present Colonial Administrative Service.

Soon after his arrival at Albany Mr Moore received a deputation from the Mohawks who had heard of his intended labours amongst them. An account of his experiences is contained in the following letter to the Secretary of the S.P.G. written on 8 March 1705:

On the 16 Nov. I arriv'd at Albany (a frontier Town ab! 50 miles from the Mohocks [*sic*]) where by my Lord Cornbury's kind Recommendation I was very civily received by the People, M! Lydius, the Dutch Minister, inviting me to his house where I now am & have been ever since. On the 22nd a Mohock Indian and his Squa[w] being in Town & hearing of my Design came & thus addresst us: "Father we are come to express our Joy at your safe arrival & that you have escapt the Dangers of a Dreadful sea which you have cross't I hear to instruct us in Religion. It only grieves us that you are come in time of war,[1] when 'tis uncertain whether you will live or dye with us."

After some time I ask't him whether he thought my coming would be welcome to the rest of his countrymen to which he answered "How should it not be welcome when they have so long desir'd it."

On the 21st December one of the Sachems & 3 more Indians came, and spake to this effect.

"Father, we are come to express our great satisfaction that God has been so propitious to us as to send you to open our Eyes which have hitherto been shut." Another told ye Interpreter that her first hearing of my coming rais'd a strange comotion in her mind and an unaccountable mixture of Joy and Fear, when she came to me amongst other [of] her congratulatory Expressions, sayd "May God support your shoulders under so great a weight (viz. that of preaching the Gospel) and may you dispel the Darkness that still overspreads us." This is but part of what I have had from them to this Effect.

I could not but be extreamly pleased to see them so sensible of the happiness that was going to be offered them, I told them that nothing should be wanting on my part & that I would devote

[1] I.e. the War of the Spanish Succession between France and England, 1701–13.

myself to their Good, & that I only staid here to learn their
Language in order to [do?] it. I had not then made any publick
proposition to them, but design'd to lay hold of the first opportunity that the weather could give me of doing it at their Castle.
But soon after there fell so great a quantity of Snow, that I was
forc't to alter my mind & to send, as I was advis'd what I had to
say to them, with a Belt of their Indian money, which is always
given to them & which they return to me upon any Proposal of
consequence. The opportunity I had of sending was three Indians
who with Snow Shoes can go in the deepest Snows. I sent them
word likewise that I would take the first opportunity of coming
myself to see them, but this Promise I could not perform till the
2ᵈ of February, but then I thank God I got safely to them with
some Difficulty. My coming indeed seem'd to be very welcome
to them of which they gave several Instances, too many & indeed
too insignificant to trouble the Society, only their manner of
receiving us I will mention which was: when they thought we
were within hearing (of which they had Intelligence of an Indian
yᵗ saw us coming) they fir'd 8 or 10 of their Guns, which being
from a high hill on which their Castle stands we heard a great way.
When we came in sight the Sachims came to meet us, & to bid us
welcome, & one of them perceiving that I walk'd with some
Difficulty led me in ye worst places; But all the walking I had was
only up this hill, for we came to the ffoot of it in sleys. When we
came to the Castle, we found one of their little houses allotted for
us, made very clean with a good ffire, which the Sachims resign'd
to me & my company & so withdrew. About 2 hours after they
return'd, & one of them after about a quarter of an hour's silence
told me that they had recd. my Message, but it was but lately, &
not having consulted with the other Castle (wch. is abᵗ 12 miles
distance) they could give no Answer to it now, but they would
consult with them, the first opportunity & send me one....¹

Armed with this assurance, Mr Moore returned to Albany
and

on the 16ᵗʰ one of them came with this answer:

The visit you made us and the Design of it was very welcome,
for which we return you our Thanks. We have always liv'd in
great friendship with our Brethren of this Province, but we have
been all along in much darkness, & our Eyes so cover'd that we

¹ 'A' MSS. Vol. 2, No. 75.

have not known what would become of our Souls after death. We saw some time ago a Light arising in Canada[1] which drew many of our Nation thither, & which was the Cause of our desiring Ministers. We can't but rejoyce that God should be so good to us as to make us this Offer, but it grieves us that the rest of our Brethren the other 4 Nations are like to have no such blessing. They have often ask't us what was the meaning of a Bell which we have, which our Fathers told us we must ring to call us together to our Devotions, but if they were so inquisitive about that, what will they think when they see their house & Church built, therefore 'tis necessary we first acquaint them (for we are all but one house) & then we will give you a positive Answer.

I was again disappointed & had new Matter for suspicion but only desir'd the Answer might be as speedy as could be. To which he immediatly reply'd, That he wondered a Minister should not be more deliberate; sudden Answers were not their Custom.

The Sachim stay'd that night in Town & the next morning I thought it advisable to return the following Answer:

Child

I have consider'd your Answer & am sorry it is not more full & satisfactory. As to what you say about consulting with the other Nations, I will believe they will rather rejoyce at your happiness than have any suspicions about it, especially when they are told that there is another Minister dayly expected for ye Oneydas & one for every other Nation, as soon as proper & willing Persons can be found. But I will stay for your Answer with the greatest patience....

I have since accidentally met with another of their Sachims, who gives me very good hopes that all will be well: he tells me he is making a Path for me, & desires me to wait with patience. I show'd him my kinsman (who is about 16 years of Age & whom I brought out of England with me) & told him that I design'd to send him very soon to live among 'em to learn their Language, which indeed he is very willing to do, at which the Sachim seem'd to be very well pleas'd. I told him I design'd to commit him to his care, to which he reply'd that he would very willingly take care of him, but that he must first propose it to the other Sachims. Thus, Sir, the Case stands with me at present, & when I receive their positive Answer your Society may expect it....[2]

---

[1] I.e. the Jesuit Missions.   [2] 'A' MSS. Vol. 2, No. 75.

Unfortunately Mr Moore's hopes were doomed to disappointment. After spending nearly a year at Albany he decided that his efforts at instructing the Mohawks were of little avail and asked leave of the S.P.G. to become an itinerant missionary in New Jersey. The following letter which he wrote from New York shortly after he left Albany sets out the reasons for his failure:

N. York, Nov: 13. 1705.

S^{r}

I am as you see by the date of my letter at N. York return'd from Albany, wch I left ye 12th of the last. I send this therefore to acquaint ye Society with it, & to give them some certain Acco^{t} of my Affairs, wch I was scarce ever able to do till now, for tho' I have been at Albany near a Twelvemonth, & have us'd all the means I could think of in order to get ye Good Will of ye Indians, that they might accept of me yet I could never get them so much as to tell me, whether they would or no, tho' I always told them I came from ye Great Queen of England, and desired their Answer might be speedy. Indeed their unreasonable Delays & frivolous Excuses for not giving me an Answer with some other Circumstances were a sufficient Indication of their Resolution never to accept me, yet I could not but hope better, & having some desire of spending my Life with them, & not knowing but that God called me to it, I overlookt all Difficultys & could not see what was ye most apparent. I continued in these vain hopes above half a year, & in ye begining of the Sum̄er, I think it was in June last, having some little Encouragment from one of ye Sachems or Governors, I bought some Biscake in order to go up into ye Country & to settle my kinsman among them, in order to learn their Language, but ye Indians refusing that, made me begin to have less hopes than before. About Two months after I had an opportunity of seeing most of ye Mohocks & their Gov^{rs} at Schenectady (a Town about Twenty miles from Albany) which opportunity I gladly accepted of to demand their Answer wch they had so long delay'd they p^{r}sently answered me they could not give it me yet,—neither did they know when they should, this when I reflected on & understood moreover by them that the soonest would be near a Twelve month, & that even then I should have, if any thing probably a positive Denial (wch I had all ye reason in the world to expect) I came to a Resolution of Leaving them, & not to give them the honour of a Refusal of ye Queens &

my offer to them, when I came to this Resolution, which indeed was sometime after, I sent them word of it, but even that would not prevail with them, so much as to come & offer to accept of me.

Indeed were Missions to yᵉ Indians of that Consequence that I believe many of yᵉ Society think & what I my self once expected, I should have had even more patience than I have had, & not left them without a positive refusal, tho' I had stay'd a Twelve month longer for it, but I am very sensible now of yᵉ contrary & for these Reasons.

1. Because our own People here have a more just right to our Care, & call for more Missionarys than yᵉ Society is able to send. Indeed so many, that were England sensible of it, there would be a greater readiness towards raising a Fund for that purpose, than I fear yᵉ Society finds.

2. Because to begin with yᵉ Indians first is pʳposterous for 'tis from yᵉ behaviour of yᵉ Christians here that they have had & still have their Notions of Christianity, wᶜʰ God knows has been & is generally such, that I can't but think has made the Indians even hate Christianity.

3. Supposing our Country-men and yᵉ Indians *cæteris paribus*, this should make us take care of yᵉ one before yᵉ other, because the English here are a very thriving growing people, and yᵉ Indians quite otherwise, they wast[e] away & have done ever since our first arrival amongst them (as they themselves say) like Snow agᵗ yᵉ Sun, So that very probably forty years hence there will scarce be an Indian seen in our America. God's Providence in this matter seems very wonderful, & no cause of their Decrease visible unless their drinking Rum with some new Distempers we have brought amongst them. Indeed yᵉ Christians selling yᵉ Indians so much Rum as they do, is a sufficient Bar, if there were no other, against their embracing Christianity.

These Sᵗ are some of yᵉ Reasons that make me very easy in my Disappointmᵗ of Living with yᵉ Indians, which are so prevalent with me & are thought so by all I converse with, that if they would accept of me now, I could not think it my duty to fling away my Life with them, I mean by spending it with so little use as I must do by living among them. Their not accepting me therefore I hope was for the best, & for yᵉ Good of yᵉ Church.

The chief Objection that I perceived yᵉ Indians had agᵗ me was that I was an Englishman, to whom they bear no good will, but rather an Aversion, having a Comon Saying among them that an English man is not good yᵉ reasons of which I find have been chiefly these.

1. The behaviour of ye English of N[ew] England towards them, which has been very unchristian, particularly in taking away their Land from them without a Purchase.

2. The Example of the Garrison at Albany (ye only English in this province that many of ye Indians ever saw) wch may justly have given them a Prejudice ag^t us not easily to be removed.

3. The continual Misrepresentations of us by ye Dutch wch are the only Inhabitants of that part of ye province that borders upon the Indians, and ye only persons that trade with them, who as they never had any Affection towards us, so they have always shown it to ye Indians, tho' I must say I have rec^d many Civilitys from some of them p̄ticularly Col Schuyler & Mr Lydius ye Dutch Minister.

These being some of ye probable Reasons of the Indians not accepting of me, I thought it not improper to mention them, & ye last so much ye rather, that ye Society may use their Interest towards making ye Dutch here better Subjects than they are, by prevailing with my Lord of London that there be no more Dutch Schools here, & with ye Queen that there be no more Dutch Ministers sent from Holland when those they have go off or dye, the Suffering of which my Lord Cornbury has told me more than once has been & is likely to be of fatal Consequence, And his Excellency was pleased to tell me but last night, that without a Com̄and, if the Queen would only give him Leave he would never suffer another Dutch Minister to come over....

I am S^r

Your real Friend and Servant

THOR. MOORE.[1]

Mr Moore's request to the Society for a transfer was granted, and in the following year he acted as missionary at Burlington, New Jersey, in the absence of the Rev. John Talbot, first Rector of that place who had gone to England. During his residence at Burlington, Mr Moore became so scandalized by the licentious behaviour of the Lieutenant-Governor, Colonel Richard Ingoldsby, that he refused to admit him to Communion. He was thereupon summoned to New York by Lord Cornbury and on refusing to obey the

[1] 'A' MSS. Vol. 2, No. 122.

warrant was arrested and imprisoned in Fort Anne, New York. After a short confinement he managed to escape with the connivance of one of the sentinels.[1] He sailed for England in November 1707, but during the voyage the ship foundered and all her passengers and crew were drowned.[2]

For nearly two years the Society's mission to the Iroquois was abandoned. Then in October 1709 the Rev. Thomas Barclay, Chaplain to the garrisons at Albany and Schenectady, was appointed to act as S.P.G. missionary to the European settlers and to give instruction to the Indians.[3] Mr Barclay had resided at Albany since his arrival in America in May 1708.[4] In July 1709 he wrote to Dr Compton, Bishop of London, reporting that besides his duties as chaplain he also preached to the Dutch congregation at Schenectady, as the Rev. John Lydius was now incapacitated by illness.[5]

In the meantime Lord Cornbury, the Governor of New York, had been recalled owing to his maladministration and financial peculations. He was succeeded by Lord Lovelace who arrived in April 1709, but died as the result of a chill six months later. A new Governor, Colonel Robert Hunter (formerly Lieutenant-Governor designate of Virginia),[6] was appointed, the administration being carried on pending his arrival by Lieutenant-Governor Ingoldsby. In 1709, during

[1] Affidavit of John Grimes, sentinel at Fort Anne, before Col. Caleb Heathcote, Mayor of New York ('A' MSS. Vol. 7, pp. 250–1).

[2] Humphreys, *History of the S.P.G.* (1701–28), London, 1730, pp. 287–91.

[3] S.P.G. Journal, Vol. 1, p. 189.

[4] 'A' MSS. Vol. 5, No. 1.

[5] *Ibid.*

[6] Colonel Hunter had fought at Blenheim with General Ross's Dragoons and was made Lieutenant-Colonel of that regiment. On his voyage to Virginia in 1707 he was captured by a French privateer and taken to France. After his release he proposed to take 3000 Protestant refugees (who had sought refuge in England) from the Palatinate of the Rhine to New York and to settle them along the Hudson. The scheme was approved and Hunter sailed with the refugees early in 1710 (cf. *Dict. Nat. Biog.*).

the interregnum, Colonel Francis Nicholson and Samuel Veitch made their disastrous expedition against Canada, which ended in a humiliating retreat due to the non-arrival of an English fleet with reinforcements. At the beginning of this abortive campaign Peter Schuyler and his brother Abraham had made strong overtures to the Five Nations to break their treaty of neutrality with the French. In this they were partially successful, but the Senecas held aloof, being won over by the influence of a French emissary.[1]

The failure of the Canadian expedition roused great resentment throughout the New England provinces and as a result of strong representations by a congress of local Governors, Nicholson and Veitch sailed for England in December to obtain sanction for a new expedition. The Home Government, however, considered the conquest of Canada too great a project, but consented to an attack upon Acadia (Nova Scotia). This proved successful, the capital Port Royal being captured in October 1710. It was subsequently renamed Annapolis Royal as a compliment to the Queen.

In the meantime Peter Schuyler had sailed to England with five of the Iroquois *sachems* in the hopes of strengthening the alliance of the league by impressing on its ambassadors the greatness of the country which had so long befriended them. Schuyler was accompanied by his brother, Captain John Schuyler, who was to act as the *sachems'* interpreter.[2] One of the *sachems* unhappily died on the voyage but the others arrived safely and they appear to have taken London by storm. They were presented to Queen Anne by the Duke of Shrewsbury and were dressed for the occasion in a strange (and somewhat incongruous) attire invented by one of the theatrical dressmakers; they were driven round London in coaches and shown over the dockyards and arsenals of the metropolis. Their portraits were painted by the Dutch artist

[1] Doyle, *The English in America: The Middle Colonies*, p. 346. Parkman, *A Half-Century of Conflict* (Centenary Edition), Vol. 1, p. 138.
[2] 'A' MSS. Vol. 5, No. 94.

Verelst, articles were written about them by Steele and Addison, and they were treated on every hand as potentates of some great foreign power.[1] Their leader, introduced to the Queen as Emperor of the Mohawks, was the redoubtable Thoyanoguen, more generally known by the Anglo-Dutch name of "King" Hendrick or Henrique, who was one of the signatories of the conveyance of the Iroquois hunting grounds to William III in 1701.[2] Hendrick was probably born before 1680.[3] During the early part of his life he had lived at the "Upper Castle" of the Mohawks, Conajoharie, but later he removed to the north side of the Mohawk River. About the year 1740 he again visited England where George II presented him with "a green coat set off with Brussells and gold lace, and a cocked hat". A great warrior, he was also a skilful diplomatist and orator and was stated by contemporary writers to "have excelled all the aboriginal inhabitants for capacity, bravery and vigour of mind, and immovable integrity united". He met his death at nearly eighty years of age in the English victory of Lake George (8 September 1755) at the head of a chosen body of Iroquois warriors.[4]

The visit of the *sachems* to Queen Anne was of definite political importance. They presented the following address in which they set forth the attitude of the Iroquois league to

[1] Cf. Parkman, *A Half-Century of Conflict*, Vol. I, p. 147.

[2] *Vide* p. 11 *supra* and Appendix A. It will be seen that the name given in the facsimile of the deed is Teoniahigarawe. This is presumably a mistranscription of the word from the original deed, or may represent an attempt of the writer of the document to reduce the sound of the name to writing.

[3] He is first mentioned in the *New York Docs.* in a dispatch by the Indian Commissioners dated June 1697 as having been to Canada, presumably upon some political enterprise. Cf. Vol. IV, p. 281. Writing in 1751, Mrs Julia Grant in her Journal *Eight Years in America* mentions him as being then "over seventy years of age".

[4] Cf. Schoolcraft's *Notes on the Iroquois*, pp. 411 *et seq.* The other three *sachems* were "John" (a brother or near relation of Hendrick), Brant (the grandfather of the famous Mohawk chief, Joseph Brant, *vide* Chap. VI, p. 132 *infra*), and Etcwa Caume.

PLATE II

"King" Hendrick (Thoyanoguen)

England and France, and added a request that English missionaries might be sent to their country:

Great Queen

Wee have undertaken a long and dangerous Voyage which none of Our Predecessors cou'd be prevailed upon to do; The Motive that brought us was that we might have the Honour to see and relate to Our Great Queen, what We thought absolutely necessary for the good of her and us her Allies, which are on the otherside the great Water.

We question not but Our Great Queen hath been acquainted with our tedious War in Conjunction with her Children (against their Enemies the ffrench) and that we have always been as a firm Wall to their Security even to the loss of our best Men, the truth of which Our Brother Queder (Col Schuyler) and Anadagariaux (Col Nicholson) will more at large inform Our Great Queen of, they having all Our Proposals in Writing, and being Witnesses to Our fidelity in the Case.

We were mightily rejoyced last year when we heard by Anadagariaux (Col Nicholson) and Anadaissa (Col Vetch) that Our Great Queen design'd to send an Army and reduce Canada, from whose mouth we readily imbraced Our Great Queen's Instructions, and as a Token of our friendship We hung on the Kettle and took up the Hatchett, and with one Consent joyned with our Brother Queder and Anadagariaux in making Preparations on the side of the Lake, by building Forts, Store houses, Battoes & Canoes.

Anadaissa (Col Vetch) at the same time raised an Army at Boston of which We had an Account by Our Ambassadors that were sent to view them as also of two great Canoes that Our Great Queen had already sent, as well as those which were expected over to joyn Anadaissa to go against Quebeck by Sea; whilst Anadagariaux, Queder and we went to Mount Real by Land.

We waited long in expectation of their Arrival, but at last were told that some important Affair had prevented Our Great Queen's designs for that season, this made us extreme sorry, least the ffrench who hitherto dreaded us, shou'd now esteem us as unable to make War against them.

We need not urge to Our Great Queen the weight that depends on the Reduction of Canada, & Mount Real, so hope for the performance after which we shall enjoy peaceable Hunting and have much Trade with our Great Queen's Children, and as a sure

Token of the sincerity of the six Nations,[1] We do in Our own and in the Names of all, present Our Great Queen with these Belts of Wampum.

We shall not add more than the necessity we realy labour under (that is) provided Our Great Queen shou'd not be mindful of her promise, that We must be forced with Our families to leave Our Countreys and seek another to dwell in or stand Neuter,[2] either of which wou'd be much against Our Inclinations.

Since We were in Covenant with Our Great Queen's Children, we have had some knowledge of the Saviour of the World, and have often been importuned by the French by Priests and Presents, but ever esteemed them as men of Falsehood, but if Our Great Queen wou'd send some to Instruct us, they shou'd find a most hearty Welcome.

We now close all in Assurance of Our Great Queen's Favour & leave it to her most Gracious Consideration.[3]

The Address was well received by the Queen, and on her instructions a copy thereof was sent by the Earl of Sunderland, one of the Secretaries of State, to the Archbishop of Canterbury who was instructed to lay it before the S.P.G. for its co-operation in the matter of sending missionaries to the Iroquois.[4] The Archbishop thereupon forwarded the copy of the Address to the Society desiring the members to appoint a committee to consider the matter and draw up an answer to the Queen. This was done, and resolutions were adopted with a view to sending two missionaries to the Iroquois, providing translations of the Scriptures in the Mohawk language, and of putting a stop to the sale of intoxicating liquors to the Indians—"this being the earnest Request of

[1] With the inclusion of the Tuscaroras, an Iroquois tribe of North Carolina, the League had become known as the "Six Nations". The date of this fusion is assumed by most authorities to have been shortly after the Treaty of Utrecht (1713), but the document here reproduced proves that it had taken place as early as 1710.

[2] I.e. "remain neutral".

[3] S.P.G. Appendix to Journal A, No. 138.

[4] Lord Sunderland's letter of 20 April 1710; 'A' MSS. Vol. 5, No. 86.

the Sachems themselves"—and the following Address to the Queen was then drafted:[1]

To the Queen's most Excel^t Maj^{ty}

The humble Representac͠on of the Society for the Propagation of ye Gospel in fforeign Parts.

May it please your Maj^{ty}

It was with very great joy that We received the Right Honorable the Earl of Sunderland's Letter written by your Majesty's Command to the most Reverend the Lord Archbishop of Canterbury, directing His Grace to lay before us the desire of the Sachems or Chiefs of the Six Indian Nations to have some Ministers sent by Your Majesty to instruct them and their People in the Christian Religion: and requiring Our Opinion about the best way of answering that request which Your Majesty did so highly and so justly approve.

We cannot but look upon it as one of the many singular Providences of God that have attended Your Majesty's Reign to have an Application of this Nature made to you. And as we are intrusted under Your Maj^{ty} with the care and ordinary means of promoting so good a design: so we hope we shall always let Your Maj^{ty} see, that We have it at heart; as we are now ready to do the utmost, that in our present Circumstances we can, toward carrying it on.

With all possible deference therefore to your Majesty We propose to send into those Countrys two Missionaries with competent Salaries at our own Charge. These Missionaries will want an Interpreter, a House to live in and a Chapel for the service of God which We are inform'd should be built within an Indian Fort for their security & defence; This we humbly submit to Your Maj^{tys} Royal Wisdom and Consideration.

We cannot but take this Opportunity further to represent to Your Majesty with the greatest humility the earnest and repeated desires not only of the Missionaries but of divers other considerable Persons that are in Communion with Our Excellent Church to have a Bishop setled in Your American Plantations (which We humbly conceive to be very usefull and necessary for establishing the Gospel in those parts) that they may be better united among themselves than at present they are, and more able to withstand the designs of their Enemies; that there may be Confirmations which in their present State they cannot have the

[1] 'A' MSS. Vol. 5, No. 85.

Benefit of, and that an easy and speedy care may be taken of all the other Affaires of the Church which is much encreased in those parts; and to which thro' Your Majesty's Gracious Protection and Encouragement we trust that yet a greater Addition will daily be made. We humbly begg leave to add that We are inform'd that the ffrench have received several great advantages from their establishing a Bp at Quebec.

As the favourable Prospect we have from the Address of these Sachems to Your Maj.^ty, gives us good hope of enlarging the Kingdome of Christ; so we do most earnestly beseech God to bless this and all Your Maj.^tys pious endeavours for the Promoting of his Honour and Worship both at home and abroad.[1]

At the suggestion of Colonel Francis Nicholson (himself a member of the S.P.G.) the *sachems* then had an interview with the Society and were informed through their interpreter that the Queen had referred the care of sending missionaries to the Iroquois to the S.P.G. The *sachems* "profest great satisfaction and promised to take care of the Ministers sent to them, and that they would not admit any Jesuites or other French Priests among them". The Society then passed a resolution "that 4 copies of the Bible in quarto with the Prayer Book bound handsomely in red Turkey Leather should be presented to the Sachems".[2]

On 2 May the *sachems* sent the following letter to the Society:

To the Ven.^ble Society for Propagation of the Gospel in fforeign Parts.

'Tis with great satisfaction that the Indian Sachems reflect upon the usage and answers they received from the Chief Ministers of Christ's Religion in our great Queen's dominions, when they ask't their assistance for the thorough Conversion of their Nations: 'tis thence expected that such of them will e're long come over and help to turn those of Our Subjects from Satan unto God as may by their great Knowledge and pious practices convince the Enemies to saving ffaith that the only true God is not amongst them. And may that Great God of Heaven succeed accordingly all the endeavours of our great Fathers for his honour & glory.

[1] S.P.G. Appendix to Journal A, No. 139.
[2] S.P.G. Journal, Vol. 1, pp. 263–4.

PLATE III

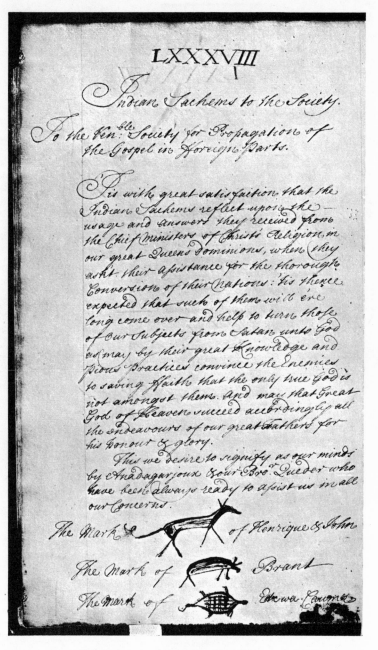

Facsimile of the *sachems'* letter to the S.P.G. (1710)
(showing *totem* signatures)

S.P.G. Archives

PLATE IV

Photo. Walker;, Brantford, Ontario

Communion plate presented by Queen Anne to the Mohawks' Chapel, Fort Hunter

This we desire to signify as our minds by Anadagarjoux [Col. Nicholson] & our Broͬ Queder [Col. Schuyler] who have been always ready to assist us in all our Concerns.

<table>
<tr><td>The Mark of</td><td>HENRIQUE & JOHN</td></tr>
<tr><td>The Mark of</td><td>BRANT</td></tr>
<tr><td>The Mark of</td><td>ETCWA CAUME.[1]</td></tr>
</table>

The Queen supported the Society's proposals, and gave orders for the erection of a fort in the Mohawk country near Albany, in which a house for the two missionaries and a chapel for their ministrations were to be built. The fort was considered necessary to safeguard the missionaries against attack from hostile Indians, and to this end a small force of soldiers was ordered to be stationed there. For the use of the chapel the Queen gave a handsome set of Communion Plate inscribed with the royal cypher and the royal coat-of-arms, and the words: "The Gift of Her Majesty Anne, by the Grace of God, of Great Britain, France and Ireland and of her Plantations in North America, Queen, to her Indian Chappel of the Mohawks." This historic treasure is still preserved by the descendants of the recipients at Tyenderoga and Brant-ford, Ontario, which became the headquarters of the Mohawks after the War of Independence. Further royal gifts included an altar cloth, a "large Cushion with Torsels [tassels] for the Pulpit, 2 Common Prayer Books, one whereof for the Clerk, and 4 of Her Majesty's Imperial Arms painted on Canvas, 1 for the Chappel, and 3 for so many Castles". To these were added "twelve large Octavo Bibles" which were presented by Archbishop Tenison, and "a Table of the Society's Seal finely painted in proper Colours to be fix'd likewise in the Chappel".[2]

[1] 'A' MSS. Vol. 5, No. 88. It will be seen that the *totem* signatures are the same as those in Appendix A. The first signature is of "King" Hendrick and his brother (?) John. The other two are Brant and Etcwa Caume.

[2] *S.P.G. Annual Report*, 1712, pp. 61–2. The plate consisted of "1 Large Silver Salver, 1 Ditto Small, 2 Large Silver Flaggons, 1 Silver Dish, 1 Silver Chalice". It was subsequently divided between two sections of the Mohawk tribe.

By the beginning of May Colonel Nicholson had concluded his negotiations with the authorities for the invasion of Acadia and set sail for New York on board H.M.S. *Dragon* accompanied by the Schuyler brothers and the four *sachems*. On 22 May Nicholson wrote to Archbishop Tenison requesting him to do all in his power to expedite the promises made by the Queen, and enclosing letters in similar terms from the *sachems* themselves to the Archbishop and the Secretary of the Society.[1] A few months after their return to America the *sachem* Brant fell ill and died.[2]

The building of the fort, chapel and house for the missionaries (in pursuance of the Queen's orders) was not put in hand until October 1711. The reason for this delay would seem to have been that the new governor, Hunter, wished to avail himself of Nicholson's experience and advice. But, as we have already seen, Nicholson took command of the invasion of Acadia (October 1710). The success of these operations induced the Home Government to further effort against Canada and in the following June Nicholson was employed in an attack on Montreal by way of Lake Champlain. A combined naval and military expedition from England, commanded by Brigadier-General John Hill (brother of the Queen's new favourite, Abigail Masham) and Rear-Admiral Sir Hovenden Walker, was to sail up the St Lawrence and capture Quebec. Through the incompetence of these two officers the expedition proved a complete failure, and Nicholson had no alternative but to retreat to Albany and disband his troops (August 1711).

Soon after his arrival at New York Nicholson was asked by Governor Hunter for his assistance in the building of the new fort, and on 11 October a contract was signed by Hunter and Nicholson and five Dutch carpenters of Schenectady for the erection of the buildings. It was also agreed that a second

---

[1] 'A' MSS. Vol. 5, Nos. 94 and 93, the latter endorsed "On board her Maj^ty's ship Draggon about 100 Leagues from the Lands End".

[2] Cf. Letter, Rev. Thos. Barclay, 'A' MSS. Vol. 5, No. 176.

PLATE V

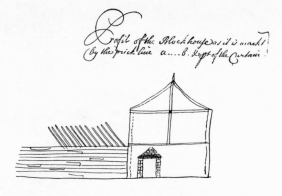

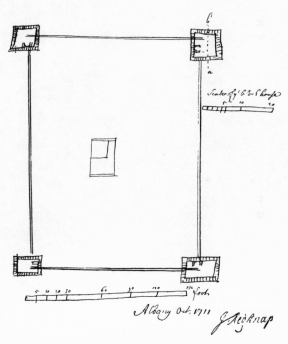

Plans of Fort Hunter
(drawn by Colonel John Redknap (October 1711))
S.P.G. Archives

fort and chapel should be built in the Onondaga country on the completion of the Mohawk fort.[1]

Two days previously, at a conference between Governor Hunter, Nicholson and the Commissioners for Indian Affairs and the *sachems* of the Five Nations, "King" Hendrick had asked Nicholson to convey a letter to Archbishop Tenison in which he expressed the thanks of the Indians to "the Great Queen for the Great Care She had taken to convert them to the Christian Religion" and requesting Nicholson to "lay their wants before their Father, his Grace the Lord Archbishop of Canterbury", to whom they sent a belt of wampum as a token of their friendship.[2]

In March 1712 the Society obtained the services of the Rev. William Andrews as its new missionary to the Iroquois. Mr Andrews had had some previous experience of America and had acquired some knowledge of the Indian language.[3] He sailed for America early in August in the ship *Four Kings* and arrived at New York on 11 October.[4] In the meantime the

---

[1] S.P.G. Appendix to Journal A, pp. 161 *et seq.* The contract specified that the fort was to be "150 feet square, ye Curtains made with Logs of a foot square one upon another and pin'd together till they reach ye height of Twelve Foot: at each Corner a Block House 24 feet square two storys high, double loop-holes, the roof to be cover'd with Boards & thin shingles, the undermost part or ground Room to be 9 foot high, the upper 8 foot, both well cover'd with Boards; the Loggs of ye Block houses to bee 9 Inches square, Bedsteads & benches in each Block house a chimny towards the Inside of ye sd. Fort, with Scaffolds 5 foot wide along each Curtain from one Block house to another, and also a Chappel in the middle of the Fort of 24 foot square one Story ten foot high with a Garret over it well cover'd with Board, and Shingled, and well floor'd, a Cellar of fifteen foot Square under it, cover'd with Loggs, and then with Earth, the whole Chappel to be well floor'd". Plans for the fort were designed by Colonel John Redknap, who succeeded Colonel Romer as Chief Engineer in America in 1706 (cf. *New York Docs.* Vol. IV, p. 1173). The plans are here reproduced from S.P.G. Appendix to Journal A, p. 163.
[2] *New York Docs.* Vol. V, p. 279.
[3] S.P.G. Journal, Vol. 2, pp. 173, 178.
[4] 'A' MSS. Vol. 8, p. 143.

"Queen's Fort", as it was called, and the chapel had been completed, and in the first week of October the Rev. Thomas Barclay visited the place and dedicated the chapel in the presence of the leading *sachems*.[1]

On 13 November Mr Andrews arrived at Albany and was welcomed by "King" Hendrick and the principal *sachems*, and on the 15th the Commissioners for Indian Affairs formally introduced Mr Andrews at a large gathering. At this meeting "King" Hendrick made a speech expressing the gratitude of the Mohawks to the Queen, the Archbishop of Canterbury, "the Spiritual Sachems of that Godly Body" (as he termed the Society) and Colonel Nicholson. Five days later Mr Andrews set out for the fort accompanied by Robert Livingston (the Mayor of Albany and son of the Secretary for Indian Affairs), Captain Matthews (one of the Church-wardens), Justice Vrooman of Schenectady and Mr Barclay. It appears that Mr Andrews' interpreter being a Dutchman[2] and not understanding English, Mr Barclay recommended his former parish clerk, John Oliver by name, to act as an intermediary interpreter from Dutch to English.[3] In a long letter written in the following March (1713) Mr Andrews thus described his experiences:

the Queens ffort near the Mohawks
Castle March the 9.th 1712
$\overline{13}$

S.r

I should have given an earlier Account of my Arrival & Reception among the Mohawks, but where my Aboad is, being so far back in the Countrey, near 200 Miles from New York, & so far to the Northward, where the Air is so Extream cold, Deep Snows so frequent for four or 5 Months which makes Travelling so Difficult, it is very rare whilst this Season continues we have an Opportunity of sending to New York.

As soon as I arrived at New York w.ch was about y.e 11.th or 12.th Day of October, I waited upon his Excellency Col. Hunter

---

[1] 'A' MSS. Vol. 8, p. 125.

[2] This was Lawrence Claessen, the official Government interpreter (cf. *New York Docs.* Vol. IV, p. 904 *passim*).

[3] 'A' MSS. Vol. 8, p. 125.

and delivered the Honble Society's Letter to him, who the next day wrote to the Com^rs for Indian Affairs to Order the principal Mohawks to come to Albany in Order to receive me when I should come there, I left New York as soon as I got a passage in a Vessell to Albany, which is counted 144 Miles from New York, which we were near a fortnight in going by reason of contrary winds; when we came near the Town, we saw the Indians upon the banks looking out for my Coming, when I came ashore they rec^d me with abundance of Joy, Every one shaking me by the hand bidding me welcome over & Over. The next day the Comissioners had a Meeting with the Sachems. There were 5 of them (there were a great many other Indians) where According to the Governours Order they recomended me to them. I then in a few words acquainted them by whom I was sent, the End & Design of my Mission &c. a Copy whereof with two of the Sachems Speeches & the Gov^rs Letter I have inclosed. Haveing dispatched my Business at Albany, I would have hastened on in my Journey to the Mohawks Countrey, but was hindered Several Dayes by a Deep Snow that fell, So that it was November the 22^d before I got to the Queens ffort there. I had m^r Barclays Company with Several others of Albany. I was p^rsently visited by a great many Indians, Men women & Children Saluting me with Abundance of Joy too & welcome to their Countrey, but altho' I was then generally well received Yet there were Some found that were dissatisfied about it, among whom one of the Sachems[1] (for which the rest have Since turned him out of his Honour) upon a Notion that I should be burdensom to them, coming in for the Tenths of every thing they had, which one of the Indians takes Notice of in his speech to which I then gave an Answer. This villainous Insinuation, Mr Barclay Supposes was made to the Indians by Some of the Dutch, & it is very probable ffor one of them who is one of the Com^rs for the Indian Affaires, was heard to Say, when he was asked by Some, why he did not Accompany me to the Mohawks Castle, haveing a great Sway among them, some of the Sachems answered, Did they think he was a Dog to follow a Priest up and down. Col. Schyler Acted all along like an honest man, who gave [the] Indians very good Advices relating to me; They are most of them Dutch that live in this part of the province but few English, and they are great Traders, with this as well as other Indian Nations, and Therefore as I have been informed never did very

---

[1] This was Hendrick, *vide* Governor Hunter's Dispatch to the Commissioners for Trade, *New York Docs.* Vol. v, p. 358.

well like of a Minister Settling among them, Except one of their
own way, for fear their Trading should be interrupted or their
Gaines lessened. It was they as I have heard since I have been in
the Countrey that Instigated those Indians against Mr Moore that
was formerly sent to instruct them. Some of them would per-
swade one if they could that they can never be made good
Christians; Indeed there is but little hopes of making those such,
who live among Xtians that see so much of their ill Lives, their
Extortion deceitfull Dealing lyeing and Cheating, how little
Conscience they make in many things they doe, but it is not so
with those Indian Nations that live more remote, who come
among the Xtians perhaps two or three times in a Year to buy
what they want. After I had a Second time declared to those
Indians that were afraid of my claiming Tenths That I desired
nothing they had but that my only Designe was to Instruct them
for the Wellfare of their Soules That I needed no Subsistance
from them, for I had a sufficient Allowance from the Society,
And therefore would have them dispose themselves of all such
Apprehensions and fears. They then seemed very well satisfied,
and ever since have been very quiet. And I find many of them
very well disposed to receive those Christian Truths, which are
delivered to them, as appears from their Diligence in coming to
the Chappel to be instructed and their seeming good Devotion
when there. The Lord grant they may be still increasing & that
day may be added to the Church Such as shall be saved. I read
prayers & instruct them every Wednesday and Lordsday, and the
Soldiers every ffriday & Lordsday. The method I have taken
hitherto and which I think to continue a While to teach them is in
a Catechetical Way, & have gone thrô briefly the Chiefe funda-
mentals of Religion as the Doctrine of God, of the Creation, of
Providence, of Mans ffall and Restoration of ffaith, Repentance
the Nature & Use of the Sacraments &c. I design next to deliver
to them an Exposition of the Church Catechism and some times
a practical Discourse from Text of Scripture. I have baptized
Several of their Children & one young man, a List whereof I have
sent. Most of the adult Indians are already baptized, some by
priests from Canada, others by Dutch Ministers, but those
baptized by the former, I am afraid are but little the better for it,
ffor as the Interpreter has told me, who lived several years among
the Indians among whom some of those priests were, That they
would baptize any that offered themselves, whether qualified or no
& took no manner of Care to instruct them before or after, & some
they brought to baptism by Threatnings and others by Presents.

I have proposed to the Mohawks the Teaching their Children to read and write, wch they very well approved of. We design to make Tryall in a Little time but whether they should be taught English or their own Language I would willingly know the Honble Society's pleasure, but in Submission to give my Opinion that have had a little Experience among them, That the best way will be to keep them to their own Language, ffor it has been observed That those that speak English are the worst, because it gives them Opportunity of converseing the more with the English as also with Dutch who speak English, and so to learn their Vices; besides here are & will be Soldiers always in the ffort, who like most other Soldiers, are given too much to Swearing & prophane Discourse, which are enough to corrupt these Indians, if there were no others. There are not above 3 or 4 of them in this Nation can speak English, and that very brokenly, and I wish they were out for they are some of the worst among them. When they get drunk, which is as often as they can get Liquor enough, They swear & use foul Language, which the other Indians are Ignorant of. If the School succeed we designe at leasure hours to turn the Primer into Indian with some Addition to it for the use of teaching the Children, but whether I should send it to England to have it printed, or to be printed at New York, I would willingly know also the Society's pleasure, And if the Hon^rble Society would be pleased to order the value of 5.¹ in some trifling things as coarse Beads, small knives, small scissers small brass Rings and the like to be sent over to give them some times it would very much Encourage them to learn their Books.

I cannot yet give an exact Account of the Number of the Adult Indians of this Nation but as informed, about 260. they have a great many Children. there are seldom above half the Indians at home together, but always going and coming. Their Chief Town or Castle as it is called, stands by the ffort, consisting of 40 or 50 Wigwams or houses, pallizadoed Round. another of their Chief Towns between 20 & 30 houses is three or four & twenty Miles distant from this. They have several other little Towns 7 or 8 houses in a Town, and single houses up and Down pretty near their Castle next to the ffort. Their houses are made of Mats & bark of Trees together with poles about 3 or 4 yards high. Their Cloathing is a Match [?] Coat like a Mantle either a blankett or a bear's skin. Their bed is a Mat or a skin. They paint & grease themselves much with bears' fat clarified, cut their hair off from one side of their heads and some of that on the other they tie up in Knots upon the Crown with ffeathers, Tufts of ffur upon their

Ears and some of them wear a Bead fastened to their Noses with a Thread hanging down to their Lips, Bead and Wampum about their Hocks and wrists. The men are sloathfull & lazie enough. The Women laborious true Servants to their husbands, carry all the Burdens, fetch the Venison home out of the Woods their husbands kill, the wood they burn, carry the Children about at their backs, hoe the Ground, plant ye Corne, waite upon their Husbands when they eat & take what they leave them. yet for all this they say, the Women court the men when they design Marriage. Their Language differs from the Language of all the other Indian Nations as they tell me, and most difficult to be learnt, their words being generally so long & much to be supplyed by the Understanding of the hearer, because of the Narrowness of it, imperfect in Adverbs conjunctions Interjections. I have set the Lords prayer & the Creed in their Language. The vices they are most Guilty of is drinking too much when they can come at any strong Liquor Especially Rum, and Changeing their Wives when they are weary of them, but [I] don't hear there are many Guilty of the latter, but that Generally they keep constantly to One Wife never Changeing till Death makes the Separation. Excepting these they are a civil peaceable quiet people. they are poor, they have but little and little contents them, Extream kind to each other, if one has any thing better than Ordinary to be sure his Neighbours must share with him. I have been at great Expences in Treating them, Especially at my first coming among them, and am still frequently giveing of them Victualls & Drink (for they are constant Visitors where they are well used) the more to engage and continue their ffriendship....

I am S^r

Y^r most humble Servt

Wm ANDREWS.

At the Queens ffort near the Mohawks Castle
March 9th 1712/13.[1]

In his next letter, written in September, Mr Andrews informed the Society that his intermediary interpreter John Oliver was contemplating opening a school for the instruction

---

[1] 'A' MSS. Vol. 8, pp. 143 *et seq.*

of the Indian children. In the same letter he gives further descriptions of his experiences:

...There is no manner of pleasure to be proposed by being here, but only the hopes of doeing some good among these poor dark ignorant Creatures. ffor in the Winter season for 4 or 5 Months we can scarce stir abroad by the reason of the Extream Coldness of the Weather and deep Snows, and in the Summer tormented with fflyes and Muschetoes, and can't stir abroad without being in danger of being stung with the Snakes, here are so many of them, Especially the Rattle Snake. In the next place the Transporting of Provisions to this place is very Chargeable. The nearest Towns to us of the Christian Inhabitants, where we buy what we want, is Skectady [Schenectady] and Albany, The one about 24 the other about 44 Miles. The Road by Land for the most part, is only a small rough Indian Path thro' the woods where we cannot ride without a great Deal of Danger by reason of the foullness of the Road with fallen Trees, Roots, Stones high Hills and Swamps. The Small River we are upon that runs to the Towns above mentioned, is generally frozen up all the Winter and almost dry in the Sumer, the Spring and ffall being the times we can make use on't for transporting any thing, and then not without Difficulty by reason of the many Rocks and ffalls in it. These are some of the Inconveniences that discourage peoples coming here to live, besides the Trouble with the Indians, who are Constant Visitors for their Bellies, and the ffear of Receiving Mischief from some of the worst sort of them upon any Disgust, or their Rebellion in General. ffor here has lately been a Report that the Onandagas Cinicars [Senecas] &c Joyning with the Tuscorory and other Indians, who have lately done so much Mischief at Carolina, were intended to make War upon the Xtians, and if so, This ffort would be one of the first places that suffered, for it could not defend it self, it is so weakly mann'd, here being not above one or two & twenty men; but if it should be so, pray God be our Protection, but I have so good Opinion of the greater part of this Nation of the Mohawks, that they would not be concerned in the Cuting us off, Except forced to it by the others. We write what we teach the Children at present. They are very apt to learn most of them, but would learn much better if we had printed Books for them. We teach them in their own Language, for they are not willing their Children should learn any other, and if they should be Thwarted by attempting to teach their Children what they do not Approve of, may spoil all; but perhaps in time [they] may be induced to let them learn English (One does already) and indeed some might be very serviceable for Translating or Interpreters, since they are so scarce in the Countrey; but Learning in their own Language will be much more Expeditious than in English; they'l learn as much in one Year as in three, and besides for the Reason I gave you in my Letter before, why it is best to let them keep their own Language, because as it has been here observed in the Countrey, That those that understand English or Dutch are Worst, because it gives them an Opportunity of Converseing the more with them and so to learn their Vices. I have sent home a Manuscript of the Church Catechism, Morning and Evening Prayer, the Liturgy, Several Psalms and Chapters of the old and New Testament, some other Prayers & Graces before and after meat, and some Singing Psalms, for they'l sing Psalms very well, and a Copy for some Horn Books in the Indian Language to be printed if the Honᵣble Society pleases. I can give you now a more exact number of the Mohawks than I did before, as having been since better informed by some of the Sachems themselves. In the Town or Castle called Teyawendarokough wᶜʰ is by the ffort are 360 Men Women & Children. In another Castle 20 Miles from this called Canojohare and another about 4 Miles further called Anadagie in both these are about 180. In another about 24 Miles from the ffort called Eskahare about 40. So that in all about 580. Some of the Indians in the distant Towns talk of sending their Children here to School when a Schoolmaster is settled....

I am Sᵣ

Your humble Servant

WILL. ANDREWS

At the Queens ffort by the Mohawks Castle

Septᵣ 7ᵗʰ 1713.

Sᵣ I have sent Duplicates. I hope one or the other will come to hand.[1]

The report mentioned in this letter that the Onondagas and Senecas were about to join the Tuscaroras in an attack on the Europeans in Carolina was at this very time being investigated by two of the Commissioners for Indian Affairs, Hendrick Hansen and Captain John Bleeker, who were accompanied

[1] 'A' MSS. Vol. 8, pp. 184 et seq.

by the interpreter Lawrence Claessen. The party left Albany for Onondaga on 10 September. On the 20th they held a great conference of the Five Nations at which they persuaded the *sachems* not to engage in a conspiracy with the Tuscaroras or any other rebellious tribe.[1] The success of this embassy is a tribute to the authority and influence of the two Commissioners, who achieved this important undertaking by the strength of their own personalities.

[1] *New York Docs.* Vol. v, pp. 372–6.

CHAPTER III
THE NEXT THIRTY-THREE YEARS
(1714–1746)

In the meantime important political developments had occurred which were to have a far-reaching significance in the relations between the English and French Governments and the Iroquois. The signal triumphs which Marlborough had obtained over the armies of Louis XIV had forced the French king to agree to the Peace of Utrecht (1713). By the terms of this Treaty, France confirmed England's possession of Acadia (Nova Scotia), Hudson's Bay and Newfoundland,[1] and acknowledged the suzerainty of the English Government over the Six Nations and their territory. Thenceforward any aggression by France against the Iroquois would be tantamount to an act of hostility against England, but unfortunately the question of the boundaries of the Iroquois country was left unsettled, to become a fruitful cause of dispute for the next fifty years. At the same time the treaty made no mention of excluding the French Jesuits, who were therefore still at liberty to continue their activities unchecked. For this reason the importance of Mr Andrews' mission as a political counterstroke to these foreign emissaries received due recognition from the New York Governor and his advisers.[2]

During the winter of 1713 and the following spring, Mr Andrews concentrated on his work at the school for Mohawk children, and on translating the Prayer Book into the Mohawk language with the assistance of his interpreter, Lawrence Claessen. He found, however, that after a few months the Mohawks grew tired of instruction and ceased to

[1] Subject to French fishing rights.
[2] As a member of the S.P.G., Governor Hunter was a strong supporter of the Society's endeavours, as may be seen from his letters in its Archives.

attend the school. He had some success with two boys whose parents agreed to allow them to stay at the fort, and this encouraged him to persevere in his difficult task.

One of the greatest difficulties which Mr Andrews experienced in converting the Indians arose from the activities of the Dutch traders from Schenectady.[1] For many years past these Dutchmen had carried on a lucrative trade by selling rum to the tribesmen, and this practice led to horrible exhibitions of drunken orgies. This "fire-water", as the Indians called it, was entirely unknown to them before its introduction by Europeans, the Indians themselves having no acquaintance of any kind with alcoholic liquor.[2] As a result, drunkenness became one of the worst vices of the Indians and in years to come it was to be one of the chief causes of the physical and mental deterioration of the Red Man.

The presence of an English missionary among the Mohawks warned the traders that his influence would naturally be exerted against the sale of liquor to his converts. The traders thereupon endeavoured to stir up trouble for Mr Andrews by telling the Indians that the forts built by the English in the Iroquois territory were a means of appropriating their lands. How far the traders were successful in their propaganda may be shown by the following circumstance: it had been the intention of the Government to build another fort in the Onondaga country, but Mr Andrews reported that the Onondaga *sachems* now refused to countenance the suggestion,[3] and the scheme was eventually abandoned.

In October 1714 Mr Andrews wrote the following letter to the Society:

S^r

...I have taught most of the children of this Castle of the Mohawks their Prayers and instructed them, and many of their Parents are very carefull in keeping them to their Duty every morning and evening as well as themselves. Here are a great

[1] Letter of 25 May 1714, 'A' MSS. Vol. 9, p. 124.
[2] Colden, *History of the Five Nations* (3rd ed. 1755), Vol. I, p. 14.
[3] 'A' MSS. Vol. 9, p. 125.

many very good Women and can give a good Acc^t of their ffaith, keep constantly to Church and Sabbath days after they have heard what is deliver'd at the Chapel, meet together at one of their Wigwams or houses and one or two of them that have better Memory than the rest repeat over again what they heard to the others. And I have been told that some of them have been heard to pray an hour together. There are but very few of the Men that are so good, they are carryed away so much wth drinking otherwise they might be managed very well; when they are sober they are orderly and civil and as I see for the generality of them will do no body any hurt; but when drunk they are ungovernable and like so many mad distracted Creatures, run about Starke naked ye wretched^t Spectacle in the world & are for doing any mischiefe; some are for burning their houses others for killing their wives and Children. And therefore when they are in this Condition the Women take care to hide their Gunns and hatchets from them for their own Security and some times for all that must goe out of ye way themselves wth their Children. When they are Sober if one ask them why they made themselves so drunk their Answer is, Why do you X^{ns} sell us so much Rum? and many of them seem to be sorey and wish that there were no strong liq^{rs} to be sold to them. The Dutch Traders or Yandlers as they are Cal'd sell rum now by wholesaile to them since ye Act of Assembly against Selling strong liquors to ye Indians is Expired and I cant find it is like to be renewed under the pretence of losing the Indian Trade, if they dont sell them strong liquors, that they will goe to other provinces as Pensilvania Maryland or Elsewhere, where there is no Law against it, And therefore it would be a good thing (Seeing these are the Excuses) And some Gentlemen have said that they wished that I would write to the Society to see if they would be pleased to use their Intrest to procure the Queens proclamation Or an Act of Parliment wth a seveere pennalty, & good Incouragem^t to ye Informer to restraine all the Country from selling strong liquors to ye Indians. It would be what most of the Indians would like because they have often desired that no strong liquors might be sold them....

This Fall the Sakamakers or Kings of all the Six nations had a Meeting wth the Gov^{rs} at Albany to [have] the Hatchet taken out of their hands as they terme it, as a peace was concluded wch was put in when that was begun (That is as much as to Say they wanted Gifts) and to renew the Chaine and Covent^t of Friendship. They had been very uneasy some time before from some storeys that had been spread among them by some French Traders, wth the Indians, wch were that the English intended to make war upon

him till X^{ns} came here; he is not angry with us, wee never did him any hurt.

I was intended to have gone this Summer againe among the Anonidian Indians but was much advis'd to the Contrary lest I should be murdered by them. The reason of this danger is, when I was among them before I baptized severall of their Children whose parents were X^{ns} either by the father or the mother's side. Since, some of them have dyed upon wch some of these Indians had a foolish conceipt that I poysned them and so reporte it among the Indian Nations. . . . Last Winter an Indian belonging to the french at Canada came here (as the Indians there are frequently coming here) who as I had a great deale of reasons to believe, by some discovery that was made of him had a designe to have kild me which, as soone as I perceived, kept out of the way and acquainted the heads of our Indians with it, who would have dismiss'd him but he prevented them by going off himself for Some rougish Tricks he played afterwards for wch he was threatned to be killed. Indeed, I live here in a great deale of danger, what of Forreign Indians that are coming here and of such of our own that are not so good as they should be, and if Instigated by some Wicked Traders who would be very glad to have me rid out of the way. But my sure trust is in Gods Good providence and protect^{n} and [I] hope by [His] Assistance [I] shall weather all opposition & difficultys and make full profe of the disposition of these people as to matters of religion. . . .[1]

In his next letter dated 17 October (1715) Mr Andrews mentioned a meeting of the Iroquois with the Governor at Albany and the defeat sustained by the French from another Indian tribe:

. . . The Six Nations of ye Indians had a Meeting again this fall with ye Governour at Albany. His Excellency proposed to them, if they were willing to goe agst ye Indians y^{t} have lately done so much Mischief at Carolina, who Answered y^{t} they were very ready to Comply wth that Proposition, & would as soon as possible dispatch their Young Men away, a great many of y^{m} are since gone & others are Intended to go next Spring. We have an account of a great Nation of Indians y^{t} were in ffriendship with ye ffrench have this last Summer broke off, & most barbarously pulld off their Skins & murdered three or four of their Priests y^{t} were

[1] 'A' MSS. Vol. 10, pp. 186 *et seq.*

sent there to Instruct y^m, upon the News of which ye ffrench at Canada immediatly dispatched an Army of 800 men away to go ag^st these Indians & Cut y^m all off, if they could. But by ye time they were got within a days Journey to y^m, they had Intelligence given them by some of ye Cynica Indians of their comming, who presently got together a great Number of them, sett upon the ffrench Army, beat y^m, took their Generall, & made such a slaughter of ye men that scarce any of them escaped. If we have Warr with ffrance again as ye News papers from England give us an Account, it is like to be another Expedition against Canada, y^t if possible, it might be taken, would be very Necessary for ye welfaire of our plantations here, Esp^ly of New England & New York which lay ye nearest to Canada; for otherwise they having still such a Strength of Indians on their side, notwithstanding ye loss of ye aforementioned, y^t they will be able to do us a great deal of damage if not cut off ye greatest part of ye aforementioned Provinces, barbarously scalping & murdering ye Inhabitants, as they use to do in time of Warr, much more now, being much stronger, as we are informed, y^n ever they were, for ye ffrench being Extream kind to their Indians y^t live about y^m at Canada, continually giving them gifts, the Priests having each 100! at a time sent y^m in Goods, as ye Interpreter has told me, to give the Indians, Cloathing every fall all the Widows & aged of y^m, upon which Acc^t a great many of ye Indians y^t belonged to us are gone to Canada & settled there, & still are going not having ye like Encouragem^t fro[m] ye English; sev^ll are lately gone from this Nation of ye Mohawks & am afraid more will goe. Here are upwards of 20 extream poor old Widows y^t belong to this Castle of Indians. I do what I can in releiving them, taking home halfe a dozen of y^m at a time every Sabath day from Church to Dinner, but to cloath y^m my Salary will not afford it, for being so much opprest with Indian Visiters, not only of these here, but also of many of ye other Nations beyond us, who pass by this way once or twice a Year to Albany to sell their Pelt & fur, & to oblige them I must give y^m Victuals & drink, & pipes & tobacco, which I cant well deny y^m, for it is what they come for, who are all in gen^ll very poor, & like so many beggars, so y^t to be giving alwayes to so many, tho but to each a little, makes my Expences great; but if I had an Allowance fro[m] ye King for supplying this ffort as Chaplain, which I have as much right to, as Mr Barclay for supplying ye Garrison at Albany, & ye Chaplain y^t Supplys ye Garrison at New York, I would do more for these poor old Widows, & give y^m blanketts every fall, & do more for ye Children to encourage them to keep to their Learning. The Indians y^t are grown Old are but very little regarded by the others, & will scarce afford y^m any relief, but perhaps ye less, because they are all so very poor themselves. I have rec^d ye five Bibles from the Governour, the Gift of my Lord A: Bishop of Canterbury for ye Use of the Indian Chappel, for which ye Chief of ye Indians desired me to return their thanks to his Grace. I am

Sr Your Most Hum:^{bl}

Servt

Wm ANDREWS

att the Kings ffort
by the Mohawks Castle
Octr ye 17: 1715.[1]

From the concluding paragraph of this letter it will be seen that Mr Andrews had a lively appreciation of the political importance of the conquest of Canada—that long-inherited dream of the New England colonists which was only to be realized by the genius of the "great commoner" Pitt in the succeeding generation.

A few months later Mr Andrews sent a message to the *sachems* of the Oneida and Onondaga tribes informing them that he would welcome the opportunity of giving instruction to their people if they would come to the fort on their periodical trading visits to Albany. He had intended to visit their country himself but was dissuaded from so doing by his interpreter on account of the hazardous nature of the journey, which lay through the country of the Tuscarora Indians. Some 500 families of this tribe had migrated to the Iroquois territory some years previously after invading South Carolina. They cherished a deep hatred of the white man and were given to cannibal practices.[2] The Oneida and Onondaga *sachems*

---

[1] 'A' MSS. Vol. 11, pp. 269–70.
[2] *Ibid.* p. 320. After describing the Tuscarora methods of torturing their prisoners, the writer makes the naïve assertion that "the Indians say a Frenchman eats better than an English man, & an Indian better than either of y^m because he is not so salt, for the Indians eat little or no salt".

declined Mr Andrews' offer on the ground that they had little hope of their people becoming converted so long as the sale of liquor continued among them. The evil effects of the pernicious trade is graphically illustrated in the following excerpt from Mr Andrews' letter:

...When drunk some of y^m are for doing all ye mischief they can, and so much disturb us as well as their own people y^t are sober (for some of y^m will not drink to Excess) y^t we can have no rest from y^m, and we cant keep y^m out of ye Garrison by shutting ye Gates, for except they are quite drunk they'll run over ye walls like so many Cats not withstanding they are 3 or 4 & twenty foot high. An Indian some Time ago was coming into ye Chapel with his hatchet to kill me while I was reading Prayers, but some of ye Soldiers took hold of him, & lately 3 others set upon ye Officer here [as he was] walking a little way out of ye Fort and would have killed him if he had not been strong enough to have kept them off; when they are sober they are quiet enough, but when drunk [they are] like mad men....[1]

As time went on Mr Andrews found that even among the Mohawks his influence was steadily declining. Their attendance at the chapel became more and more meagre and in the following year he reported that he had been forced to debar several of his converts from Communion "because of their scandalous lives". In general the parents were willing to bring their children to be baptized but allowed them to lapse into their heathenish customs as they grew up.[2] Apart from his frequent disappointments in his work, the good missionary had to contend with libellous reports about himself made to the Society by the officer of the fort, Captain Charles Huddy, on account of Mr Andrews having refused to give him a certificate of good character. Fortunately, Huddy's continued malpractices (which included the sale of rum to the Indians) came to the ears of Governor Hunter who forthwith dismissed him from his office.[3]

[1] 'A' MSS. Vol. 11, p. 322.
[2] Letter of 17 September 1717, 'A' MSS. Vol. 12, pp. 338 *et seq.*
[3] Letter of 20 April 1716, 'A' MSS. Vol. 11, p. 326.

For the next few months Mr Andrews remained at his task, which daily became more difficult owing to the general inclination of his converts to relapse into heathendom. He had now spent six years of extraord..ary hardship among the Mohawks, his only European companions being a disreputable English officer and twenty hard-swearing soldiers, a Dutch interpreter who could not speak English, and the English interpreter-cum-schoolmaster who was ultimately dismissed for incompetency by the Governor.[1]

Mr Andrews' disappointment at the ill-success of his labours, and the loneliness of his position, which would have been sufficient to deter the most stout-hearted, induced him in October 1718 to ask the Society if he might be removed to a more congenial locality.[2] Having arranged with the commandant of the fort, Captain John Scott (who had relieved Captain Huddy), to take charge of the furniture, plate, and fittings of the chapel, and having sent the Society's books to the Rev. Robert Jenney,[3] Chaplain to the garrison at New York, Mr Andrews resigned from the mission in June 1719 and went to reside in Virginia.[4] He only survived two years, and died on 27 August 1721.[5]

For the next eight years the mission to the Iroquois was suspended, the Society feeling that their efforts for the conversion of the Indians were unlikely to achieve any permanent results. The garrison was still maintained at the fort (now known as "Fort Hunter", after the Governor), which was used as a political post by the Administration. The fort was, however, not considered capable of withstanding an attack,

---

[1] Letter, Governor Hunter to S.P.G. 3 June 1718, 'A' MSS. Vol. 13, p. 331.

[2] Letter, *ibid.* pp. 333 *et seq.*

[3] Rev. Robt. Jenney, LL.D. (1687–1762), formerly chaplain R.N. (1710–14). In 1714 he became an S.P.G. missionary and was stationed at New York in 1715. In 1742 he became Rector of Christ Church, Philadelphia.

[4] Letter, 'A' MSS. Vol. 13, pp. 468, 469.

Cf. Memorial of James Brown (Mr Andrews' executor), 'A' MSS. Vol. 15, p. 28.

as it was only defended by wooden palisades.[1] As has often happened in isolated posts, the soldiers of the garrison were prone to become lax in discipline, and complaints were laid by the *sachem*, "King" Hendrick, to the Indian Commissioners that the new commandant was openly selling rum to the Mohawks.[2]

During the next few years the Mohawks became more civilized through their intercourse with the neighbouring Europeans of the Albany district, and in 1727 the S.P.G. decided to reopen the Indian mission. As the mission at Albany had become vacant some years previously owing to the mental derangement of the Rev. Thomas Barclay, the Society appointed the Rev. John Miln to serve both places, with his headquarters at Albany.[3] Mr Miln arrived early in December and soon afterwards paid his first visit to Fort Hunter. Here he received a warm welcome from the more enlightened Mohawks, and shortly after his arrival he reported that he had administered the Holy Communion to thirteen Mohawk converts and four of the English soldiers.[4]

Towards the end of the following year, Mr Miln reported further success among the Mohawks who used to meet him "with acclamations of joy at some distance from their castle where they discharged volleys of shot". He found that Mr Andrews' labours had not been in vain, and that his converts had in fact been well grounded in the fundamental principles of Christianity.[5] Encouraged by these manifestations of the willingness of the Mohawks to receive instruction, Mr Miln made a practice of visiting Fort Hunter four times a year, and the number of the regular communicants soon increased. To help him in his work the Administration allowed him to use the Government interpreter, who assisted Mr Miln in translating "discourses" into the Mohawk language and

[1] *New York Docs.* Vol. v, p. 556.
[2] *Ibid.* p. 569.
[3] S.P.G. Journal, Vol. 5, p. 140.
[4] Letter, 20 June 1728, 'A' MSS. Vol. 21, pp. 412 *et seq.*
[5] Letter, 3 November 1729, 'A' MSS. Vol. 22, p. 357.

PLATE VI

The old church of St Peter, Albany (1715–1820)
(From a contemporary painting)

preparing candidates for Baptism.[1] The Government's evident appreciation of Mr Miln's services may be gauged from the certificate given to him by Lieutenant Walter Butler, then commandant of Fort Hunter, who stated that through Mr Miln's teaching the Mohawks had become "greatly civilized". This certificate was authenticated by Captain William Duck, the commanding officer of a company of troops at Albany, who had himself accompanied Mr Miln on some of his visits to Fort Hunter.[2]

For the next four years Mr Miln continued his labours at Albany and Fort Hunter until finally his health broke down under the strain, and he was obliged to return to England to recuperate.[3] Some months later he was at his own request appointed missionary in Monmouth County, New Jersey, where he remained for a further eight years. His success among the Indians was again certificated by Lieutenant Butler, who testified to "the Industry & Pains taken by the Rev.ᵈ Mr John Miln in teaching and instructing the Mohawks in the Christian Religion".[4]

In April 1735 the Society appointed Mr Henry Barclay, son of the Rev. Thomas Barclay, as Catechist to Fort Hunter. Having been born and bred in America and having a great interest in the Indians, Mr Barclay had acquired some knowledge of the Mohawk language. He also possessed the added advantage of being able to speak Dutch, which he had learnt from his mother, Anna Dorothea Draeyer. This lady was the daughter of Andries Draeyer, formerly commandant of Fort Orange, New York, who became an Admiral in the Danish Navy.[5] Although too young to be ordained, Mr Barclay was anxious to devote his services to the Mohawks in a subordinate capacity. He had graduated at Yale and had

[1] Letter, 4 November 1730, 'A' MSS. Vol. 23, p. 85.
[2] *Ibid.* pp. 381, 382.
[3] S.P.G. Journal, Vol. 6, p. 307.
[4] Cf. Affidavits of Lieutenant Butler sworn before James de Lancy, Mayor of New York, on 26 October 1735, 'A' MSS. Vol. 26, p. 4.
[5] Brodhead, *History of New York*, Vol. II, p. 224.

studied theology under the celebrated Dr Samuel Johnson, the Society's missionary at Stratford, Connecticut, and later the first President of King's College, New York.[1]

On receipt of the Society's instructions Mr Barclay took up his residence at Fort Hunter. He was well received by the Mohawks and soon exerted a favourable influence over them. After the first eighteen months of his labours he reported to the S.P.G. that he had forty Indian children at his school in addition to a "Catechetical" night school which was attended by adults also. Mr Barclay made a practice of visiting the "Upper Castle" of the Mohawks, situated some twenty miles distant from the "Lower Castle", and he was thus able to preach to the more distant members of the tribe. These journeys he made on horseback, having purchased a horse for the purpose.[2] His great success was certified by the Commissioners for Indian Affairs who testified that "the Indians expressed a great Love and Esteem for him and that they had very much reformed since his residing among them". As a commentary on the influence of the Dutch community in official circles, it may be mentioned that with the exception of Robert Livingston and Edward Holland (the Mayor of Albany), six of the nine commissioners were of Dutch descent.[3]

Towards the end of 1737 Mr Barclay went to England to take Holy Orders and was ordained deacon and priest in January 1738. After a short stay in the Home Country he sailed for America and arrived at Albany in April.[4] On instructions from the Society he now undertook the post of missionary at Albany in addition to that of Fort Hunter, and divided his time between these two places. At Albany his congregation was materially increased by the settlement of some Protestant Irish who appeared to be "very honest,

[1] S.P.G. Journal, Vol. 6, pp. 235, 236.
[2] Letter, 31 August 1736, 'A' MSS. Vol. 26, pp. 283, 284.
[3] Ibid. p. 285. The signatures are Robert Livingston, Mijndert, John and Philip Schuyler, Edward Holland, Nicholas Bleeker, John de Peyster, J. Rensselaer, Reyer Gerritson.
[4] New York Docs. Vol. VI, p. 88.

PLATE VII

The Rev. Henry Barclay, D.D.
(From a contemporary painting)

sober, industrious and religious". Besides ministering to these newcomers, Mr Barclay frequently preached to the Dutch townsfolk and settlers of Albany in their own language.[1]

In August 1740 the acting Governor of New York, George Clarke, held a conference of the Six Nations at Albany at which Mr Barclay attended. At this meeting the *sachems* pledged themselves to renew the "ancient Silver Covenant Chain which had so long united their Forefathers" to the English Government.[2] At the conclusion of the conference Mr Barclay preached a sermon to the Mohawks in their own tongue in the presence of the acting Governor and several members of the Council, and the Mohawks made their responses in the service "in so devout a manner as agreeably surprised all who were present".[3] Mr Barclay's evident success in his mission was warmly appreciated by Governor Clarke who sponsored a special recommendation to the New York Assembly for the rebuilding of the Fort Hunter chapel which had fallen into great disrepair. A subscription list for this purpose was opened at New York and distributed by members of the Council, and in November 1741 Mr Barclay was able to report that the new building—"a neat Stone Church"—was nearing completion. In the same letter he informed the Society that the Indians' prevailing vice of drunkenness had greatly diminished.[4]

During the next year Mr Barclay opened schools at the Upper and Lower "Castles" of the Mohawks. He obtained the services of two Christian *sachems*, Daniel and Cornelius, to act as schoolmasters, and the latter occasionally read prayers at the Fort Hunter chapel when Mr Barclay was absent at Albany. By this time the whole Mohawk tribe were (at least nominally) Christian, there remaining only two or three of the number who were unbaptized.[5]

[1] Letter, 'B' MSS. Vol. 7, Pt. II, No. 139.
[2] *New York Docs.* Vol. VI, p. 176.
[3] Letter, 'B' MSS. Vol. 7, Pt. II, No. 139.
[4] Letter, 'B' MSS. Vol. 9, No. 81.
[5] Letter, 'B' MSS. Vol. 10, No. 112 and Vol. 11, No. 155.

In the meantime affairs of great importance to America had taken place in Europe. In 1740 the War of the Austrian Succession had broken out in which France and the other powers repudiated their promise to the Emperor Charles VI to support his daughter Maria Theresa. The invasion of Silesia by Frederick the Great provoked England into championing the Austrian Empress out of distrust of Prussia, whose proximity to Hanover alarmed George II. As a result of these complications, all Europe became embroiled and France and England became ranged as antagonists. The battle of Dettingen followed (1743) at which a seventeen-year-old ensign named James Wolfe (who was destined to become the conqueror of Canada) distinguished himself as acting adjutant of the 12th Foot.[1]

The participation of England in this campaign had its natural repercussions in America. In the spring of 1744 France formally declared war, and in May, Duquesnal, the French Commander of Louisburg, attacked and took Canseau, an English fishing post on the north-east coast of Acadia (Nova Scotia), and unsuccessfully endeavoured to capture Annapolis Royal.[2] As a result of these expeditions the French emissaries reopened their anti-English propaganda among the Iroquois, and in January an alarm of a French expedition against the New York province was concocted by their adherents. The following account of this occurrence was given by Mr Barclay in a letter to the S.P.G.:

...I am Just returnd from the Mohawks, where I have Spent Two Months in a very disagreeable Manner. About the Middle of January five or Six Indians comming home from Schenectady, Alarm'd the whole Indian Town in the Dead of The Night, telling them that the White People were Comming with a Considerable force to Cut them All in Pieces; The Poor Creatures in a Fright fled—most of them into the Woods; as soon as I heard of

[1] Wolfe was promoted Lieutenant and Adjutant, on the Duke of Cumberland's recommendation, a fortnight after the battle (cf. Beckles Willson, *Life and Letters of James Wolfe*, p. 39).

[2] Parkman, *A Half-Century of Conflict*, Vol. II, pp. 60, 61.

It, I call'd as Many of them Together as I could and Endeavour'd
to Convince them of the Groundlessness of their Fears, which had
a good Effect on Many of them, who Joyn'd their Endeavours
with Mine to pacify the Rest: But the Authors of The Sedition
Oppos'd us with Violence, Said that the Plot against them was
certain, that a Man of Good Repute in the Township of Schenectady had Assurd them of It, and warn'd them to be on Their
Guard, and that I was the Chief Contriver of the Destruction
intended against them, That Notwithstanding my Seeming Affection for Them, I was a very Bad Man and in League with the
Devil who was the Author of All the Books I had given them.
Very Few however of the Lower Mohawks could be Brought to
Believe this Idle Story, But the Upper Town was all in a Flame,
Threatning to Murder the Inhabitants setled about them, And
had Sent Expresses to All the Six Nations. In the Mean time I
gave notice to the Commissioners of Indian Affairs Who came
up Immediatly to the Lower Towne and with Great Difficulty
prevaild with the Upper Mohawks to come down and Treat with
them But could not persuade them to discover the Author of This
Disturbance. But they promised to lay aside all thōts of It for
the Future and parted with the Commissioners seemingly well
satisfyd. But the Villains who first occasion'd This Disturbance
Endeavour'd for some time to Kindle the Fire Anew, but met
with Little Success and Seem now Much out of Credit. This
Affair, which has given us great Uneasiness, and been A Considerable Charge to the Country, we have at last discovered to
have been Occasiond by the French who have had some Emisarys
Endeavouring to Corrupt the Indians. As this is the First So I
hope It may prove the Last remarkable Discouragement I Shall
meet with....[1]

After the excitement had died down one of the traders
started a rumour that the alarm had been fabricated by some
of the leading residents of Albany, including a member of the
Governor's Council and Mr Barclay. The matter formed the
subject of an inquiry held at Albany by the Governor, the
Hon. George Clinton, and the Indian Commissioners. At
this conference, the Mohawk "King" Hendrick accused a
French emissary named Joncaire as the inventor of the story,

[1] 'B' MSS. Vol. 13, No. 314.

but no definite proof was forthcoming.[1] Although the authorities were able to reassure the tribesmen of the falsity of the rumour the incident had a detrimental effect on Mr Barclay's mission by the immediate falling off in attendance at his school at the "Upper Castle" of the Mohawks.[2]

Meanwhile the capture of Canseau by the French and their expedition against Annapolis Royal had influenced the authorities in Massachusetts and New Hampshire into striking a counterblow by an attack on Louisburg, the most strongly fortified harbour in America, situated on the southeastern shores of Cape Breton Island. A force of over 4000 men was assembled under the command of William Pepperell, a prosperous New England landowner, assisted by a local fleet of thirteen small vessels. The co-operation of an English fleet under Commodore Peter Warren rendered material assistance, and Louisburg fell on 17 June. An attempt to recapture the fortress in 1746 ended in disaster, and a second expedition in the following year was negatived by the defeat of the French fleet off Cape Finisterre by Anson and Warren.

While these important events were taking place the French on the Canadian border were busily engaged in intrigue amongst the Iroquois, and in October 1745 a mixed force of French and Indians attacked a settlement on the Massachusetts frontier.[3] Encouraged by this exploit a series of raids were made in the New York province, and Saratoga, the farthest settlement of the colony and the only defensive post between Albany and the frontier, was captured and burnt.[4] The following graphic description of these incursions was given by Mr Barclay in his next letter to the Society:

About the middle of November 1745 The French Indians came to an Open Rupture with Us, and with a Party of French fell upon a Frontier Settlement which they laid in Ashes, and made

[1] *New York Docs.* Vol. VI, pp. 293 *et seq.* Chabert de Joncaire was the son of a French officer and a Seneca squaw. He lived among the Senecas, with whom he had great influence.

[2] Letter, 'B' MSS. Vol. 13, No. 316.

[3] *New York Docs.* Vol. VI, p. 303 (dispatch of Governor Clinton).

[4] Cf. Parkman, *A Half-Century of Conflict*, Vol. II, p. 210.

most of the Inhabitants, to the Number of above a Hundred, Prisoners; ever Since which Time, they have Kept us in a continual Alarm by Sculking Parties, who Frequently murderd and carry'd off the Poor Inhabitants, treating them in the most Inhumane and Barbarous manner, by which means the Lately Populous and Flourishing County of Albany is become a Wilderness and Numbers of People who were Possess'd of good Estates are Reduc'd to Poverty. In the mean Time Our Indians could not be prevail'd upon to Enter into the War but have deceived us with Fair Promises from Time to Time, whilst we were Convinc'd by undenyable Proofs that they Kept a Correspondence with the Enemy.[1]

In October 1746 Mr Barclay was offered the incumbency of Trinity Church, New York, which had become vacant by the death of the Rev. William Vesey in the previous July, and feeling that there was now no prospect of being of further service to the Indians owing to the distracted state of the province, he decided to accept the appointment.[2] He arrived at New York in November and reported that:

Since my Arival at this Place which was about a fortnight ago, a Party of Mohawks arrived here with Eight French Prisoners and four Scalps which they had taken near *Montreal* in *Canada*. As this was the first Instance of their Ingageing in the War they were receivd with great Joy but It was much Allay'd when We learn'd from the Prisoners, and the Confession of the Indians, that the French Indians had been privy to, and assisted in the taking of them, which puts It beyond All Doubt, that these Savages are in League with Each Other, to Destroy both English and French, and to Observe a Strict Neutrality between themselves. I had a long Conversation with these Indians who happen'd to be some of the Better Sort. I frankly told them the Reason of My Leaving them to which they could make no Reply, but said they were Sorry for what had happen'd. I then told them that if they behaved like Men and Christians I would interceed with the Honble Society and endeavour to find some Young Gentleman to succeed me as Soon as the War was Ended.

The State of my Parish at Albany when I left It was Truly Deplorable, Several of the Inhabitants having been Oblidg'd to

---

[1] 'B' MSS. Vol. 14, No. 95.
[2] *Ibid.*

Seek New Habitations, And another Such Year as the last will I fear Reduce It to a Garrison Town....[1]

With the transfer of Mr Barclay to New York the Society's mission to the Mohawks was again left without a minister. Until such time as a new missionary could be obtained the Mohawks were thrown upon their own resources, and it speaks well for their initiative that they sent a deputation to New York to assure Mr Barclay that they would do all in their power to keep religion alive among their people by reading prayers on Sundays as they had been taught to do. On this Mr Barclay promised them a monetary gratuity for the services of their "lay-readers" and this obligation met with a sympathetic response from the venerable Society.[2]

[1] 'B' MSS. Vol. 14, No. 95.
[2] S.P.G. Journal, Vol. 10, pp. 213, 214.

CHAPTER IV
THE CONFLICT FOR CANADA
(i) (1747–1755)

THE temporary abandonment of the Society's Mission to the Iroquois in consequence of Mr Barclay's transfer to New York occurred at a time of danger and difficulty to the American Colonies. The destruction of Saratoga was followed by further hostile raids by the French and their Indian allies, and for the next two years the frontiers of New York, New Hampshire, and Massachusetts were subjected to numerous incursions by the enemy. To make matters more complicated, a strong party in New York was opposed to the war because of its detrimental effect on trade with Canada, and Governor Clinton's measures for the protection of the frontiers were frustrated by the New York Legislative Assembly. This body claimed to control the militia, and on several occasions the troops refused to march at the Governor's orders on the grounds that a special Act of Assembly would first be required.[1] The position was further aggravated by the failure of a scheme which had been proposed by Clinton and Governor Shirley of Massachusetts for a comprehensive attack on Canada after the English capture of Louisburg. To this end strenuous preparations had been made by the colonists and their Iroquois allies, but owing to the futility of the Duke of Newcastle in not sending a promised fleet from England, the project had to be abandoned.[2]

---

[1] Cf. *New York Docs.* Vol. VI, pp. 340 *et seq.*

[2] The amazing inefficiency of Prime Minister Newcastle is well illustrated by Smollet in his contemporary novel *Humphrey Clinker*: "Captain C. treated the Duke's character without any ceremony... 'In the beginning of the [Seven Years'] war (said he) the Duke told me in a great fright that 30,000 Frenchmen had marched from Acadia to Cape Breton. Where did they find transports? said I— Transports! cried he, I tell you they marched by land.—By land to the island of Cape Breton!—What, is Cape Breton an island?—

This occasioned a bitter resentment in the minds of the colonists and as a result of the widespread disaffection Clinton found himself unable to enforce his authority for the adequate protection of the province. The fort at Saratoga, which had been rebuilt after its destruction by the French, was abandoned by its commanding officer—Colonel Peter Schuyler—for want of supplies, and the Governor thereupon ordered it to be burned as indefensible. This made a deep impression on the Mohawks, who considered the act as a display of inexcusable weakness if not of positive cowardice.[1]

The French were not slow to turn this circumstance to their own advantage and redoubled their propaganda among the Iroquois. Although the Five Nations were still attached to the English Alliance the French succeeded in keeping the Senecas from co-operating with the English, through the skilful efforts of their agent Joncaire. Fortunately for the English Colonies a young Irishman named William Johnson had already begun to acquire that great influence amongst the Five Nations which later made him the acknowledged leader of the Iroquois tribesmen. His father, Christopher Johnson —a former cavalry officer who suffered lifelong disablement from a wound received at Oudenarde[2]—had married a sister of Admiral Warren, and at twenty-three young Johnson had gone to America to act as agent for his uncle's estate of Warrenburgh in the Mohawk Valley.[3] He soon gained an

Certainly.—Ha! are you sure of that?—When I pointed it out on the map, he examined it earnestly with his spectacles; then, taking me in his arms,—My dear C. cried he, you always bring me good news. Egad! I'll ɣo directly and tell the King that Cape Breton is an island!'" (quoted by Parkman in *Montcalm and Wolfe*).

[1] Cf. Hendrick's taunt at a conference with the New England Commissioners in 1754: "You burnt your own Fort at Seraghtoag (Saratoga) and ran away from it, which was a shame & a scandal to you" (*New York Docs.* Vol. vi, p. 870).

[2] Cf. A. C. Buell, *Sir William Johnson*, pp. 4–5.

[3] Sir Peter Warren, K.B., received his knighthood after the victory off Finisterre. He married Susannah, daughter of Stephen de Lancy of New York, and purchased under royal grant a large tract of land south of the Mohawk river.

ascendancy over the Indians by his honesty and fair-dealing, and by adopting their customs of dress and war-paint like one of their own *braves*.

When the Indian Commissioners of Albany resigned in 1746, Governor Clinton appointed Johnson "Colonel of the Six Nations", and soon afterwards he was made Commissary of New York Indian affairs. In the following year Johnson sent out some Indian "war-parties" into Canada under "King" Hendrick and other *sachems*, and thus made a timely diversion in the French activities.[1] He had recently been given the command of the local forces for the defence of the frontier and had drawn up a plan of campaign for a strong attack on the Canadian outposts. But before his scheme materialized, news came of the Peace of Aix-la-Chapelle which had been signed by the belligerent Powers in October 1748. Under the terms of this treaty Cape Breton was restored to France in return for the trading post of Madras. Thus the conclusion of the war left the French colonies in America unimpaired while the English suffered considerable loss of prestige from their failure to follow up the capture of Louisburg, which was now arbitrarily handed back to their enemies by the short-sighted diplomacy of the home authorities.

In the meantime the question of the reopening of the Society's Mission among the Mohawks had occupied the attention of Mr Barclay, who reported that while the war continued there was little prospect of doing anything among the Indians, more especially since "the intended Expedition against Canada being laid aside, has given the Indians a very mean Opinion of us and our Power, and should they forsake our Interest, the Consequence will, I fear, be much worse than the Government at Home can imagine".[2] At the same time Mr Barclay mentioned that the Rev. John Jacob Oël (a German immigrant from the Palatinate who had received Anglican Orders in 1722 and was living on a plantation some

[1] *New York Docs.* Vol. VI, p. 361.
[2] 'B' MSS. Vol. 15, No. 123.

eighteen miles from Fort Hunter) was working among the Mohawks, and recommended him to the Society's notice.

In October 1748 Mr Barclay suggested the appointment of John Ogilvie, "a young Gentleman who understands the Dutch Language, a very necessary Qualification, and hath been educated at Newhaven", as missionary to the Mohawks.[1]

John Ogilvie was born in New York and was educated at Yale where he came under the influence of the Rev. Dr Samuel Johnson, then Rector of Stratford, Connecticut. In 1747 Dr Johnson employed him as a lay-reader during the doctor's frequent absences on other duties,[2] and in the spring of 1748 the Churchwardens and Vestry of the neighbouring parish of Norwalk wrote to the Society requesting that Ogilvie might go to England for Orders with a view to becoming their missionary.[3] This request was recommended by Dr Johnson and the Revs. Joseph Lamson and John Beach, the Society's missionaries at Fairfield and Newtown.[4]

Early in the new year Mr Ogilvie sailed to England taking with him a recommendation to the Society for his work among the Mohawks from Governor Clinton, who himself had recently become a member of the S.P.G.[5] Mr Ogilvie was ordained by the Bishop of London soon after his arrival, and sailed for New York in the early autumn. After a ten weeks' passage he arrived at his destination, but his health having been severely tried on the voyage, he stayed some months with Mr Barclay and began to study the Mohawk language under his tuition.[6] While staying at New York, Mr Ogilvie preached at Elizabeth Town, New Jersey, where

---

[1] Letter, 'B' MSS. Vol. 16, No. 55.
[2] Letter, 'B' MSS. Vol. 15, No. 28.　　　　[3] *Ibid.* No. 41.
[4] S.P.G. Journal, Vol. 11, p. 43. The Rev. J. Lamson had only recently been appointed to Fairfield and Ridgefield. He had been captured by an enemy ship in 1745 on his way to England for Orders and was kept prisoner for 5 months in France and Spain. He served at Fairfield and Ridgefield until his death in 1773. The Rev. John Beach was Rector of Newtown for 50 years, 1732–82. He was a staunch Loyalist in the Revolution and died in 1782 at the age of 81.
[5] S.P.G. Journal, Vol. 11, p. 101.　　　　[6] *Ibid.* p. 200.

PLATE VIII

The Rev. John Ogilvie, D.D.
(From a contemporary painting)

he met Thomas Bradbury Chandler, then a young catechist in the Society's employ, who was destined to become one of the outstanding leaders of the American clergy.[1]

In March Mr Ogilvie left New York and proceeded to Albany, and in July he wrote the following account of his activities to the Rev. Dr Philip Bearcroft, Secretary of the S.P.G.:

Albany, July 27, 1750.

Rev⁴ Sir,

I should have been earlier in acquainting the Venr. Society with my arrival & reception at Albany, but did not know the time of the ship's sailing before it was too late.

As soon as the season of the year would admit it, I left New York & arrived at Albany the last [day] of March. I was recommended by his Excell: our Governour to the countenance and favour of the commanding officer of Fort Frederick in this City, & was received by him & many of the principle gentlemen with the strongest expressions & respect.

The Congregation in Albany is very much decreased occasioned by the removal of many of the principle English families to New York on account of the late war. The number of people that attend divine service in the Church on Sundays (besides the Garrison) far exceeds my expectations. I administred the holy Communion on Easter Sunday to 15 persons, & have admitted two since, Persons of unblemished character. Besides preaching twice on Sundays I have prayers & catechise on Wednesdays, many of the inhabitants send their children so that I've near 50 that attend catechetical instruction constantly.

Many of the Negroes are very desirous of Instruction, to encourage this good disposition I constantly catechize them on

[1] Rev. T. B. Chandler, Hon. D.D. Oxon., was born at Woodstock, Mass., in 1726. Brought up as a dissenter he graduated at Yale in 1745, and became an S.P.G. catechist and (1751) Rector of Elizabeth Town. He became famous for his pamphlets—*Appeal to the Publick* (1767) and others—in which he championed the appointment of bishops for America. At the outbreak of the Revolution he was compelled to seek refuge in England, and at the conclusion of the war he was nominated the first colonial bishop (Nova Scotia, 1783). He was unable to accept the offer because of ill-health and, returning to America in 1785, he resumed the incumbency of Elizabeth Town. He died in 1790.

Sundays after divine service in the afternoon. Since my arrival here I have baptized eight children two of which were negroes.

The Indians being at this time from home I did not immediatly proceed to Fort Hunter, but waited for their Return. In the mean time many of the Indian women visited me at Albany, expressing the greatest pleasure at my arrival. In Easter Week I went to the Mohawks & was kindly received by Col. Johnson, a gentleman of the greatest influence & interests in these parts. I visited the few who were at home & promised to declare my intentions when the rest returned. I preached to a very large congregation on Sunday the 22nd. of Apr: & baptized three children one of which was an Indian Child. I waited at Albany till the 5th of June & then went up with the Interpreter of the Province; we were met by two of the principle Sachems, who in the name of the rest, congratulated me upon my arrival, expressed great thankfulness to the Society for sending them a Minister upon the conclusion of the Peace, promising they would use their endeavours to influence the Indians to be attentive to my instructions, & do all in their power to make my life agreeable.

These congratulatory expressions were very pleasing to me, & things seemed to appear with a promising aspect. But alas! I am sorry I'm obliged to say I find them universally degenerated. Since the war they are intirely given up to Drunkenness. Many seem to have lost all sense of religion, and the best are in a state of indifferency. However I find a good foundation laid by my worthy predecessor [Mr Barclay]. I hope God will succeed my endeavours to build thereon. My hopes are intirely fixed on the rising generation, the children are universally disposed to learn, & if we can lay a good foundation by the education of the youth, the conversion of the heathen will be very much facilitated to succeeding missionaries....

I can truly say I rejoice that there are any measures taken to instruct the Indians in our language, but can by no means approve of their making themselves popular by entering into the Society's labours. Therefore in justice, to the Ven: Society (who have always done their utmost to promote the conversion of these nations, & being satisfied that they would encourage this disposition in the Indians to learn English) I refused my consent to send the children, promising the Indians that I would acquaint the Society with their desire of having a schoolmaster. I am persuaded a Schoolmaster in these parts may do extensive good not only to the Indians but other of the inhabitants. The children here have no education, but the little they receive from their parents, & even many of them not able to read & very few who understand the English language. I would wish there was proper encouragement given for a young gentleman from Yale College to act in the capacity of a Schoolmaster, it would be very acceptable to the Indians, & as I'm obliged to be half my time at Albany in my absence he may still be carrying on the good work, & by learning their language & customs may hereafter be an instrument of promoting the Society's pious intention to the Indian Nations. In the mean time to encourage this good disposition in the Indians I act as Schoolmaster myself and every day I have near twenty Indian children to teach reading besides some of the young men who learn to write.

I preach to the Indians twice every Sunday by the help of an Interpreter whom I hire for that Purpose, & read most of our Liturgy to them myself in their own language. On Sunday the 24th of June I administred the holy Sacrament to 13 of the Indians, who seem to have preserved some sense of religion on their minds, & have behaved very soberly since.

Beside care of the Indians I have divine service and preach twice to the Garrison & other of the inhabitants who attend in the Indian Chapel. On Sunday the 8th of July I visited the upper Castle [Conajoharie] about 38 miles above Fort Hunter.

Here things have a better appearance, & I find some who are not so much addicted to drunkenness, which has been greatly prevented by a very pious Indian whose name is *Abraham*;[1] this Indian has for some time past intirely neglected his hunting in order to instruct his Brethren in the principles of Religion, & to keep up divine service among the aged people & children whilst the others are in the woods. He has likewise visited some of the upper Nations to instruct them; & seems intirely devoted to the interest of Religion. I mention this Indian because I apprehend some notice taken of his services, may have good effects.

While I was at this place the Indians received a belt of money from a popish priest settled at a place call'd Cadraghque [Cataraqui].[2] The substance of the message was to invite them to embrace the true religion, expressing a most tender concern at their being Hereticks, promising kind entertainment at his Habitation &c. The Mohawks refused compliance with the strongest intimation of resentment; I was quite pleased with their

---

[1] This was a brother of "King" Hendrick.
[2] Cataraqui or Fort Frontenac, the Indian and French names of Kingston, Ontario.

behaviour upon this occasion. I am informed by some of our Indians that he has made considerable impressions upon the *Onandagas* & many others in our alliance. I very much fear (if some measures are not taken to prevent it) that the French priests by their craft & policy will lead away most of the Indians into the French interest. Since the 5th of June I've baptized in y^s Branch of ye Mission 9 children, 3 of which are Indian Children. The number of the Mohawks is very much decreased within these few years, as will appear by the accounts transmitted by my Predecessors. The castle at Fort Hunter consists at present of 204, & the upper Castle of 214. This from the best information is chiefly owing to the Numbers who have gone over to the French Interest & settled in their territories.

I wish I could be more sanguine in my hopes of success, but the want of Missionaries & Schoolmaster; the opposition of the Romish priests; the ill examples of Christian professors; the Indians' strong propensions to strong liquors, are such impediments to this glorious work, as fills me with very dark apprehensions;...

May God in His Providence ever smile upon the Venr. Society to raise them generous benefactors to support them in this noble design is the fervent prayer of

Revd. Sir their

& your most obedient

& humbe. Servt.

JOHN OGILVIE.[1]

This letter was received some two months after a communication from Governor Clinton stating that Colonel Johnson suggested that an allowance should be made by the Society to the *sachem* Abraham—"a very honest, sincere, sensible old man...who has been of vast Service to the Welfare and Security of these Parts doing his utmost in keeping the Indians firm in their Friendship and Alliance to us". Johnson also recommended Abraham's son, Petrus Paulus, to be appointed as a salaried schoolmaster to the Mohawks which would "much engage his uncle Hendrick, who we are all sensible has been of the most material Service

---

[1] 'B' MSS. Vol. 18, No. 102.

during the late War, and is the chief leading Sachem among the Five Nations".[1] The Society accordingly granted a gratuity to Abraham and informed Mr Ogilvie that Petrus Paulus was to be appointed Schoolmaster under his supervision.[2]

A year later Mr Ogilvie sent the following letter to the Society:

Albany, August 7, 1751.

Revd. Sir,

I received your favour of the 27th of Octbr. with the greatest pleasure, & most lively sentiments of gratitude to the Venerable Society for their kind notice of this Mission.

I have informed Mr. Oël[3] and given him directions for drawing [his salary?] & put him into a method of instructing the Indians at Canijohare as far as his age & infirmities will admit.

I have directed Abraham to draw for his money & hope this benefaction to him will have a good effect. As to Petrus Paulus,[4] I never heard of such an Indian unless it be a son of Abraham's that has been dead some years since. I have not recommended any other Indian as Schoolmaster upon account of the strong inclination there seems at present in most of them to have their children in..:tructed in the English language. There might be a great deal of good done among them, if there was proper encouragement given for something of that nature.

The Government of Boston are sensible of this & are concerting a scheme for educating the Indian children upon their frontiers, & are lik'wise soliciting the Mohawks to relinquish their own habitations & settle in their Government. Our province in general

[1] S.P.G. Journal, Vol. 11, pp. 258–9.
[2] *Ibid.* pp. 299, 300.
[3] Rev. J. J. Oël had been appointed as Mr Ogilvie's assistant (cf. S.P.G. Journal, Vol. 12, p. 68).
[4] There is a curious discrepancy about Petrus Paulus. Ogilvie's statement is corroborated by the Rev. H. Barclay in a letter to the S.P.G. of 29 April 1751 in which he says he knows nothing about him as Abraham never had a son unless he adopted one after he (Barclay) left the Mohawk mission (cf. S.P.G. Journal, Vol. 12, p. 46). In a later letter Ogilvie asked for the appointment of one Paulus "instead of Petrus Paulus, who has been some time dead" (cf. S.P.G. Journal, Vol. 12, pp. 308–9). This Paulus, whose Indian name was Sahonwadie, was the son of "King" Hendrick (cf York Docs. Vol. vii, p. 112).

dislike the Indians' Removal as it would lead to divert the trade from us & leave our frontiers naked & defenceless in case of another War; but I sincerely wish they would express their dislike, by contributing generously to a scheme of the like nature in this Province. For my own part I am against the Indians going from hence upon no other reason than an apprehension that their coming to the knowledge of the unhappy divisions subsisting among the Protestants may so prejudice their minds as to render them a more easy prey to the craft of Popish Missionaries.

I am informed that Sr. Peter Warren[1] has something under his direction for the education of some Mohawk children. I make no doubt Sr. Peter would chuse to have any thing of that kind under the direction of the Venr. Society & that the Indians should be instructed in their own country upon the frontiers of this Province. I can truly say I rejoice in any Measur's that have the least probability of promoting the conversion of the Gentiles tho' concerted & executed by the Dissenters but I must say I always desire to see the five nations under the patronage & direction of the Venr. Society.

I hope my letter of the 14th of Apr. is safe come to hand since which nothing of moment has occurred. I am Revd. Sir with fervent prayers for the Venr. Society & sentiments of the most perfect regard to you,

> Your very affectionate Servant & Brother,
>
> JOHN OGILVIE.[2]

Meanwhile the French activities which had necessarily been prevented from becoming open hostilities by the Treaty of 1748 were still directed towards the subversion of the Six Nations from their English alliance. The Abbé Piquet, a clever and far-sighted schemer known among the French as the "Apostle of the Iroquois", had recently founded a mission station called La Présentation at the junction of the Oswegatchie and the St Lawrence. From its situation at a point where the rapids ceased and navigation was open to Lake Ontario the new station had an obvious strategic importance by its command of the main river. The new mission was intended to serve as a means for winning over the Onon-

---

[1] Colonel Johnson's uncle (*vide* p. 62 *supra*).
[2] 'B' MSS. Vol. 19, No. 72.

daga, Cayuga and Seneca tribes who were believed to be more amenable to French influence than the Mohawks. In the course of several months La Présentation became transformed into a fort with a garrison of twenty soldiers and five pieces of ordnance.

In 1752 Piquet suggested raising a war-party of 4000 Canadian and Iroquois Indians which was to expel the English from the Ohio and attack the Cherokee tribe on the Virginian border. Fortunately this project did not materialize although it received the sanction of the French Governor. Nevertheless Piquet had in the previous year visited all the French outposts on Lake Ontario and obtained many Indian recruits. His object was to persuade the Iroquois to attack the English fort at Oswego on the south-eastern shore of Ontario by persuading the tribesmen that Oswego was an encroachment on the part of the English which would be used in time to come as a means of taking possession of the Iroquois territory. With the exception of Oswego all the forts round Ontario belonged to the French, the key position being Fort Niagara (built in 1726) which controlled the passage from Ontario to Erie and the Great Lakes beyond. It was therefore essential for the French to keep Niagara in their hands, and in 1751 the French Governor[1] erected a new fortified trading post at the farther end of the Niagara portage.[2] On receipt of this information Governor Clinton wrote a strong representation pointing out that this was an encroachment on the country of the Iroquois who were declared "subjects of Great Britain" by the Treaty of Utrecht.[3] The French Governor, however, refused to demolish the post, and denied that the Iroquois were English subjects.[4] There the matter

[1] The Marquis de la Jonquière.
[2] *New York Docs.* Vol. VI, p. 608.
[3] *Ibid.* p. 711. The question of the boundaries of the Iroquois territory had in fact never been settled either at the Peace of Utrecht or the Treaty of Aix-la-Chapelle. A joint commission at Paris had endeavoured to find a solution following the latter Treaty, but their efforts proved abortive.
[4] *Ibid.* pp. 731 *et seq.*

rested as Clinton did not feel able to back his demands by force unless and until war should again break out between the parent countries.

In the meantime the Society's mission to the Mohawks was undergoing a difficult phase owing to the resumption of the sale of rum to the Indians. In July 1752 Mr Ogilvie reported that:

Their strong & still growing propension for spirituous liquors, proves the most fatal obstruction to the Progress of the glorious Gospel of Christ, among that unhappy people. The disolute lives of the greatest part of those who converse with them upon account of trade, seem to have a very ill-effect upon yᵣ Minds, & I fear in a great measure influences them to think that Christianity is not of that importance that the Missionaries represent it of.

The generality of the Professors of Christianity, who have any considerable dealings with the Indians by yᵣ conduct give the most convincing proof that they regard them only as meer Machines to promote yᵣ secular interest; & not as yᵣ fellow creatures, rational & immortal agents, equally dear to the Father of spirits, capable of the same Improv'ments in Virtue, & the purchase of the same precious Blood; in short, *the salt of the earth hath* (in these parts) *lost its savour*; & [there is] not one thing that I can mention, as a circumstance of encouragement, in this momentous undertaking. I have made use of everything that had the least probability of being serviceable to the main end. I've only been (as it were) rowing against [the] stream, & have not been able to stem the torrent by reason of the extravagant quantities of rum, that is [*sic*] daily sold to those poor creatures.

It is impossible for me to express, in a proper manner the shocking effects of strong drink upon these people; they commit the most barbarous actions; they grow quite mad, they attempt to burn yᵣ own little hutts, threaten the lives of yᵣ wives & children, abuse yᵣ neighbours & cast off all signs of regard to every body. Upon these occasions I shun them, & as soon as they are sober, I severely reprove them, & set before them, the fatal consequences of this detestable vice; they seem penitent and promise amendment but upon the first opportunity fall to the same extravagancies.

As I am now entered into the married state,[1] my removal from

---

[1] Mr Ogilvie had married, as his first wife, Susanna Symes, of New York. He subsequently married Margaret, widow of Philip Philipse, of New York.

Albany to Fort Hunter is attended with more trouble and expence but notwithstanding I go punctual as usual. I stayed with them throughout the last winter, & proceed regularly with the same method of instruction, that I informed the Society of before.

Since my letter of the 7th of August, I've baptized at the Mohawks, 17 white, 18 Indians, & 2 negroe Children.

Mr. Oël by letter informs me, that from Jany. yᵉ 1rst. 1751 to June yᵉ 25th he had baptized 50 children white and Indians, and that on the 20th of May, he administred the holy Communion to 29 persons; 5 Indian men, 20 Indian women & 4 white persons. I returned to Albany about Easter & no sooner had I left them, but they fell to drinking in yᵉ excess, barbarously murdered a worthy woman, the wife of a Sachem, who officiates as reader in Church, during my absence. I tremble for the consequences of this fact because it was committed by an Indian of a considerable large family, & no doubt, agreeable to yᵉ constant custom in such cases, the life of the murderer will be pursued, & so we shall be constantly perplexed with the broils of these families. I have encouraged them to attention by little gratuities, which with the charge of paying the Interpreter & other contingent expenses, obliges me to be very frugal in my family, or I should soon run behind in my interest.

I had almost forgot the death of a great Sachem known by the name of *Seth* a Communicant of yᵉ Church, which was likewise the effect of a drunken frolick; for in his intemperance he fell into the fire, & was burnt to that degree, as in a short time proved the cause of his death. I cannot well express the Sentiments I feel, while I am writing these unpromising facts; & my only relief is the promise of God that the Kingdom of this world, shall once become the Kingdom of God and Christ; & tho' so many benevolent attempts to this purpose have failed, yet we have sufficient reason to expect that the purposes of divine grace shall be accomplished in the bringing in the heathen world [to] the fellowship of the Gospel.

As to the Church of Albany, [there is] no great alteration only that I've received five persons to the Communion & baptized 22 white & 4 black children & two adult negro women, who had passed thro' a regular course of catechetical instruction, & brought a Certificate of yʳ good behaviour from yʳ masters.

The good people of yᵉ Church in this place, have in the last year rebuilt the Church which was very fallen to decay; & by the generous contribution of his Excellency Govr. Clinton, & the Honle. Council & most of the principle inhabitants of Albany, have erected a handsome steeple, & purchased a very good Bell & other ornaments of the Church, so that the publick offices of Religion are attended with circumstances of Dignity & Solemnity....[1]

In his next communication (July 1753) to the Society Mr Ogilvie reported that he had obtained the services of the Mohawk Paulus (Sahonwadie, a son of "King" Hendrick) to teach the Indian children at Fort Hunter and to act as clerk and lay-reader during Mr Ogilvie's visits to Albany. On these occasions Mr Ogilvie "preach'd twice every Lord's Day besides a Catechetical Lecture on Frydays", and baptized several Europeans and a number of negro slaves from the neighbouring farms.[2]

Meanwhile the antagonism between French and English had received an added stimulus by the erection of the French forts at Presqu'isle on Lake Erie and Fort le Bœuf some fifteen miles farther south, and the seizure of an English trading post at Venango in the same vicinity. Robert Dinwiddie, the Lieutenant-Governor of Virginia,[3] immediately sent a letter of expostulation to the French commander by the hands of a young major of militia named George Washington. The French officers received Washington courteously but made it clear that they had no intention of evacuating the post, saying that "it was their absolute design to take possession of the Ohio, and by G——, they would do it".[4] On the return journey Washington narrowly escaped death while floating down the Alleghany on a raft. The river was full of floating ice and he was jerked into the stream and only saved himself by catching hold of a log as he was being swept away. Had this accident terminated differently, it might well have changed the subsequent history of America.

As a result of the French defiance, Dinwiddie sent a force

[1] 'B' MSS. Vol. 20, No. 55.

[2] S.P.G. Journal, Vol. 12, pp. 307–9.

[3] The Governor, Lord Albemarle, remained in England, his appointment being a sinecure.

[4] Washington's Journal, quoted by Parkman, *Montcalm and Wolfe*, Vol. 1, p. 139.

of several hundred men under the command of Colonel Joshua Fry and Washington to occupy the valley of the Ohio. In the meantime the French had occupied the English trading post at the junction of the Ohio and the Alleghany, which they renamed Fort Duquesne.[1] On hearing this news Washington advanced to within 40 miles of the French position and built a fort at Great Meadows. From there he attacked and defeated a small advance detachment under Ensign Jumonville, but was himself attacked in turn by a strong French force and compelled to surrender his post (July 1754). He was, however, permitted to march out at the head of his troops with the honours of war on condition that no other English fort should be built on the Ohio for the period of a year.

The failure of Washington's expedition had an evil result on the English relations with the Indians. Unlike the Six Nations, the tribes of the Ohio valley had no binding alliance with either of the hostile powers, but were prepared to co-operate with whichever side should prove the strongest. Thenceforward the French were able to win them over as their allies and thus commanded the allegiance of hordes of savages from Acadia to the Mississippi, the Ohio, and the Illinois. Had it not been for the English alliance with the Iroquois, now firmly cemented by the far-reaching influences of the Society's missionaries and the personality of William Johnson, there would have been a grave danger of the French overrunning our northern colonies. Such a catastrophe would, moreover, have automatically precluded the future conquest of Canada.

As a result of the now open hostility between France and England in America, the English Government decided to send two regiments to Virginia, although the two countries were still nominally at peace. The command was given to Major-General Braddock, an elderly protégé of the Duke of Cumberland, who had entered the Army in 1710. A counter-expedition was organized by France, consisting of a fleet of

[1] So called after the Governor of Canada.

eighteen warships under Admiral de la Motte and six infantry battalions commanded by Baron Dieskau, a German who had served under Marshal Saxe. A new Governor, the Marquis de Vaudreuil, accompanied the expedition.

On his arrival at Hampton Roads, Virginia, in February 1755, Braddock convened a council of local governors and it was decided to send four expeditions—three of colonial forces to the north against Niagara, Crown Point, and Acadia (Nova Scotia), and one to the south against Fort Duquesne. This latter expedition consisted of the two English regiments and a body of 450 Virginian provincials; it was commanded by Braddock, who appointed George Washington as one of his aides-de-camp.

The story of Braddock's terrible reverse is well known. Relying on his knowledge of how *European* campaigns should be conducted, and discounting the advice of Washington and other provincial officers as to the methods of American warfare, the general marched into an ambush and his troops were overwhelmed by the French and their Indian allies. Braddock himself received his death-wound in the mêlée, and the remnants of his ill-starred force retreated in the utmost disorder to Fort Cumberland. But for the bravery and resource of Washington and the Virginians who covered the retreat, it is probable that the English regiments would have been annihilated.

In the meantime plans for the expedition to Crown Point had been proceeding. By agreement between the local legislatures a force of over 3000 provincials was raised and placed under the command of William Johnson. In the last week of June 1755 (a fortnight before Braddock's disaster) Johnson held a conference at his own house with the Six Nations to enlist their aid in the expedition.[1] Mr Ogilvie attended at Johnson's request and among the interpreters was a certain Daniel Claus who afterwards married Johnson's younger daughter Mary. After three days of interminable speech-

---

[1] *New York Docs.* Vol. VI, pp. 964 *et seq.*

PLATE IX

"King" Hendrick and Sir William Johnson
(Statue in the State Park, Lake George)

making, Johnson made this impassioned appeal to the *sachems*:

I am ordered to go with a considerable number of your Brethren from the neighbouring Provinces over whom I am appointed to the chief Command with great guns and other implements of war, to drive the French from their encroachments on your hunting grounds in this Province; if you will treat me as your Brother, Go with me—My war kettle is on the Fire, my Canoe is ready to put in the water, my Gun is loaded, my sword by my side, and my Axe sharpened. I desire and expect you will now take up the Hatchet and join us, your Brethren, against all our Enemies. By this large Belt I call upon you to rise up like honest and Brave Men and join your Brethren and me against our Common Enemy, and by it I confirm the assurances I have given you.

With these words Johnson gave the war-belt to the *sachem* Abraham ("King" Hendrick's brother) and the conference broke up.[1]

On 8 September the main force of Johnson's army (numbering some 2000 troops) came up with the French near Lake George towards the southern end of Lake Champlain. The French force under Baron Dieskau mustered about 1000 whites and 700 Indians, but although inferior in numbers to the English colonists they underrated their enemy, remembering how easily Braddock had been defeated. At the beginning of the action Johnson made a serious error by sending two detachments of 500 men to take the French in flank and rear. "King" Hendrick at once pointed out the mistake by demonstrating the weakness of a divided force, and the detachments were then united into one.[2] The main force of the colonists was now posted behind a rough barricade and a few pieces of cannon were hauled into position to command the approach. In the meantime the flanking detachment had marched into an ambush and had been mowed down by scores. Hendrick, mounted on Johnson's charger, led his warriors in an endeavour to assist the colonists, but his horse was shot under

---

[1] *New York Docs.* Vol. VI, pp. 973, 974.
[2] Parkman, *Montcalm and Wolfe*, Vol. I, p. 312.

him and he was bayoneted before he could rise.[1] For a few moments there was a panic but some of the Mohawks and a small body sent by Johnson held the enemy in check until the survivors of the flanking party could reach the barricade. Encouraged with the success of their ambush the French advanced against Johnson's main body but were met with a storm of musketry and grape which did terrible execution. They fell back to the cover of the trees and kept up a well-sustained fire for several hours. "It was the most awful day my eyes beheld, there seemed to be nothing but thunder and lightning and perpetuall pillars of smoke", wrote Surgeon Williams to his wife.[2] During the terrific firing Johnson was wounded and Dieskau was shot in the leg and taken prisoner. This was the turning point of the battle and the French, losing heart at the loss of their commander, fled in disorder.

The following letter, written by one of the English gunners to his cousin, gives a spirited account of the action which may warrant its inclusion here:

Lake George 10 Sep[r] 1755.

Dear Cousin,

On the sixth one of the Sachems[3] dreamed a dream, and ordered prayers to be read (a prayer was read in the Indian Camp), and the Sachems ordered no person to go out on the left of the Camp, which was obeyed. On the seventh at 4. P.M. three Mohawks came in who went [as] Scouts, and told us a great body of Men was come from Crown point. A Council of War was held, and orders was [sic] given for 1000 Men to be ready to scour the Woods next morning, which was accordingly done, under the command of Coll: Williams, Lieu[t] Coll: Whiting and our Mohawks, with King Hendrick, Capt[s] Farrell, Stoddart, McKinnis. About 3 or 4. miles from the Camp we begun the attack which was about the hour of eight in the morning, they fought and retreated to the camp, when the French thought to go thro' all, but was [sic] much surprised with our Artillery which made Lanes, Streets and Alleys thro' their army; they fought the front two hours, and then came on the right wing, which was commanded by Coll: Tidcomb, and

[1] *New York Docs.* Vol. VI, p. 1008.
[2] Quoted by Parkman, *Montcalm and Wolfe*, Vol. I, p. 317.
[3] Probably Abraham.

attacked two hours there, and back to the front again and thought
to come in on the rear of our army; but the General perceiving
danger, ordered me to throw some shells, which accordingly I
did, and some 32 pounders, which soon made them shift berths;
they retreated in sad disorder, and with shouts of Victory we got
the day. About 700 French and Indians got back to their old
place of encampment, where they met with Capt^ns Magines and
Folsom with a party of 170 Men, and after an attack of about two
hours intirely defeated the Enemy. We had a Muster, and find our
loss not to exceed 170 and 30 wounded. Our Genl is wounded,
but thank God, not mortal, both him and his Aid-de-Camp with
other officers distinguished themselves by their bravery. The loss
on the other side was computed to be near 700. We have the head
General prisoner and its thought mortally wounded and his Aid-
de-Camp. Their Major-Genl was killed,[1] he was the same who
commanded at Ohio. His last words [were] "fight on boys, this
is Johnson not Braddock". They say they lost four Capt^ns, and
how many other Officers they cannot tell. We lost the following
brave Officers

> Coll: Williams
> Coll: Tidcomb
> Cap^n of Indians and King Hendrick
> Farrel, Stoddard, McKinnis. Provincials.
> Capt Tice.
> Captn Maginnis in the pains of death

On their retreat they killed what prisoners they had taken and
scalped them. We found the poor creatures tyed to each other by
threes and fours. Our Blacks[2] behaved better than the Whites.
My love to all friends, excuse haste, we are buysied burying the
dead; I wish we had fresh supplys before its too late. I am ettc.

P.S. we have various accounts about the numbers we engaged
with, but by the Captn of Pioniers I am told for a certainty 700
Indians 1250 Whites.[3]

The result of this victory (for which Johnson was rewarded
with a baronetcy) had little beyond a moral effect on the
general military situation. Johnson made no effort to follow
up his advantage and the French retreated to Fort Ticon-

---

[1] Jacques Legardeur de Saint-Pierre who commanded the Indian
allies in the battle.

[2] I.e. Indians.　　　　　[3] *New York Docs.* Vol. VI, p. 1005.

deroga on Lake Champlain. Crown Point, the original objec-
tive of the expedition, had not been captured, and the proposed
expedition against Niagara (under the command of Governor
Shirley of Massachusetts) had been abandoned on the arrival
of French reinforcements.

By the death of Hendrick England lost her most powerful
and influential ally among the Six Nations.

There was a time, in our settlements [wrote the historiographer
of the Iroquois], when there was a moral force in the name of
King Hendrick and his Mohawks which had an electric effect; and
at the time he died, his loss was widely and deeply felt and
lamented, even in Great Britain....As a diplomatist and orator,
he was greatly distinguished, and divided the palm only with his
brother Abraham of pious memory, who was exclusively devoted
to civil pursuits...,From the New York Mercury, under date of
September 22, 1755 [i.e. a fortnight after the battle of Lake
George] I glean the following additional particulars. The whole
body of the Iroquois in alliance with England were greatly exas-
perated against the French and their Indians, more particularly
on account of the death of "the famous Hendrick, a renowned
warrior among the Mohocks [*sic*], and one of their Sachems or
kings. His son on being told that his father was killed, gave the
usual groan, and suddenly putting his hand on his left breast,
swore that his father was still alive in that place, and stood there
in his son. It was with the utmost difficulty Gen. Johnson
prevented the fury of their resentment taking place on the body
of the French General, Dieskau, whom they would have sacrificed
without ceremony, but for the interference of Gen. Johnson."[1]

Hendrick's son here mentioned was Paulus (Sahonwadie),
who, as we have seen, had been appointed the Society's
schoolmaster two years before. He had accompanied the
Mohawks on the expedition in his former role of a warrior
and with the dramatic instinct of his race had thus proclaimed
himself the avenger of his dead father. Paulus succeeded
Hendrick as *sachem* of Conajoharie,[2] the "Upper Castle" of
the Mohawks. Some years afterwards he was seen by

---

[1] Schoolcraft, *Notes on the Iroquois, or Contributions to American
History, Antiquities, and General Ethnology*, pp. 414 *et seq.*, Albany,
1847.   [2] Cf. *New York Docs.* Vol. VII, p. 255.

Mrs Grant,[1] the authoress of the *Memoirs of an American Lady*, who thus described her interview:

It was the fortune of the writer of these memoirs...to see that great warrior and faithful ally of the British Crown, the redoubted King Hendrick, then sovereign of the Five Nations, splendidly arrayed in a suit of light blue, made in an antique mode, and trimmed with silver lace, which was probably an *heir loom in the family*, presented to his *father* by his good ally and sister, the female king of England.

It is obvious that Mrs Grant was in fact referring to Hendrick's *son*, the error having evidently arisen owing to her having written her memoirs "unassisted", as she says, "by written memorials", more than thirty years after she returned to Scotland from America. The "female king"—as the Indians themselves called her—was Queen Anne, to whom Hendrick had been presented when he visited England in 1710.

[1] Mrs Grant was born in 1755, the year of Hendrick's death. She left America in 1768 at the age of 13 and published her *Memoirs* in 1808 (cf. *Dict. Nat. Biog.*).

CHAPTER V
THE CONFLICT FOR CANADA
(ii) (1756–1760)

MEANWHILE Mr Ogilvie, who we last mentioned at Sir William Johnson's conference with the Six Nations, had returned to his mission, although he was very anxious to go with the expedition to Crown Point as the Mohawks' chaplain. In a letter of 25 December (1755) he gave an account of his activities, and requested the Society to confirm the appointment of Hendrick's son, Paulus, as schoolmaster. (The original letter and some of Mr Ogilvie's other letters are unfortunately no longer extant, and the résumé thereof in the Society's Journal is therefore given):

...Dec.ʳ 25ᵗʰ 1755, acknowledging the receipt of yᵉ Secretary's Letter of May yᵉ 2ᵈ, & acquainting, that his best Endeavours have not been altogether unsuccessfull; many of the Indians of both Castles seem to have a serious & habitual sense of Religion; they regularly attend Divine Worship & participate frequently of the Lord's Supper, and tho' at this season they are all out upon yᵉ Hunt several of yᵉ principals come near 60 miles to communicate at Christmas; there are now between both castles about 50 Communicants. Mʳ Ogilvie wrote to yᵉ Society the 25ᵗʰ of June 1755, acquainting them that Genˡ Johnson was then holding a treaty preparatory to yᵉ intended Expeditions,[1] that he was like to engage a considerable number of Warriors in our favour, that Mʳ Ogilvie himself was giving all yᵉ assistance he could for yᵉ publick good; & in the same Letter gave an account of yᵉ success of the School, & the diligence of Paulus in his Office, but is extreamly sorry to find that this Letter was never sent from New York, thro' the negligence of yᵉ person to whose care it was committed. Mʳ Ogilvie referrs to the Minutes of Indian Affairs transmitted to Lord Halifax,[2] a Worthy Member of the Society,

[1] I.e. of Braddock and Johnson.
[2] George Montague Dunk, 2nd Earl of Halifax. In 1748 he became President of the Lords of Trade. Halifax, Nova Scotia, founded in 1749 as a rival to Louisburg, was named after him.

to prove that he has not been remiss in his Duty. Of 12 principal men of our Mohawks which fell in the action at Lake George 6 were constant Communicants of ye Church. The Indians when they took the field were very desirous Mr Ogilvie should go out with them as their Chaplain, but as there was no provision for that purpose he was obliged to decline it; but Gen! Johnson says that Good Old Abraham performed Divine Service every morning & evening. From ye 28th of August 1754 to ye date of his Letter Mr Ogilvie had baptized in Albany 49 White & 20 black Children, & received 4 new Communicants: at ye Mohawks he had baptized 30 white, & 18 Indian Children, & admitted 4 Indians to the Communion, who gave a very good Account of the Christian Faith. The Church at Albany is very much crouded, occasioned by Col! Dunbar's Regiment[1] posted there, so that there is a great deal of occasional Duty to do. Mr Ogilvie intends for ye Mohawks very soon, where he punctually performs his usual Duty, which consists of 4 different Services every Lord's day. Paulus is diligent in his Office as Schoolmaster; he teaches above 40 Children every day, several begin to read, & some to write: they learn ye Church Catechism, & have made a considerable Progress in Psalmody. The Indians of ye lower castle have signified their desire to have a Schoolmaster, as they formerly had; & Mr Ogilvie thinks it would be of considerable service, as there are a large number of promising Children; if this is agreeable to the Society, he would be glad to have no particular Indians named to that Office, only ye same Salary that is granted to ye upper Castle, to be paid by Mr Ogilvie (or any one ye Society shall think proper) to ye person who duly executes that Service; Mr Ogilvie's reason for this is, that he knows an Indian well qualified for this Service, but he is much addicted to strong drink, & therefore should be employed only upon condition he keeps himself sober. The six united Nations seem at present to be in good temper not withstanding the Craft & Intrigues of ye French, who by their Priests are extreamly industrious at this critical conjuncture of Affairs. Gen! Johnson is indefatigable, & no doubt will prevail on numbers of them to join us next Season; Mr Ogilvie is much obliged to ye General for ye countenance he gives him. Last

[1] Colonel Thomas Dunbar, of the 48th Foot, had accompanied Braddock's expedition and was left to follow on with the rearguard. After the defeat Dunbar destroyed the remaining artillery and stores and retreated to Fort Cumberland. In 1756 he was made Lieutenant-Governor of Gibraltar.

Summer Mr Ogilvie had a good deal of fatigue & Charge, as ye Indians were constantly passing thro' Albany; he had ye care of providing for all ye War-parties of Indians that went thro' that place, by order & at ye Expence of Gen! Johnson, which he performed to ye Gen!^s entire satisfaction. Mr Ogilvie adds that he pleases himself with the hopes of seeing (after these disputes are ended) an effectual Door opened to introduce Missionaries into most of ye Castles of ye six Nations, for nothing will contribute more to make them firm friends than uniting them to Us by ye sacred ties of Christianity.[1]

The writer's reference towards the end of this letter to Sir William's "entire satisfaction" is corroborated by a letter of Johnson's to the Lords of Trade, dated 6 March 1756:

I beg the liberty to mention to your Lordships the Reverend Mr Ogilvie, Missionary to the Mohawk Indians, who has upon all occasions done everything in his Power for the promotion of true Religion; this Gentleman's Salary both for this place [i.e. Fort Johnson] and the City of Albany is very inconsiderable; some further Encouragement to him by some Addition to his Sallary [*sic*], would be of Service to the common Interest, as it would enable him to proceed in his mission with greater Spirit, & to support the Expences that must attend the keeping up of common Hospitality among so mercenary a people.[2]

On 18 May the "War of Outposts", which had now lasted for nearly two years in America, was placed on a recognized footing by England's formal declaration of hostilities. New plans were set on foot by the energetic Governor Shirley for an attack on Lake Ontario and the important post of Ticonderoga on Lake Champlain. But before the expeditions were ready, the English Government intervened by appointing Lord Loudon as Commander-in-Chief of the American forces.[3] A man of hot temper, always appearing ready to

---

[1] S.P.G. Journal, Vol. 13, pp. 182–5.

[2] *New York Docs.* Vol. VII, p. 43.

[3] John Campbell, 4th Earl of Loudon (1705–82), had raised the 54th Regiment for suppression of the '45 Rebellion. On 17 February 1756 he was appointed Captain-General and Governor-in-Chief of Virginia, and a month after Commander-in-Chief in America. He arrived at New York on 23 July.

advance but never starting, Loudon was satirized by Benjamin
Franklin as being "like St George on the sign-posts: always
on horse-back but never rides on".[1] Loudon was no match
for the new French commander, the Marquis de Montcalm,
who had arrived at Quebec with reinforcements of two
battalions of infantry in May. In August Montcalm captured
and burned Oswego, and a year later he attacked Fort William
Henry at the southern extremity of Lake George. The commander, Lieutenant-Colonel Monro, was forced to surrender,
a large number of his garrison being prostrate with smallpox.
A terrible tragedy followed the capitulation: the Indian
auxiliaries got out of hand, and despite the efforts of Montcalm
and his officers to stop them, barbarously murdered numbers
of men, women and children in their mad lust for blood.[2]

Towards the end of this disastrous year Mr Ogilvie sent
a further communication to the Society, which is thus
recorded in the Journal:

From the Rev. John Ogilvie (undated) [Read at a meeting of the
S.P.G. held on Dec. 17th, 1756]...he writes, that immediatly
after Christmas [1755] he went to the Mohawks & continued there
till the Sunday before Easter, proceeding in his usual method of
Instruction, & in the last half year preceding he had baptized
10 White & 9 Indian Children, two of which were the Children of
the famous Indian half-King[3] who distinguished himself so much
in the fatal Expedition under Gen! Braddock—he is now settled
with his Relations & family at the Mohawks to the number of
40 Persons, some of them Christians & most of them well disposed
to the Christian Religion. Early in the Spring about 140 of those
persons inhabiting the Frontiers of New Jersey came up to ye
Mohawks—these poor Creatures were intirely uninstructed in
Religion, tho' many of them speak the English Language, &

[1] Quoted by Sir J. G. Bourinot in *Canada*, p. 237.
[2] A detailed account of the massacre is given by Parkman,
Montcalm and Wolfe, Vol. I, pp. 519 *et seq.*
[3] The half-King, *alias* Scarouady, a chief of the Ohio Indians,
was with Washington at Great Meadows in 1754 (cf. *New York
Docs.* Vol. VII, p. 270). I have been unable to discover in what
manner he distinguished himself in General Braddock's expedition
as mentioned by Ogilvie.—AUTHOR.

Mr Ogilvie will endeavour to instruct them. Mr Ogilvie says he has almost more Duty at Albany than he is able to do, by reason of the great number of Strangers & Soldiers quartered there, he performs three Services on Sunday, as the Church will not contain every body at one time; he has baptized 16 White & 6 Negro Children, & 2 Adult Negroes, at Albany, since Christmas last. At this time (Mr Ogilvie adds) he finds it hard to support his Family as every thing is as dear again as it was, tho' he is King's Chaplain at Albany[1] with 50£ Sterling P. annum upon which there are considerable deductions; if by any means he could get his Salary increased to the same Value with that at Boston, Viz^t 100£ P. annum, it would enable him in a great measure to support the unavoidable expences he is at in this important Mission; it is mere necessity (he says) compells him to mention this, for he has had no Assistance from his Parishioners, who are not indeed able to help him. There is at present a great call for Comon prayer books, & Mr Ogilvie would be glad of some Copies of the Soldiers' Monitor, & some practical Tracts for the use of the Hospital, as the Grand Hospital of the Army is fixed at Albany, & he constantly attends it & he adds that the School Master is diligent in his Office.[2]

In recognition of his services the Society gave Mr Ogilvie a gratuity of £30 "in consideration of his great Labours... & to encourage him to persevere in them".[3]

Some months later Mr Ogilvie was given a chaplain's commission in the Royal American Regiment (a new corps which had been raised in the colonies with English officers), as appears from his next letter:

...June 25th 1757, in which he writes, that ye Indian Affairs in General have taken a most unfavourable turn, but not withstanding ye danger he has still visited ye Mohocks [*sic*]; he was there ye whole Month of Aug^st & returned in Sepr to officiate to ye Garrison at Albany, which was very numerous & had no Chaplain: he went up again in Jan^y & staid 'till March, but bad Example, frequent use of Strong Drink, & their excursions at this time, take

[1] The chaplaincy to the troops at Albany appears to have been conjoined with the rectory. It was so held by the Rev. Henry Barclay and his father before him.
[2] S.P.G. Journal, Vol. 13, pp. 202–4.
[3] *Ibid.*

off their attention to Religion; in yᵉ last year Mʳ Ogilvie baptized in this part of his Mission 25 White & 16 Indian Children, & 2 Adult Indians. The Congregation at Albany is numerous, occasioned by yᵉ great number of Merchants & others who follow yᵉ Army; he continues to have 3 Services on Sundays, that all Ranks of people may have yᵉ benefit of Divine Worship; he administered yᵉ Communion on Christmas Day to 70 Persons, & on Easter Day to 60, & had baptized in this City of Albany last year 89 White & 10 Negro Children. And yᵉ Earl of Loudon observing Mʳ Ogilvie's daily calls to officiate to yᵉ Army was pleased to give him a Commission as one of the Chaplains of yᵉ Royal American Regiment; Mʳ Ogilvie hopes this will be agreeable to yᵉ Society, & that they will indulge him in holding it, so long as it interferes not with yᵉ Duty of his Mission.[1]

Meanwhile political events of the first importance to America were taking place in England. In November 1756 an accumulation of disasters which included the loss of Minorca, Braddock's defeat, Surajah Dowlah's capture of Calcutta and the unspeakable horrors of the "Black Hole", forced the Duke of Newcastle to resign. He was succeeded by the Duke of Devonshire, with William Pitt (the virtual Prime Minister) as Leader of the House of Commons. But owing to the dislike of the old King (George II) for Pitt and the eagerness of the Duke of Cumberland for the formation of a new ministry before he left for Hanover to take over the command of the Electoral forces, Pitt was suddenly dismissed from office in the following April. For the next eleven weeks no ministry was appointed until at the end of June the King found himself forced by popular clamour to recall Pitt. George insisted, however, on reappointing Newcastle as the titular Premier, the "Great Commoner" Pitt being made Secretary of State, with supreme control of the war and foreign affairs. For the next four years Pitt's genius, in the words of a great historian, "made England the first country in the world".[2]

It was America which first claimed Pitt's attention: the

[1] S.P.G. Journal, Vol. 14, pp. 6, 7.
[2] Macaulay, *Essays*, Vol. II, p. 198.

recapture of Louisburg and the reduction of Ticonderoga and Fort Duquesne, which would place the conquest of Canada within his reach, were his immediate objectives. Pitt's first move was to recall Loudon in favour of Major-General James Abercromby,[1] the next in seniority, under whom was Brigadier Lord Howe, an able and experienced officer, who had proved his ability in several minor expeditions on the Canadian frontier.[2] Abercromby was given the command of the Ticonderoga expedition, while the attack on Louisburg was entrusted to the newly promoted Major-General Amherst,[3] assisted by Brigadiers Whitmore, Lawrence and Wolfe, and a fleet under Admiral Boscawen.

Early in July (1758) Abercromby and Howe advanced on Ticonderoga, but unhappily Howe was killed at the first encounter. His death was the prelude to disaster, for without his advice Abercromby was almost helpless. The French held an unassailable position defended with barricades against which Abercromby ordered a frontal attack. The result was a hopeless failure followed by a disorderly retreat.

Meanwhile on 8 June the attack on Louisburg had been begun by a brilliant landing of the troops from the fleet led by Brigadier Wolfe, and on the 25th the town was invested. For the next four weeks the English kept up a continuous bombardment and on 26 July the garrison surrendered. The reduction of Louisburg gave England the key to the St Lawrence and made possible Pitt's great project of capturing Quebec.

---

[1] Abercromby had been sent to America in 1756 to take over from Governor Shirley before Lord Loudon arrived.

[2] George Augustus, 3rd Viscount Howe; he was a brother of General (William) Lord Howe, Commander-in-Chief during the first part of the American Revolution, and of Admiral (Richard) Earl Howe.

[3] Sir Jeffrey, afterwards Baron, Amherst, K.B. (1717–97). Served at Dettingen and Fontenoy and (on the Duke of Cumberland's staff) at Lauffeld and Hastenbeck. Promoted Lieutenant-Colonel of the 15th Regiment in 1756. In 1776 he received a Barony, and was made a Field-Marshal in 1796 (cf. *Dict. Nat. Biog.*).

In the meantime the expedition against Fort Duquesne
had set out at the end of June. The command was given to
Brigadier John Forbes, an able Scotch soldier, who was
accompanied by Washington, now Colonel of the Virginia
Regiment. As a preliminary to the campaign Forbes believed
it essential to obtain the alliance (or at least the neutrality) of
the Indians of the Ohio Valley. To accomplish this important
undertaking he was fortunate in securing the services of a
Moravian missionary, Christian Frederic Post, who had for
some years past gained the confidence of the tribes. That
Post was no ordinary character is shown by his absolute dis-
regard of personal safety. Having held a conference with three
Delaware chiefs he was obliged to go with them to Fort
Duquesne itself where he put forward his proposals to the
other chiefs in the presence of the French garrison. On his
arrival the French immediately demanded that he should be
handed over to them, but this the Indians refused, and bade
him stay close to their camp-fire. The brave missionary (to
use his own words):

Stuck to the fire as if I had been chained there. On the next
day the Indians, with a great many French officers, came out to
hear what I had to say. The officers brought with them a table,
pens, ink and paper. I spoke in the midst of them with a free
conscience, and perceived by their looks that they were not pleased
with what I said.[1]

As a result of Post's mission a great convention of English
and Indians including some envoys from the Iroquois met at
Easton and a formal treaty was made. Post was then sent to
convey the message of peace to the more distant tribes and to
invite their participation. In this he was successful and the
French had the mortification of seeing their former allies won
over by the English. Some years later Post became an S.P.G.
Catechist on the Moskito Shore (Bay of Honduras) where he
had long been engaged in preaching to the Indians and the

[1] Journal of C. F. Post, quoted by Parkman, *Montcalm and
Wolfe*, Vol. II, p. 152.

English. Here he served the Society for nearly twenty years and died in harness in 1785.[1]

Post's success with the Indian tribesmen broke the resistance of Fort Duquesne, and on 25 November Forbes' army found the place deserted and dismantled. A new fort was at once erected and a small garrison left to defend it. It was renamed Pittsburgh in honour of the great minister, and became the nucleus of the great manufacturing city which has since grown up on its site.

The French evacuation of Fort Duquesne, following upon the capture of Fort Frontenac by a force under Colonel John Bradstreet two months before, did much to counterbalance Abercromby's defeat at Ticonderoga. Thenceforward the valley of the Ohio was secured to England, and the English now held an important post on the north-eastern shore of Lake Ontario. Although Fort Niagara still remained in French hands its days were already numbered and in due course its conquest was to be added to the English laurels.

Meanwhile the Society's mission to the Mohawks had been greatly retarded by the effects of the war. Writing in May 1758, Mr Ogilvie reported:

...at present the Mohawk's River is a Scene of all the Horrors of War, and continued circumstances of the most horrid cruelty; notwithstanding which he [Mr Ogilvie] has visited his Mission, and stayed there two Months in the Winter; in which time he Preached to the Garrison at the German Flats and Preached and Administred the Sacrament at Canajohare; while he was there the French and Indians came down upon the Settlement, burnt three Houses, and Captivated the families: While things are in such a Melancholy state Mr. Ogilvie does not think it proper to appoint a Schoolmaster, and has done that Duty himself during his stay among them; in that part of his Mission since the 25th of June 1757 he has Baptized Twenty white and Sixteen Indian Children. As the Troops were taking the field and there was no Chaplain to Attend Six Regiments of Regulars (Except a Deputy Chaplain to the Highland Regiment) and as the Mohawk Indians are to take the

[1] S.P.G. Archives.

field M! Ogilvie was resolved to go with them, and he hopes the Society will approve of it. At Albany his Duty is Extensive, and he trusts not without good effect; he administred the Holy Sacrament to Ninety Persons at Christmas, to Sixty at Easter and has Baptized Seventy Six White and Seven Negro Children; he has likewise Baptized an Adult Negro and his Wife, after previous instruction, and admitted them to the Holy Sacrament. M! Ogilvie adds that M! Oël has in the last year Baptized 30 Children.[1]

As will be seen in this letter Mr Ogilvie had been confirmed in his appointment as Chaplain to the Royal American Regiment. It does not appear, however, whether Mr Ogilvie accompanied the regiment with Abercromby's disastrous expedition to Ticonderoga, although his intention to do so is expressed in his letter. When he next wrote to the Society (in the following February) Mr Ogilvie was at his mission, which had suffered from the absence of the schoolmaster Paulus who "was so taken up with War-parties that he had greatly neglected the Instruction of the children".[2] From this it is evident that Paulus was following in the footsteps of his famous father Hendrick, whose death had been a grievous loss to the Mohawk warriors.

The *annus mirabilis* of 1759 opened with Pitt's final scheme for the conquest of Canada. A combined naval and military force was to sail up the St Lawrence and capture Quebec, while a second army was to invade Canada by way of Ticonderoga and Crown Point, re-establish the evacuated fort at Oswego and unite with the victorious army at Quebec in the very centre of the enemy's country. If this could be accomplished successfully the British flag would inevitably be raised over Montreal and French rule in Canada would be extinguished.

With his genius for choosing the right man Pitt gave the command of the Quebec expedition to Vice-Admiral Charles Saunders and Wolfe, while Amherst, the Commander-in-Chief, was ordered to lead the attack on Central Canada. As

---

[1] S.P.G. Journal, Vol. 14, pp. 106, 107.
[2] *Ibid.* p. 186.

a preparatory measure Amherst decided to capture Niagara and to reinforce Pittsburg (Fort Duquesne), which as we have seen, had been left with a small garrison. The attempt on Niagara was accordingly entrusted to Brigadier Prideaux while the main army under Amherst advanced against Ticonderoga, Crown Point, and Montreal.

The fort at Niagara, garrisoned by some 600 men under Captain Pouchot, was situated a mile and a half below a second fort known as Little Niagara held by the half-breed Chabert de Joncaire and a number of Indians. This post being only built of wood was incapable of withstanding an assault and Joncaire therefore evacuated it and joined the main force at Niagara.

Brigadier Prideaux's force was augmented by over 900 Mohawk and Iroquois warriors led by Sir William Johnson. They were accompanied by Mr Ogilvie who had received the Society's approbation of his appointment as chaplain. The siege began early in July, but at the first bombardment a fragment of shell from one of his own guns killed Prideaux. The command devolved upon Johnson who carried on the attack with great energy. After two or three weeks the fort became untenable, but on 24 July some French reinforcements arrived from Presqu'isle. The French commander thereupon resolved to make a sortie. A hand-to-hand encounter followed in which the French were repulsed, and Pouchot had no alternative but to surrender the fort.[1] Two days later, on the night of 26 July, Amherst captured Ticonderoga, and on 1 August he occupied Crown Point which had been evacuated by the enemy.

Meanwhile the expedition under Saunders and Wolfe, which had successfully negotiated the passage up the St Lawrence, had come to a virtual standstill before Quebec. On 31 July Wolfe's army had sustained a severe repulse at the falls of Montmorency, and the French Governor Vaudreuil had written that he had no more anxiety about the safety of

---

[1] A detailed account of the operations will be found in *Montcalm and Wolfe*, Vol. II, pp. 252–8.

the city.[1] For the next six weeks the army lay inactive and
Wolfe himself, worn out with anxiety and ill-health, became
dangerously ill towards the end of August. The problem which
confronted him appeared to be wellnigh insuperable. Quebec
stands on a rocky promontory overlooking the St Lawrence.
The city's fortifications had been greatly strengthened for
some years back and were now guarded by 14,000 men. Of
these some 4000 lay entrenched on high ground extending
six miles from the St Charles River (to the south-east of the
city) to the place where the glittering cataract of the Montmorency cascades into the river far below. Directly beneath
Quebec the French had placed large floating batteries in the
St Lawrence, and above the city several miles of precipitous
cliffs overlooking the river gave it a further natural protection
from attack. The only solution seemed to lie in the possibility
of scaling the Heights of Abraham above the city, which
would compel the French army to give battle. As is well
known this was achieved by the finding of the narrow winding
path leading from the Anse du Foulon (now known as
Wolfe's Cove) to the summit of the Heights.

The accounts of the discovery of the ever-famous pathway
have been variously described. According to some authorities
Wolfe himself first saw it while surveying the cliffs through
his telescope from the opposite shore of the St Lawrence,
while the biographer of Major Robert Stobo (who had been
given as a hostage five years before and had recently arrived
from Halifax) states that it was this officer who was Wolfe's
informant.[2] This claim is, however, of doubtful authenticity
and is generally discredited by modern historians. The point
has never been satisfactorily elucidated, but there are strong
grounds for believing that the Rev. Michael Houdin, then
acting as Chaplain to the 48th Regiment,[3] was the person
who gave the information.

[1] Vaudreuil to Brigadier Bourlamarque, quoted in *Montcalm and
Wolfe*, Vol. II, p. 243.   [2] Cf. *Memoirs of Major Robert Stobo.*
[3] Cf. S.P.G. Journal, Vol. 13, pp. 183, 184, which records: "A
Letter from the Rev. Mr Barclay, Rector of Trinity Church in the

Houdin was a French ex-Roman Catholic priest who had been the Superior of a convent in Canada. In 1747 he conformed to the Anglican Church by making a public recantation of Roman Catholicism in Trinity Church, New York.[1] A few years later he was appointed an itinerant missionary of the S.P.G. in New Jersey, and in 1757 he was made Chaplain to the English army and served under Loudon and Abercromby. In the following year he accompanied the Louisburg expedition and on 28 July (two days after the surrender of the fortress) he wrote to the Society "that he was obliged to sail with the Fleet before Cape Breton at the instance of Genl. Abercrombie, who had no Chaplain to send from that part of the Army".[2] Thereafter Houdin joined Wolfe's army before Quebec, where he acted in the capacity of an intelligence officer to the general. In a letter of 23 October, some five weeks after the famous battle, he wrote as follows:

Quebec. October 23, 1759.

Revd. Sir,

I am in hope that my absence from my Mission will not bring me under the displeasure of the Venble. Society, what I have done from the beginning was to obey the orders of my Lord Loudon and other commanders in chief after him who depended much upon my being well acquainted with all the country I could be of service to them. The desire I had for the good success of his Majesty's arms, hath given me strength above my age and constitution, to bear all the fatigues of such campanes [*sic*], and, blessed be God, that he hath been pleas'd to crown our labour this year beyond, I can say, our expectation. I asked leave, after

City of New York, dated May 24.th 1757, in which he writes that yᵉ Rev. M! Houdin...at yᵉ especial Instance of His Excellency the Earl of Loudon has been obliged to leave his Mission for a few months; Lord Loudon has bought out yᵉ Chaplain of yᵉ 48.th Regiment & made a Compliment of y! Commission to M! Houdin...."
In the Champlain Society's edition of Knox's *Historical Journal*, Vol. II, p. 28, Dr Doughty makes a note of those chaplains who appear to have been at Quebec, including "Michael Houdin of the 48.th, appointed April 29, 1757".

[1] Letter, Rev. Henry Barclay, 'B' MSS. Vol. 15, No. 123.
[2] 'B' MSS. Vol. 14, No. 105.

the reduction of Quebec, to return to my Mission, but General Murray, our Governour, ordered me to stay with him, telling me he had no properest [i.e. properer] person, as the Country was not yet reduc'd, to depend upon for intelligence of the French proceeding[s]. He promised me he would acquaint the Society of it, and of the reason thereof. I am entirely deprived of my expectations by the Death of our brave General Wolfe, who promised me to remember my labours and services, and as they are unknown to General Murray, he keeps me here this winter without any advantage....

I am

Your humble Servant

MICHAEL HOUDIN.[1]

In this letter Houdin's reference to his "labours and services" which were "unknown to General Murray" is very significant. Monckton, Wolfe's senior Brigadier, had been wounded in the battle and had returned to England with Brigadier Townshend, the next in seniority, and the command had thus devolved upon Brigadier Murray. It is a well-known fact that Wolfe's relations with Townshend and Murray had been definitely strained for some weeks before the battle, and this may well account for Houdin's statement that Murray was unaware of Wolfe's promise to him. There is no doubt from Houdin's letter that he had on several occasions communicated important intelligence to Wolfe (as also to the previous commanders, Loudon and Abercromby), and it would seem highly probable that the chief item of this intelligence concerned the pathway from the Anse du Foulon which Houdin would almost certainly have known from his many years' residence in the country. In this connection the entry in Townshend's diary that "By *some intelligence* the General hath, he hath changed his mind as to the place he intended to land" is extremely suggestive.[2]

[1] 'C' MSS. (Canada).
[2] In the December 1935 number of *United Empire* (the Journal of the Royal Empire Society) an article by me entitled "Wolfe's French Intelligence Officer" was published, which gave a detailed account of Houdin's services. Since then I have found the following

The battle which followed the memorable ascent by the British troops of the Heights of Abraham is one of the most dramatic episodes of our military history. Soon after daybreak the French began to muster from their camp, and before ten o'clock they had formed themselves into three bodies and had begun their advance, firing and shouting as they came, against the British line which stood ready to receive them. Our troops had been trained to a superb discipline by Wolfe, who had never forgotten the lesson he had learnt as a youth at Dettingen of the necessity for well-ordered musketry fire.[1]

As the French came within musket shot, many gaps were made in the British ranks but no answering fire was returned. The files closed up silently, waiting with levelled pieces, stiff and motionless as if on parade. Then, when the enemy were within thirty-five paces Wolfe gave the order, and like a single monstrous cannon shot the deafening roar of the volley shook the heavens. Before the smoke had lifted a second volley burst from the red-coated ranks and the whole front line of

corroboration of my theory in a short sketch of the Rev. John Ogilvie by the late Professor A. H. Young, D.C.L., of Trinity College, Toronto: "Among the signal services performed by Houdin, it has been said, was that of informing Wolfe of the possibility of scaling the bank of the St Lawrence above Quebec." (It is regrettable that Professor Young did not give any authorities for this suggestion.)—AUTHOR. It is a curious circumstance that in the picture "The Death of Wolfe", painted by Benjamin West (whose brother served in the campaign) from eye-witnesses' descriptions, there is a clergyman standing on the extreme right of the group in an attitude of prayer. The names of the chief persons represented are given in a key to the picture but the clergyman's is not given, and is apparently not known. Whether in fact this clergyman was Houdin must remain a tantalizing conjecture.

[1] Cf. Wolfe's letter to his father written a week after Dettingen describing his regiment being attacked by the French infantry: "The Major & I, for we had neither Colonel nor Lieut-Colonel, were employed in begging & ordering the men not to fire at too great a distance, but to keep it till the enemy should come near us, but to little purpose. The whole fired when they thought they could reach them, *which had like to have ruined us*" (quoted by Beckles Willson, *The Life and Letters of James Wolfe*, pp. 36, 37).

PLATE X

"The Death of Wolfe"

Photo. Rischgitz Art Agency

the French lay crumpled in a huddled mass. No human beings could have withstood the shock, and as the dazed survivors recoiled from the deadly hail, Wolfe's Grenadiers and High-landers were upon them with the bayonet and the claymore. At their head raced the tall youthful figure of the General, armed with a musket like his men.[1] A bullet from some sharp-shooters hidden in the bushes shattered his wrist but he ran on. A second bullet hit him, he staggered and by a supreme effort kept his feet. A moment later a third shot struck him in the breast and he sank down. "Don't let my brave lads see me", he murmured as he was carried to the rear. A few minutes passed and a young ensign ran up waving his hat and shouting the words used by Cromwell at Dunbar:[2] "They run: I protest they run." The dying General half raised himself: "Who run?"—"The enemy, Sir; Egad they give way every-where." "Then go one of you to Colonel Burton and tell him to march Webb's regiment down to Charles river and cut off their retreat by the bridge" Wolfe feebly commanded, and having murmured "Now God be thanked, I die in peace", in a few moments expired. He was only thirty-two.

A few months later Mr Ogilvie sent the following letter to the Society concerning the Niagara expedition of the previous year:

Albany, February 1, 1760.

Revd. Sir,

I beg leave to congratulate the Venble. Society upon the great Successes with which it hath pleased the Supreme Disposer of all events, to crown the arms of our most gracious Sovereign by sea & Land, both in *Europe & America*. May the issue of all these

---

[1] *Vide* the pencil sketch of Wolfe made by his aide-de-camp, Captain Hervey Smith, just before the battle. He has a musket slung over his shoulder and carries a sheathed bayonet at his belt. (This sketch is reproduced in *The Life and Letters of James Wolfe*, quoted above.)

[2] Cf. *Memoirs of Captain Hodgson*, p. 148, quoted in *Dict. Nat. Biog.* under "Oliver Cromwell".

important events tend to the Glory of God, the Honour of our King, the Security of the protestant Religion and the Peace & Happiness of our Nation & its Colonies.

I have the Pleasure to acquaint the Society that my duty as their Missionary has hitherto been intirely compatible with my Chaplaincy in ye Army & particularly so the last summer. I attended the royal American Regiment upon ye Expedition to Niagara; And indeed there was no other Chaplain upon that Department, tho' there were three regular Regts. & ye provincial Regt. of New York. The Mohawks were all upon this Service, and almost all the six Nations, they amounted in ye whole to 940, at ye time of ye Siege. I officiated constantly to ye Mohawks & Oneidoes [Oneidas] who regularly attended divine service. I gave them Exhortations suitable to the Emergency & I flatter myself my Presence with them contributed in some Measure to keep up Decency & Order amongst them: the Oneidoes met us at the Lake near their Castle, & as they were acquainted with my coming, they brought ten children to receive Baptism; and young women, who had been previously instructed in ye Principles of Christianity, came likewise to receive that Holy ordinance. I baptized them in the presence of a numerous Crowd of spectators, who all seemed pleased with the attention & serious behaviour of the Indians upon that solemn occasion; and indeed, bad as they are, I must do them the justice to say, that whenever they attend the offices of religion it is with great appearance of solemnity & Decency.

During this campaign I have had an opportunity of conversing with some of every one of ye Six Nation Confederacy & their Dependants and of every nation I find some who have been instructed by ye priests of Canada, & appear zealous roman Catholicks, extremely tenacious of ye Ceremonies & Peculiarities of that Church; and from very good authority I am informed, that there is not a Nation bordering upon ye five great lakes, or the Banks of ye Ohio, the Mississipi, all the way to Louisania [sic], but what are supplied with priests & Schoolmasters, & have very decent Places of Worship, with every splendid utensil of their Religion. How ought we to blush at our coldness & shameful indifference in ye propagation of our most excellent Religion. *The Harvest is great but the Labourers are few*. The Indians themselves are not wanting in making very pertinent Reflections upon our inattention to these points!

The possession of the important Fortification of Niagara, is of the utmost consequence to the English, as it gives us the happy opportunity of commencing & cultivating a friendship with those numerous tribes of Indians who inhabit the Borders of *Lake Erie*, *Huron, Michigan* & even *Lake Superiour*; And the Fur trade which is carried on by these tribes, which all centers at Niagara, is so very considerable, that I am told by very able judges that the French look upon Canada [as] of very little importance without the possession of this important Pass; it certainly is so and must appear obvious to any one who understands the geography of this country. It cuts off & renders their Communication with their Southern Settlements impracticable. In this Fort, there is a very handsom Chapel, & the Priest who was of the Order of St. Francis, had a Commission as the King's Chaplain to this Garrison. He had particular instructions to use the Indians who came to trade, with great Hospitality, (for which he had a particular allowance) and to instruct them in yᵉ Principles of the Faith; the service of the Chʰ here was performed with great ceremony & parade. I performed divine service in this Church every day, during my stay there, but I am afraid it has never been used for that Purpose since, as there is no Minister of the Gospel there; this neglect will not give the Indians the most favourable Impression of us.

We have now, by the Blessing of Heaven, obtained the whole object of the war upon this Continent, and upon the Conclusion of a Peace, if we may only keep those places, to which we have an undoubted right, by grants from the natives, & confirmed by solemn Treaties, particularly by that of *Utrecht*,[1] and Niagara is certainly one of those places; I think we shall have it in our power to frustrate the extensive & ambitious views of the Court of France upon this Continent of America, by effectually securing the alliance of all the Indian nations.

And as the situation we shall be in, in all probability, if we obtain an honourable Peace, will give us the happy opportunity of sending Missionaries not only to the six Nations, but to yᵉ other tribes, in their Alliance, I pray God the Government may think it an object worthy of their attention.

My Mission is in much the same Circumstances, as when I wrote last Febr; only that my Indian Congregation is very much decreased by the late Mortality that prevailed amongst the Mohawks. I shall soon transmit an account of the Numbers baptized in both branches of my Mission. In the mean time with

[1] Ogilvie was quite incorrect in thus mentioning the Treaty of Utrecht, which left the boundaries of the Five Nations unsettled (*vide* p. 42 *supra*).

prayers to almighty God for a Blessing upon the pious endeavours of the Venl. Society for the Promotion of true Religion & Virtue,

I am, Revd. Sir,

with the most dutiful sentiments

their & your most devoted

Humble Servt.

JOHN OGILVIE.[1]

A few weeks after Mr Ogilvie had written to the Society, the French made a determined attempt to recapture Quebec. Montcalm's second-in-command, the Chevalier de Lévis, assembled a strong force to attack the city, and in April Quebec was besieged. Towards the end of April Murray, who commanded the British troops, marched out of the fortress and attacked the French at St Foy. He was repulsed with heavy losses and the city was closely invested. But unknown to de Lévis relief was at hand, and on 15 May a fleet of six English ships sailed up the St Lawrence and obliged the French to withdraw to Montreal.

In the meantime Amherst had passed the winter at Crown Point intending to advance on Montreal in the spring. The failure of the French to retake Quebec enabled him to devise a comprehensive scheme for attacking Montreal by three separate armies which would join forces at the city. Accordingly Murray was ordered to advance up the St Lawrence from Quebec, Brigadier Haviland to march from Lake Champlain to Montreal, while Amherst himself led the main force down the St Lawrence from Lake Ontario. Towards the end of May the preparations for the invasion were nearing completion, and on the 20th Mr Ogilvie wrote from Albany that:

We are now all preparing to take the field, which we shall do in a few days; As the Mohawks all go, I imagine the Genl.[2] will expect my attendance, which I hope will be agreeable to the Venl. Society, as I shall still be in the Way of Duty as their Missionary.

The issue of the Campaign, I trust in God, will be the compleat

---

[1] 'B' MSS. Vol. 2, No. 105.   [2] I.e. Amherst.

Conquest of Canada. We have a very promising Prospect, before us, of bringing the affairs of America to a safe & honourable issue.

Every thing is kept a profound secret by the Gen¹ but from very good circumstances, we conjecture that the Grand Expedition will be by way of Oswego, & so down the river St. Lawrence to the Town of Montreal; whilst Brigadier Gage¹ will operate with a considerable Army by the way of Crown Point, & so down the Lake Champlain. We have lately had some accounts by some Deserters from Canada that the Govr. of that country with all his force were just going to make a grand effort for the retaking Quebec.² If the Intelligence be true, & the scheme should prove abortive, 'tis generally thought we shall meet with little Resistance, for, from the deplorable situation they must be in, one would imagine they would make the best Terms for themselves they can. I pray God, the supreme Disposer of all events, to direct & bless the public Counsels at yˢ important Conjuncture, that he would be both with our Fleets & Armies, & smile upon our Nation's interests & bring this war to a speedy & honourable issue. That the peaceable Kingdom of the Blessed Jesus may flourish from the rising, to the setting sun, & that the labours of yᵉ Venbl. Society may be prosper'd to this blessed Purpose.

This is the prayer of him who has the Honour to subscribe himself, Revd. Sir, with the most dutiful respect,

Their & your most obedient

Humble Servt.

JOHN OGILVIE.³

In July Amherst's army (consisting of 10,000 men and 700 Indians under Sir William Johnson) had marched from Crown Point and concentrated at Oswego where Mr Ogilvie joined them in his capacity of chaplain. On 10 August the

¹ Hon. Thomas Gage, second son of Thomas, Viscount Gage (1721–87). Served under Braddock at Fort Duquesne as Lieutenant-Colonel of the 44th Regiment. Promoted Brigadier-General in 1758, he commanded the rearguard in Amherst's advance on Montreal. He became military Governor of Montreal after its capitulation, and in 1763 he was appointed Commander-in-Chief of North America (cf. *Dict. Nat. Biog.*).

² I.e. de Lévis' abortive attempt, which, unknown to Ogilvie, had already failed.

³ 'B' MSS. Vol. 2, No. 106.

troops embarked on Lake Ontario in a flotilla of *bateaux* and whaleboats, escorted by a number of armed gunboats, which were to transport the army to Montreal. On the day before Mr Ogilvie wrote the following letter to the Society:

Oswego, August 9, 1760.

Rev. Sir,

...By this I beg leave to inform the Society that I left Albany the 24th of June in order to join the Army, who were proceeding under Gen¹ Amherst to Oswego. I tarried at Fort Hunter three days, I preached twice during that time, and administred the Sacrament of Baptism to several white and indian children. The Mohawks were preparing for the Field, & told me they should overtake me near the Oneida Lake,¹ at which place a considerable number of Indians join'd us. Gen¹ Amherst being at the *Oneida* Lake on the preceeding Sunday went up as far as the Oneida town, upon his arrival there he found them at their worship and expressed a vast pleasure at the Decency which the Service of our Church was performed with by a grave Indian Sachem. They applied to the Gen¹ to leave directions for me to come to the Castle upon my arrival at the Lake.

Agreeable to the General's directions, I went to the Oneida Town the 19th day of July; I had sent a Mohawk Indian before, so that upon my coming into their town I found a large congregation met for divine service, which was performed with great solemnity. Six adults presented themselves to be examined for Baptism, who all of them gave a very satisfactory account of the Christian faith & appeared to have a serious sense of Religion, I baptized them & immediatly after join'd them in Marriage, they were three principle Men, & their wives who had lived many years together according to the Indian Custom. I baptized 14 Children, & in all join'd nine couple in the holy Bands of Marriage.

I was much pleased with this day's solemnity, it would have been a noble subject for the pen of one of the Jesuites of Canada. I would to God, we had Labourers in this Part of the Vineyard to keep alive the spark that is kindled among some of these Tribes, & spread the glad tidings of the Gospel among the numerous Tribes with whom we have now a free communication.

Beside my duty in the Army, I attend the Indians, & give them prayers, as often on Week days, as the public service of the Camp

¹ Situated to the south-east of Lake Ontario.

will admit, and on Sunday, the Gen[1] always gives public orders for divine service among the Indians.

I hope soon to congratulate the Venr. Society upon the intire Conquest of Canada, and I pray God that by that means, there may be a more effectual door open'd for the Propagation of the blessed Gospel amongst the Heathen.

I beg your candour in excusing the Inaccuracies of this letter, for I am now embarking for the River St. Lawrence.

I am, Revd. Sir, with the most respectful
& Dutiful Sentiments the Venr. Society's
and your most obedient
Humble servant,
JOHN OGILVIE.[1]

On 23 August Amherst captured Fort Lévis, which stood on an islet near the rapids. The fort had been built a year before and was commanded by Pouchot, the former commandant of Niagara. The most difficult part of the expedition now began with the descent of the rapids. Forty-six boats were destroyed and over eighty men were drowned during this dangerous passage, but the remainder passed safely through the raging torrent and landed at Isle Perrot below Montreal. The following day Amherst advanced to La Chine nine miles above the city and the next day Murray's army reached the same place, while Haviland's force, which had captured Isle-aux-Noix some days before, lay a short distance away on the southern shore of the St Lawrence. The junction of the three British armies (totalling some 17,000 men) made the fall of Montreal inevitable. The French commander, Vaudreuil, had less than 3000 troops, and on the morning of 8 September he surrendered. Thus, after half a century of conflict Canada passed to Great Britain and the dreams of Champlain and Frontenac were for ever dispelled.

By the terms of the capitulation the French Canadians were allowed the free exercise of their religion, and certain specified fraternities (excepting the Jesuits, Recollects and Sulpicians until the orders of the King-in-Council were made

[1] 'B' MSS. Vol. 2, No. 107.

known) were guaranteed the possession of their constitutions and privileges. At the same time the local cures and missionaries were allowed to continue their parochial ministrations and to receive their customary tithes.[1]

The great rejoicings at the conclusion of the campaign were reflected by Mr Ogilvie in a letter written to the Secretary of the S.P.G. a few weeks after the surrender of Montreal. He had returned to his mission at Albany at the end of September, having received the necessary permission from General Amherst.

Albany, October 14, 1760.

Rev? & Dear Sir

It is with the highest Pleasure that I congratulate the Venr. Society upon the success of his Majesty's arms both by sea & land, and more especially upon the glorious Conclusion of this Campaign in America, by the intire reduction of Canada to the obedience of our most gracious Sovereign; An event so deeply impressed with such obvious characters of its own importance, that every sincere Lover of his Country must feel his mind transported with admiration, Gratitude & Joy upon this happy occasion. May these remarkable smiles of divine Providence upon our national Interest make such a lasting impression upon the minds of all the subjects of the British Government, that a universal Reformation of Manners may be the Tribute of our gratitude to the supreme Regent of the Universe!

I left Albany [at] the beginning of June, & returned (after a very fatiguing campaign) the 30th of September. I did myself the Honor of writing to the Venr. Society the 20th of June from Oswego, giving them an account of the good disposition I found the Oneidoes in, & of my services among them. Would to God there might be a due encourag'ment given to proper persons to undertake the Propagation of the blessed Gospel among the natives of this Country! There seems now to be a fair Prospect for this generous work, from our great successes upon this Continent. During this campaign, I have been particularly attentive to perform the offices of Religion among the Indians, great Numbers attended constantly, regularly, & decently. During our stay at Oswego I baptized six Indian & four white children.

It is with real concern I am obliged to inform the Venr. Society

---

[1] Cf. Articles of Capitulation, Nos. 27 to 35 inc.

that by express Order from Gen[1] Amherst, I am preparing to return to Montreal for the Winter Season. The Gen[1] seemed extremely sensible of the Inconveniency of removing me from my Mission for so long time. But was pleased to say that he could by no means dispense with my Absence, as the Honor of the protestant Religion must be kept up, in a Town where all the inhabitants were of a contrary persuasion, by the regular & decent performance of the public offices of our Church, & that he had fix'd upon me for that Purpose. He was extremely sensible of the necessity of a Minister in this City, & therefore directed me to endeavour to procure some Clergyman to do the Duty here. I have therefore partly engaged the Revd. Mr. Jacob Townshend,[1] formerly resident upon the Frontiers of Virginia, to do my duty this winter. He is now gone to New York in order to settle his affairs for his return to this place. Upon his punctual performance of the Duty I have promised him the Society's allowance during his stay, upon condition of the Society's approbation. He is likewise to visit the Mohawks as often as possible. As I hope to return early in the Spring, I flatter myself the Society will still consider me as their Missionary, and should I be obliged to quit their service, (in which I should be glad to have the honour to spend my life) I shall give the earliest Notice, & consult with my worthy Predecessor the Revd. Mr. Barclay & the Rev. Dr. Johnson, to procure a proper Person to succeed me in this important Mission. By the terms of Capitulation, the Society will observe, that the Priests are all left in their respective Parishes amongst the Indians as well as the French Inhabitants. I shall do all in my power to recommend our excellent religion by the public & constant performance of the duties of divine worship, & by keeping up a friendly correspondence both with clergy and Laity, to answer which good purpose I could wish for a number of French Bibles & common prayers and some plain Accts. of the protestant religion, wherein the points in dispute between us are treated of, with a spirit of Moderation & Christian charity. Surely these might be distributed to very good purpose. The french Mohawks & other Tribes of Indians in this Neighbourhood are all zealous roman Catholicks, however I shall endeavour to contract an Acquaintance with them, & gain an Interest among them, & do all I can to promote the generous designs of the Society.

[1] Mr Townshend did not in fact take over the Albany and Fort Hunter Missions, which were entrusted to the Rev. Thomas Browne, an ex-army chaplain.

I observe all the Lands upon the Island of *Montreal & Isle Jesu* are vested in the Church, the soil is good the country well cleared & cultivated & should our Stock of consequence be so great, that at the settlement of a general peace we may be able to retain this most valuable acquisition, I make no doubt but a proper attention will be paid to the establishment of Religion, & a sufficient provision made for the support of a regular & orthodox Clergy; and if I might be indulged the thought I could wish to see part of these valuable lands vested in the venr. Society in order to enable them to propagate true Christianity among the numerous tribes of Indians who inhabit this extensive country.

Upon my arrival at Montreal, I shall do myself the honour of writing to the Society, & give all the Intelligence I can collect of the state of Religion in this country. I am able to express the universal Joy & Triumph that prevails among us at this period of public success. How remarkably has God in His Providence sustained the Cause, & restored the honour of our country, By the successes of the last & the glorious conclusion of this year. The Inhabitants of this northern Region of America are now happy in the quiet possession of their estates. *No more leading into Captivity*, a Captivity big with danger & Horror, *no more complaining in our streets*.

May all these happy events conspire to bring about a speedy, safe & honourable peace! May the peaceable Kingdom of the Redeemer universally prevail among Mankind, and all the World know the *only true God & Jesus Christ whom he hath sent*! And that the pious labours of the Venr. Society may be instrumental in bringing about this Happy event is the prayer of their

Most dutiful Missionary,
& humble Servt.
JOHN OGILVIE.[1]

---

[1] 'B' MSS. Vol. 2, No. 108.

CHAPTER VI
THE YEARS BETWEEN
(1761-1774)

THE conquest of Canada was followed by a period of transition which saw the establishment of the English administration in the former French possession, and the gradual union of the English "Thirteen Colonies" prior to the Declaration of Independence.

It was more than a coincidence that the birth of the United States followed so comparatively soon after the termination of the French rule in Canada. One of the strongest ties which bound the Colonies to England was the ever-present fear of French aggression which was doubly magnified in the absence of an ocean boundary between the two territories. England's insularity had proved an agelong safeguard to her people, but her colonists could only view with apprehension the presence of a foreign power separated from them by artificial barriers. As early as 1748 the Swedish traveller Kalm had opined that the presence of the French in America would most effectually ensure the Colonies' obedience to England,[1] and at the close of the Seven Years' War the Duc de Choiseul (the negotiator of the famous "Family Compact") warned the English envoy at Versailles that the colonists would assuredly declare their independence as soon as France relinquished Canada.[2] Nevertheless these emphatic warnings were disregarded, the Home Government conceiving that the increased prosperity consequent upon the English absorption of Canada would serve to bind the "Thirteen Colonies" more closely to the parent country.

[1] Kalm, *Travels in North America*, Vol. I, p. 207; quoted in *Montcalm and Wolfe*, Vol. II, p. 418.
[2] Parkman, *Montcalm and Wolfe*, Vol. II, p. 418. Cf. also *The Cambridge History of the British Empire*, Vol. I, p. 686.

The new government was inaugurated by the division of the territory into three districts, Quebec, Three Rivers, and Montreal, which were placed under a military régime. This was, perhaps, unavoidable as the negotiations for a peace treaty continued for many months.

Meanwhile in February 1762 Admiral Rodney had captured Martinique and some other French islands in the West Indies, and in August the Earl of Albemarle and Admiral Pocock reduced the Spanish island of Havana.[1] These fresh disasters following upon their losses in India, West Africa, and the capture of Guadaloupe and Dominica induced the French Government to resume negotiations for peace and on 10 February 1763 the preliminaries were signed. By the terms of the treaty France ceded Canada, Cape Breton and all her possessions in North America east of the Mississippi (excepting New Orleans and the neighbouring area) and renounced her claims to Acadia (Nova Scotia). She was, however, permitted to retain the small islands of St Pierre and Miquelon and to exercise certain fishing rights on the coast of Newfoundland. In the West Indies France ceded Grenada and the Grenadines in return for Martinique and Guadaloupe, and in Africa and India she gave up almost all her possessions. Spain surrendered Florida to England in return for Havana, and France later gave New Orleans and the great region of Louisiana to the west of the Mississippi to Spain as compensation to her unfortunate ally.

The cession of Canada produced an unexpected disquietude among the former Indian allies of the French. They had shown no open resentment at the surrender of the French posts on the Great Lakes to the English Government, but the wholesale transfer of their territory which accompanied the English occupation turned their growing discontent into flagrant rebellion. Led by the Ottawa chief, Pontiac, a confederation of the Algonquin tribes suddenly rose and seized the forts built by the French on the Ohio, the Great Lakes, and in the Illinois country. On 10 May (1763) Pontiac

---

[1] War had been declared against Spain on 4 February 1762.

attacked Detroit and only the gallant defence of a small force under Major Gladwin saved it from destruction. In the space of six weeks the only posts which remained in the western Ohio country were Fort Pitt,[1] Green Bay and Ligonier, and of these Green Bay had to be abandoned. Fortunately, through the efforts of Sir William Johnson most of the Iroquois remained loyal, but the Senecas, who had always shown themselves amenable to French influence, joined in the rebellion. The frontier settlements of Virginia and Pennsylvania were soon devastated by hordes of painted savages who burned the homesteads of the hapless settlers and massacred their occupants. The Rev. Thomas Barton, the Society's missionary at Lancaster, Pennsylvania, reported that

the Barbarians have renewed their Hostilities and the Country bleeds again under the savage Knife. The dreadful news of murdering, burning, and scalping is daily convey'd to us and confirm'd with shocking additions.... Our Garrisons have been invested, and some of them obliged to surrender. About fifty miles of the finest country in America are already deserted, and the poor People,...are reduc'd to the most consumate distress.[2]

In July the Rev. William Thomson, S.P.G. itinerant missionary in York and Cumberland Counties, Pennsylvania, wrote that

...the Indians...are killing, scalping, and butchering all who are so unhappy as to fall into their hands. There are upwards of 1,500 Plantations evacuated, the People daily crouding towards the Interiour Parts of the Province for Refuge....[3]

He himself was forced to fly to Carlisle, a small fortified post on the road to Fort Pitt. It was the subsequent relief of this latter post by Colonel Bouquet[4] with a force of 500 men which did much to check the rising. Bouquet had succeeded in

---

[1] I.e. the fort outside Pittsburg.
[2] 'B' MSS. Vol. 21, No. 13.   [3] 'B' MSS. Vol. 6, No. 282.
[4] Brigadier Henry Bouquet had been appointed Lieutenant-Colonel of the Royal Americans in 1756, and served under Brigadier Forbes in the expedition against Fort Duquesne in 1758 (*New York Docs.* Vol. VII, p. 352 footnote).

defeating the enemy at Bushy Run, where (to quote Mr Thomson)

he was warmly engaged with ye Savages for two Days, but to his eternal Honour be it spoke, he routed them, disconcerted their Designs & put them to Flight, and carried his important Convoy to the Relief of the poor distressed People at Fort Pitt....[1]

In the following year Bouquet marched into the enemy's country while a force under Colonel John Bradstreet co-operated by threatening the Indians on the banks of Lake Erie. Pontiac and his followers were overawed by this un-expected display of force and soon sued for peace. This was finally made through the influence of Sir William Johnson who drafted the necessary treaties with the representatives of the rebellious tribes,[2] and finally concluded a treaty with Pontiac in 1766.[3] Thereafter Pontiac's power was broken and he soon lost all influence with the tribes. He met his death in 1769 at the hands of an Illinois Indian who is said to have been bribed by an English trader.

Soon after the outbreak of Pontiac's rising the Home Government had issued a proclamation (October 1763) setting up four new governments in America at Quebec, East and West Florida, and Grenada. Under this order the governors were empowered to convene representative assemblies and to set up Courts of Justice. In the Quebec province the French Canadian population declined to take the oaths of allegiance and supremacy (which were made a condition for election to the assembly) and as a result the Governor, General Murray, administered the government by an officially nominated executive council. This led to much dissatisfaction, which was enhanced by a general uncertainty as to whether the two European races should be subject to the laws of their parent countries—a matter of considerable importance arising from the wide divergence of French and English jurisprudence.

[1] 'B' MSS. Vol. 6, No. 283.
[2] New York Docs. Vol. VII, pp. 650–3 et passim.
[3] Ibid. p. 781.

A secondary part of the proclamation related to the Indians who were now to be protected in the enjoyment of their prescriptive hunting grounds. It was enacted that in future the Indians would only be permitted to alienate their land with the special acquiescence of the Governor-in-Council, and further, that all traders with the Indians must obtain a licence from the authorities before embarking on their projects. In this manner the Indian territories would be reserved in security for their owners—a far-sighted and equitable policy which has been justly described as being "in harmony with the best traditions of British Colonial government".[1]

In the meantime the Society's missions at Albany and Fort Hunter were left without a minister,[2] Mr Ogilvie having returned to Montreal at General Amherst's request.[3] At the suggestion of Dr Barclay[4] the Society endeavoured to obtain a successor for Mr Ogilvie.[5] The Rev. Thomas Browne, then serving as a chaplain to the 27th Regiment under Amherst, applied for the post and received a temporary appointment from the Society. He officiated at Albany during the year 1761 but left in November to serve with the expedition against Martinique.[6] On the cessation of hostilities he returned to Albany (May 1762) where he remained for the next four years, but in 1766 he resigned from the mission and removed to Maryland.[7]

The next communication (as recorded in the Journal) which the Society received from Mr Ogilvie was written at Montreal in July 1763:

...since he [Mr. Ogilvie] left Albany he has been officiating in this City, where the British Merchants with the Garrison make a considerable Congregation, who assemble regularly for divine

[1] Cf. *The Cambridge History of the British Empire*, Vol. 1, p. 643.
[2] The Rev. J. J. Oël was still resident in the Mohawk country but was not in charge of the mission.
[3] S.P.G. Journal, Vol. 15, p. 133.
[4] The Rev. Henry Barclay had recently received the honorary degree of D.D. Oxon.   [5] S.P.G. Journal, Vol. 15, p. 134.
[6] Letter, 'B' MSS. Vol. 3, No. 103.
[7] S.P.G. Journal, Vol. 17, p. 320.

Worship on Sundays and other Festivals. He has baptized since y.ᵉ 1.ˢᵗ of Nov.ʳ 1760 to the date of this Letter 100 Children, and administred the holy Communion to 30 or 40 Persons at a time. As by the Capitulation there is no Provision made for a place of Worship for the Established Church, they are under a Necessity of making use of one of the Chapels, which is the cause of much discontent; but hopes this will soon be remedied by the Government. The Jesuits, he says, have a small College and a Church adjoining, as yet unfinished: could this be procured it would be extremely convenient, and could be put in order at a small Expence. At present it only serves as an Habitation for one Jesuit Priest and two or three Lay Brothers: In the Government of Montreal there are 36 Parishes, 10 of which are upon the Island. The property of the Soil of the Island and two other Parishes in the Government, is vested in the Seminary of S.ᵗ Sulpice in Paris, whose Affairs here are negotiated by a Branch of said Seminary, consisting of about 20 Priests, whose Mansion House is in this City, from whence they supply the Parishes upon their Estates as Curate-Miss.ʳⁱᵉˢ. The annual Income of their Estate is computed at near 3000£ sterling: They have a vast Influence upon the People, are exemplary in their Lives, and extremely attached to the Ritual and external Parade of their Church. In every point of view this is a Body of Priests, whose Influence ought, by means consistent with Truth and Virtue, to be lessened as much as may be: for They and the Jesuits (who have a large Estate likewise) will ever keep up a Spirit inconsistent with the genius of a British Government. The Superior of this Community and grand Vicar of this Government, Mons.ʳ Montgolfier,[1] comes over by this Conveyance. He is a Gentleman of considerable Knowledge & polite Address: his design is to solicit the Affairs of their Church in general, and their own Estate in particular; in either case it is interesting and must have a great Influence upon the state of religion in this Country, should he succeed in his Views. M.ʳ Ogilvie thought it his Duty to give the Society this Notice, that this Gentleman may be observed in his Application to the Government by some Persons of Interest and Influence. In this City they have one Convent of Recollects, consisting of four Priests and as many

[1] The Rev. Étienne Montgolfier was the Superior of the Seminary of St Sulpice and Grand Vicar of Montreal. With the connivance of the English Government he was allowed to accept the appointment of Bishop of Quebec in succession to Henri Marie Dubreuil de Pontbriand, the last Bishop of the French régime.

Lay Brothers. There are three religious Houses for Women, one of which is a kind of Boarding School for Girls, the other for the Accommodation of the Sick, and one for Lunaticks and Foundlings. Within 9 miles of this there is an Indian Mission supplied by two Jesuits, and at the distance of 40 miles, there is another supplied by two Priests of the House of S! Sulpice. These Savages are extremely attached to the Ceremonials of the Church, & have been taught to believe the English have no Knowledge of the Mystery of Man's Redemption by Jesus Christ. As these Indians speak the Mohawk Language, M! Ogilvie has endeavoured to remove their Prejudices, and by shewing them the Liturgy of our Church in their Mother Tongue, has convinced many of them that we are their fellow Christians.

A School and an Exemplary Clergyman from this Town is absolutely Necessary: and should the Society have the supplying this Country, M! Ogilvie humbly begs their particular remembrance for the City & Island of Montreal, where he has already formed a decent Congregation. He is apprehensive his half-pay will be incompatible with the Chaplainship at Albany, and the Mission without it would not be a sufficient Support. His Services are at the Society's Command, if they may be of any Consequence to the Protestant Cause in this Colony. Upon this occasion he begs leave to give a hint relative to the raising a Support for the Protestant Clergy here. The Jesuits are dissolved as a Body in France, and consequently so here, and their Estates here of course devolve to the Crown. If this be the case, surely an application from the Society for a Provision from hence would have its due weight, and merit consideration from the Government. While inattention to the weighty concerns of Religion prevails but too much among them, he is bound in Justice to mention the exemplary Conduct of Gen! Gage, who is a constant Attendant upon the Offices of Religion, & endeavours to support its Influence in its present low Estate, the Church having no Provision for any of the decent Appendages of divine Worship. He hopes the Society will excuse this Liberty in one who is not properly speaking in their immediate Service.[1]

In the following month Mr Ogilvie's chaplaincy terminated on the reduction of his regiment, but instead of returning to Albany he remained for another year at Montreal to minister to the English congregation of the city in a voluntary

[1] S.P.G. Journal, Vol. 16, pp. 45–8.

capacity.[1] In August 1764 Dr Barclay died and was succeeded as Rector of New York by the senior curate, the Rev. Samuel Auchmuty, who had been in charge of the Society's Negro Mission in that city since 1747.[2] The congregation of Trinity Church thereupon invited Mr Ogilvie to become their assistant curate, and at a subsequent meeting of the Vestry he was unanimously elected to that post.[3] Dr Ogilvie[4] remained at New York in this capacity until his death, which occurred in November 1774, within a few months of the outbreak of the American revolution.

With the resignation of the Rev. Thomas Browne, the Society's missions at Albany and Fort Hunter again became vacant, and early in the following year the Rev. Harry Munro was appointed on the suggestion of a clerical convention at New York under the presidency of Dr Auchmuty.[5] Mr Munro had formerly been a Presbyterian minister and had served as a chaplain to a Highland Regiment stationed at New York.[6] He took Anglican Orders in 1765 and was then sent as the Society's missionary to Philipsburg, New York, the home of Colonel Frederick Philipse who had recently built a church on his manor. Mr Munro arrived at Albany in April when he reported that the congregation was scattered and reduced to a very small number.[7]

In the following January Mr Munro informed the Society that he had visited Sir William Johnson to discuss with him the future of the Mission to the Mohawks. In the meantime at Sir William's request Mr Munro agreed to devote part of

---

[1] Letter, 'B' MSS. Vol. 2, No. 109.

[2] The Rev. S. Auchmuty was the second son of Judge Robert Auchmuty and was born in Boston, Mass., in 1722. He was educated at Harvard and Oxford (Hon. D.D. Oxon.) and was a firm loyalist in the revolution. He died in 1777 as a result of privations and anxiety during Washington's occupation of New York.

[3] Berrian, *History of Trinity Church, New York* (1847).

[4] He had received the honorary degree of D.D. Aberdeen in 1769 and of King's College, New York, in 1770.

[5] S.P.G. Journal, Vol. 17, p. 366.

[6] *Ibid.* Vol. 16, p. 222.   [7] 'B' MSS. Vol. 3, No. 266.

his time to Fort Hunter, although he expressed a fear that "his ignorance of the language and his broken constitution made him ill qualified for the office".[1]

The great interest which Sir William showed in the work of the S.P.G. is a revealing sidelight on the character of that remarkable man. In 1766 he had been elected a member of the Society[2] and from then until his death he devoted much of his time and talents to the furtherance of its objects, as may be seen in the many carefully thought-out suggestions contained in his letters to the Secretary. Sir William's meeting with Mr Munro occurred shortly after the baronet's great conference with the Six Nations and the tribes of the Ohio at Fort Stanwix to settle the boundaries between the English Colonies and the Indians' territories, under instructions from the Home Government.[3] Over 2000 Indians assembled at this important gathering, which deliberated for nearly two weeks, and on 5 November a formal deed was signed by Sir William Franklin[4] (Governor of New Jersey) and commissioners from Virginia and Pennsylvania, and six of the principal *sachems* headed by the Mohawk Abraham.[5] The

[1] 'B' MSS, Vol. 3, No. 268.
[2] *Vide* S.P.G. Journal, Vol. 17, p. 109.
[3] Cf. *New York Docs.* Vol. VIII, pp. 111 *et seq.*
[4] Sir William Franklin (1731–1813) was a son of the celebrated Benjamin Franklin. He served with distinction as a captain at Ticonderoga, and in 1757 visited England with his father who was then Colonial Agent of Pennsylvania. In 1762 he was knighted and appointed Governor of New Jersey. During the revolution he took the opposite side to his father and became one of the leading loyalists. He was taken prisoner in 1776 and exchanged in 1778 when he emigrated to England (*vide New York Docs.* Vol. VII, p. 837 footnote). He became a member of the S.P.G. in 1771 (*vide S.P.G. Annual Report*, 1771, p. 21).
[5] It appears from a study of the New York Colonial Documents that this was "Little Abraham", son of Abraham (the brother of "King" Hendrick) who is generally referred to as "Old Abraham". The latest reference to "Old Abraham" is in June 1756 at a conference held by Sir William Johnson at Onondaga (*New York Docs.* Vol. VII, p. 146). In May 1756 both are mentioned as being present at a conference at Fort Johnson and are there spoken of as "Abraham,

deed was witnessed by Sir William Johnson, and a map showing the agreed boundary line was prepared by Colonel Guy Johnson (the baronet's nephew), then acting as Deputy Indian Agent to his uncle.[1]

In his next letter (14 July 1769) Mr Munro reported that he had now visited the Mohawks on several occasions, and had also been to Schenectady where a new church had recently been erected. Mr Munro officiated at the opening of this building and Sir William Johnson and his family attended the ceremony.[2]

The need for a resident minister at Fort Hunter, Schenectady and Johnstown had now become urgent. The latter village had been laid out by Sir William some years previously and possessed "a neat stone Church" which Johnson had built.[3] In 1764 the baronet had built Johnson Hall—a wooden mansion still standing in the village of Johnstown—which he made the headquarters of the great domain of the 100,000 acres on the north bank of the Mohawk River granted to him by the King for his services in the conquest of Canada. In the course of a few years a number of European settlers had taken up their residence at Johnstown, which had now become too large a parish for a single clergyman to supervise in addition to Albany, Schenectady and Fort Hunter. Of these, the mission at Fort Hunter was rightly considered the most important for the evangelization of the Iroquois from the convenience of its situation and its long association in the minds of the tribesmen.

the chief Sachem of Conajoharrie castle and young Abraham, a chief Sachem of the lower Mohawk Castle" (*ibid*. p. 115). The subsequent references are simply to "Abraham" or "Abraham, chief Sachem of the lower Mohawk Castle", from which it may be presumed that "Old" Abraham was now dead. The last speech recorded of "Old Abraham" ends with these words: "We are inviolably attached to our Brethren the English"—a fitting sentiment from one who had done so much to foster the alliance.

[1] *New York Docs.* Vol. VIII, pp. 111–37.
[2] 'B' MSS. Vol. 3, No. 269.
[3] Letter, Sir William Johnson, 'B' MSS. Vol. 2, No. 87.

PLATE XI

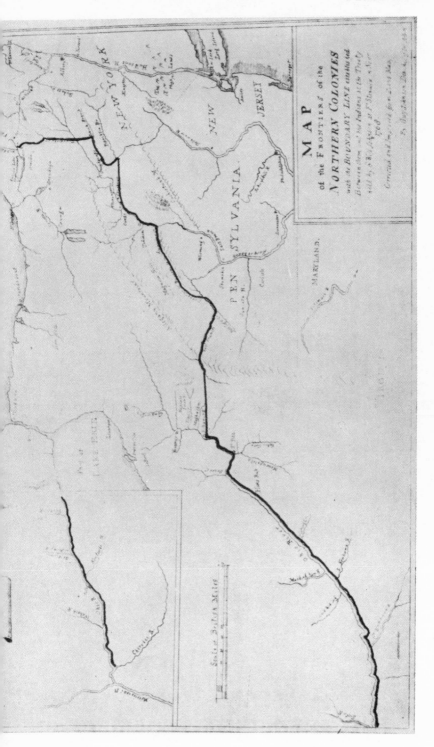

The appointment of a suitable missionary for Fort Hunter had occupied Sir William's attention since the resignation of the Rev. Thomas Browne in 1766. In October of that year Sir William wrote to the Society pointing out the great importance of the Mission on the grounds that certain Dissenting missionaries were now making proselytes of the Indians, and were not only undermining the Mohawks' loyalty to the Crown but were exercising a demoralizing influence on the young warriors who were thereby in danger of "becoming a gloomy race & losing their Ability for hunting, & spending their Time in Idleness". In the same letter he suggested that an Indian training school should be established so that young Mohawks of ability could become qualified to teach their own people.[1]

The Dissenting missionaries referred to by Sir William were adherents of the Rev. Eleazer Wheelock, D.D., a Congregationalist minister. Some years previously, Dr Wheelock had opened a free school for Europeans and Indians at Lebanon, Connecticut, known as Moor's Indian Charity School after Joshua Moor, the donor of the lands and buildings. In 1769 the school was removed to Hanover, New Hampshire, and incorporated as Dartmouth College in honour of the Earl of Dartmouth, Chairman of the Trustees, Dr Wheelock becoming the first President. The most successful of Dr Wheelock's pupils was the Rev. Samuel Kirkland,[2] who served for forty years as a missionary among the Senecas and Oneidas, and founded the Hamilton Oneida Academy (afterwards Hamilton College).

A few weeks after the Treaty of Fort Stanwix Sir William wrote to the Society concerning the difficulties he experienced from the Dissenters, especially with regard to the Indian

[1] 'B' MSS. Vol. 2, No. 86.
[2] During the War of Independence Mr Kirkland adhered to the revolutionists and in 1779 he became Brigade Chaplain in General Sullivan's campaign against the Indians of Western New York. He died in 1808 (cf. *New York Docs.* Vol. VIII, p. 631 footnote).

boundary, and his intended gift of land for the use of the Church:

...I cannot help Lamenting the unhappy disadvantages...thro' the want of an Episcopate in America. The Reasonableness of such Establishment, & the Distresses which are occasioned thro' this want have been so fully described that I need not enlarge upon them, but I become daily more sensible of these truths from the Conduct of those of other Denominations whose Religious Principles are so far from being adapted to our Constitution that they cannot omit any oportunity of raising and Strengthening themselves 'till they finally acquire a Superiority in all Matters Religious & Civil, the event of which may be easily forseen, and a variety of Disputes, perhaps a Religious War in [the] future, can only be prevented by giving the Established Religion such present Countenance and Support as there is no reason to think they will ever make a bad use of, for (different from the views of others) they will have all they want in possessing their own Religion according to its Rights and Institutions. In short we cannot have a Clergy here without an Episcopate, and this Want as it has occasioned many to embrace other persuasions, will oblidge greater Numbers to follow their Example, of which the Dissenters are very Sensible, and by pretended fears of an Episcopal power, as well as by magnifying their own Numbers and lessening ours give it all possible Opposition. The Fund they lately raised in England will answer various purposes, they have long had an Eye on part of Pensilvania in virtue of an absurd Claim, & they Seldom lose sight of a favourite object, of which I shall give a recent Instance.

The late Treaty for the Boundary Line was thought the only Salutary measure for preventing disputes about Encroachments, I received his Majesty's Orders for the Settlement of it, and the same was much desired by yᵉ Colonies Concerned, Nevertheless Missionaries came up from N[ew] England with a view to Obstruct it, One of them strongly recommended to me by Mr Wheelock of Connecticut with his Collegue Memorialled me that the Line should not be Extended to the North or West, but reserved for yᵉ purposes of their Religious Plan, previous to which they went amongst the Oneidas, and used all the Arguments in their power to disswade them from agreeing to the Line proposed, & afterwards on Several Occasions, publickly avowed they had done so, n the presence of Several Gentlemen of Character who attended he treaty, to whom they declared that they would Still continue to give it all the Obstruction in their power in which they were as good as their Words, 'tho I prevailed over all their Artifices, obtained a Secure Boundary, & an advantagious & Extensive Cession of Lands to the Crown. The Arguments they made use of in private amongst the Indians, their Misrepresentations of our Religion, & the Extraordinary private Instructions of Mr Wheelock, of which I am accidentally possessed would shew them in a very odd Light. I write this for the Society's Information knowing at the same time that if it were public it would draw upon me a great deal of Scurrility of which they are but too Liberal, whenever their Schemes are Attacked, or laid open to the Publick.

I think I have now fallen upon a Measure for Obtaining a very Handsome & Valuable Tract for ye purposes of Religion in this Province. Some Gentlemen having applied to purchase a very large Tract of Land adjoining to my Estate here & Extending from the Rear of the Pattented Lands near Conajohare to Sacondaga (a Branch of Hudson's within twelve Miles of the Mohawk River) I became concerned with them, with a view to obtaining a part in so Valuable a Scituation for the use of the Church, & have Settled the purchase, my Share in which cost £100, and is about Twenty Thousand Acres. There are many Gentlemen who would now give a large Sum for the Indian purchase, and take out the Patent themselves, but as I have reason to think that the Society have Interest enough to obtain the King's Grant for it, with a remission of the verry high Fees paid here on taking out Patents, & that as I presume they might obtain it free of Quit Rent, or on some Slender Acknowledgement, I will, in case they can Obtain His Majesty's Grant freely make a gift of the Indian purchase to be vested in the Society until the Appointment of an Episcopate, & then to go towards a provision for that Establishment; If this is approved of, I will send them a full Description of the Land, to enable them to take out the Grant, and I am sensible from its quality and Scituation it will yield at least £100 Sterg P Ann within 10 years, probably in much less time. Whenever the Boundary Line is closed to the Northward a Larger Tract may be obtained, but this is so much better Scituated that it is more immediatly worth Attention. I find it is Extremely difficult if not impracticable to get Clergymen here to Supply the Missions. I wish Mr Seabury[1] may incline to accept of one of them, but I imagine he has a better Living where he is Settled. Another

---

[1] The Rev. Samuel Seabury, S.P.G. Rector of West Chester, New York; consecrated the first American Bishop in 1784.

Difficulty arises about Schoolmasters who are Extremely necessary, particularly at the Mohawks & Conajohare, but I find none who are in the least qualified that would undertake that office for less than Twenty five Pounds Ster!ᵍ P Annum, as their Diet & Lodging would make a great hole in that Sum. However as I write to Dʳ Auchmuty on this Subject, I may for the present decline adding any thing further than that I am with Sincere Regard

Sir

Your most Obedient & Very Humble Servant

W. JOHNSON.[1]

In the matter of the need for a Colonial Episcopate—a need which had been repeatedly stressed by the S.P.G. from the time of its foundation—Sir William naturally felt very strongly. The Colonial Church suffered many grave disadvantages from the entire lack of bishops, who alone could have exercised an organizing and controlling authority among the widely scattered clergy and congregations. An equally important aspect of the case lay in the necessity for candidates of American birth to go to England for ordination. A large proportion of the American clergy were colonial born and were thus forced to incur the expense of a transatlantic voyage. The dangers of this journey can hardly be appreciated to-day, for in the middle years of the eighteenth century it was estimated that approximately five out of every twenty of the men who went to England for Ordination were lost at sea by reason of shipwreck, capture by pirates or the French, or illness contracted on the voyage.[2] Nevertheless despite the many urgent representations by the Society and the leading ecclesiastics in England, the Home Government declined to inaugurate a colonial Episcopate until the great upheaval of the War of Independence and the consequent influx of many thousands of American loyalists to Canada induced Parliament to grant this long-delayed relief.[3]

[1] 'B' MSS. Vol. 2, No. 89.   [2] *Vide* S.P.G. records.
[3] An account of the Society's endeavours to establish an American Episcopate and the politico-ecclesiastical controversy which occurred in the American Colonies on this important matter will be found in the author's *Life and Letters of Charles Inglis: His Ministry in America and Consecration as First Colonial Bishop, from 1759 to 1787*, Chaps. I and III, S.P.C.K. London, 1936.

In December 1769 Sir William Johnson informed the Society that he had obtained the services of two schoolmasters, Messrs Colin McLeland and Edward Hall, for Fort Hunter and Johnstown, and that Mr William Andrews, a prospective ordinand, had been recommended to him for the mission of Schenectady where some of his relations were residing.[1] These three gentlemen were accordingly appointed at a meeting of the Society held in the following April (1770).[2] In the same month Sir William again wrote to the Society recommending the bearer of the letter, John Stuart (a graduate of Philadelphia College), who was "well represented by the clergy of Virginia for a Mission", with a view to receiving ordination preparatory to taking over the mission of Fort Hunter.[3]

Meanwhile the important question of the Society's work among the Iroquois had claimed the attention of the Rev. Charles Inglis, formerly S.P.G. missionary at Dover, Delaware, and now an assistant curate at Trinity Church, New York. In May (1770) he visited Sir William Johnson to discuss various schemes for the Mohawk mission, taking with him the Rev. Myles Cooper, D.D., President of King's College, New York, who was anxious to obtain some Indian youths as students at the College. The day after their arrival at Johnson Hall, a deputation of Mohawk elders came to see them, headed by Little Abraham (referred to by Inglis as "the present reigning Sachem"), whose young nephew was there baptized by Dr Cooper, Mr Inglis standing as godfather.[4]

[1] 'B' MSS. Vol. 2, No. 92.
[2] S.P.G. Journal, Vol. 18, pp. 371–2.
[3] 'B' MSS. Vol. 2, No. 92. Stuart was 30 years old and is thus described by the Rev. Charles Inglis in a letter to the Rev. Dr Samuel Johnson: "He is 6 Feet 4 Inches high, of a robust Constitution, a good Scholar and of unblemished Character" (New York Historical Society's Collection). He was the son of Andrew Stuart, a Scottish Covenanter, who emigrated to America prior to 1740 (cf. Monograph, *The Rev. John Stuart and his Family*, by the late Professor A. H. Young).
[4] Letter, Inglis to Rev. Dr Samuel Johnson (New York Historical Society's Collection).

On their return to New York the two clergymen wrote the following joint report to the Society:

New York. 12 June. 1770.

Rev.ᵈ Sir,

The Subject of the following Relation being, as we apprehend, of great Consequence to the Interest of Religion in this Province, we beg Leave to communicate it to you, and, by your means, to the Society for the Propagation of the Gospel, to whose attention, with all imaginable Respect and Deference, we take the Liberty to recommend it.

About three weeks ago, we took a Journey of between two and three Hundred miles, to pay a visit to S.ʳ William Johnson, in the Mohawks' Country, whom we have just Reason to look upon as one of the most able, as well as most willing Laymen on this Side the Atlantic, to promote the Interest of the Church to which we have the Happiness of belonging.

The Day after our Arrival at Johnson Hall, we were not a little surprized at a formal Deputation of Indians from the lower Mohawk Castle, to the number of nine; of which Three were principal Men in their Nation. After being conducted into the apartment where Councils etc. are generally holden, and when yᵉ accustomary Comps: had reciprocally passed, by the Mouth of an Interpreter, the chief Sachem, by the same Medium, spake to the following Effect—

"That the Mohawks, who in general entertained the highest Regard for the Church of England (as far as they could be supposed to be acquainted with the Doctrines which She taught) were thankful to the Society for their former Goodness, in sending Missionaries to propagate the blessed light of the Gospel amongst them; tho' they could not but lament, that these Teachers had seen cause to leave them, almost as soon as they had well learned their language, and were thereby rendered capable of being more extensively useful to a forlorn unenlightened people. That they still more lamented, that such Ministers had never yet had any successors in their Mission, and were greatly surprized at being of late, and for several years past, so much neglected, notwithstanding S.ʳ William's repeated Applications, and the promises they had received, by his Means, of a speedy, and effectual Supply. But more than all,

"That their Amazement was encreased at yᵉ Information they had but lately received of the Government's Indulgence of a

Missionary to the Tribe of their Popish Brethren, who had, all
along, till the Conclusion of the late war, been inveterate Enemies
to the Crown and People of Great Britain; whilst They themselves
who had ever been our unshaken Friends, in Times of the greatest
Danger and Distress, and had shed the purest Blood in their
Nation in our Cause, and for our Defence, should, in Their
Opinion be so undeservedly left to wander out of the way, and
have the Mortification to find that all their Applications for a
Clergyman had hitherto been rejected.

"That they intreated us, however, to do all we could to second
S.ʳ William's Endeavour for the obtaining of their Request, and
were not yet utterly without Hopes of Success; especially as a
Missionary, with a tolerable Income from home, might now live
very comfortably among them, as a good House and Glebe were
prepared for his Reception, where they hoped a good man, who
was intent on the welfare of their Souls, might be induced to
end his Days, with much Advantage to them and Satisfaction to
Himself."

Such was the purport of their Talk; and then, in Token of
Amity, and in Confirmation of their good Disposition to the
Church of England and ourselves, They presented us with a Belt
of Wampum: and we, in promise of making Representations in
their Favour, returned them another, which S.ʳ William had
supplied us with for that purpose. Their's we beg leave to present
to the Society for some of y.ᵉ same Reasons that the Indians
gave it to us: it will be delivered to you, along with this, by
M.ʳ David Griffith,[1] whom we have recommended to the Society's
Service.

On our Return an Indian Child, which had been born since
M.ʳ Munro had been there, was brought to us from Fort Hunter,
which one of us baptized, the other being a Sponsor. The Mother,
and the other women that attended, were very decent, well
behaved people, and expressed an earnest Desire of having a
Minister once more appointed, regularly to officiate at their
Churches.

Such was the Behaviour, and such were the Requests of his
Majesty's best Indian Allies—the faithful Mohawks—whose Case
we think truly worthy the Attention of Government; which we
cannot but hope that y.ᵉ worthy Society, especially in such Circumstances, have Interest sufficient to Commend: and we are

[1] The Rev. David Griffith, S.P.G. missionary at Gloucester and
Waterford, N.J., 1770–1.

confident that they will take such Steps, as their superior Judgments shall deem necessary—

We are, Revd Sir, your and Their most obedient
and very humble Servants

MYLES COOPER.

CHARLES INGLIS.[1]

By the same packet Mr Inglis wrote a covering letter to the Secretary of the S.P.G.:

New York, June 15, 1770.

Revd Worthy Sir,

By this Conveyance you will receive a joint Letter from the Rev. Dr. Cooper, the worthy President of King's College in this City, and myself in Behalf of the Mohawk Indians. As the Circumstances which gave Rise to our Application are particularly related in that Letter, I shall not repeat them here. One principal Reason for my going to Sir William Johnson's, where the Mohawks requested Dr. Cooper & me to write to the Society in their Favour, was to converse with Sir William about the State of the Indians & get what Intelligence I could from him, as well as by seeing the Indians and their Situation....

I have thought much of this Subject lately, & consulted all that were capable of giving me Information about it; particularly Sir William Johnson, who, from his thorough Knowledge of Indian Affairs, is the best qualified perhaps of any to form a proper Plan. He is a Zealous Churchman. Sensible how closely the Honour of the Church & Welfare of the State are connected with the Execution of such a Scheme, he promises his hearty Concurrence, & to do every Thing in his Power to further it. He thinks, that a Representation of the State of the Indians, setting forth the Advantages that would arise from their Conversion—that a regular Plan judiciously formed, in which he will lend his assistance—that this laid before the Public, & supported by the Society & other Friends of the Church, here & in England; Would draw the Attention of well disposed Christians & awake their Charity— That such a Plan would bid fair to succeed at this Juncture, when so many Circumstances concur to favour it here; such as the Dependence of the Indians on the English, the general Peace that now prevails, & the Inclination which appears in many Tribes to embrace Christianity. To these I may add the very great Influence

[1] 'B' MSS. Vol. 3, No. 339.

which Sir William has over the several Tribes of Indians, the Confidence they repose in him, the Earnestness he expresses to have the Design carried on, & the Vigour with which I am persuaded he would support it.

Sir William has communicated to me in Writing a Sketch of such a Plan. Conscious that I am not sufficiently acquainted with Indian Affairs to form it myself, & that its Success, humanly speaking, could only be insured by a strict Attention to Circumstances, & making them subservient to the Design; which Circumstances could only be known by a long Intercourse with the Indians: I applied to him on this Head, as his good Sense and thorough Knowledge of Indian affairs enabled him to form an accurate Judgment of it. I have collected some Materials relative to the State of the Indians, & other Matters that should be considered; but before any Thing further was done, I thought it necessary to consult the venerable Society. Without their Approbation I would not presume to go on; & if they approve it, I must beg their Direction. I have no End in View, besides the Extension of our Saviour's Kingdom, the Honour of the Society, & of that Church to which I have the Happiness to belong.

It is much to be lamented that the present Dissentions in the State,[1] & the violent Opposition to Government, are unfavourable to any such Measure & must draw the Attention of the Ministry from it. Yet Things may take another Turn; and if this political Ferment should subside, weighty Arguments are not wanting to evince the Expediency of Christianizing the Indians. The Savages on this Continent are a numerous, fierce & Warlike People. It is of the utmost Consequence to the Colonies to secure their Friendship & attach them to our Interest. Reason and Experience demonstrate this cannot be so effectually done as by proselyting them to Christianity, as professed by the Church of England. The Mohawks are an uncontestible Proof of this. The Popish Missionaries are numerous & active—zealous as ever to draw them into the Bosom of their Church. Their Labours meet with Success, & they have the greatest Influence over the Proselytes. Dr. Wheelock has his Missionaries, such as they are, at Work among them. One of them in particular, who is settled among the Oneidas, a numerous Tribe that received some Impressions of Christianity from the Society's Missionaries, is becoming popular, & gains

[1] This refers to the increasing ill-feeling between the American Colonists and the English Government since the Stamp Act of 1764.

Ground.[1] He has enough of those Missionaries at Command; for indeed they make no Sacrifice by settling among Savages. And altho the Indians discover a greater Inclination to be instructed by the Society's Missionaries or Clergy of the Church than by these; yet if the latter continue among them, & none of the former visit them, Wheelock's Missionaries will succeed; & I can averr on the best & most authentic Evidence, that the Principles inculcated by them, are by no Means favourable to Government. Let these Circumstances be weighed, besides many more of a similar Nature that might be added; & any Person of Discernment must see that they may & probably will, in Time to come, produce the most allarming Consequences—Consequences which it is the Wisdom & Interest of Government to prevent by a timely Interposition. Whether the Government would not do so & afford its Aid in the present Design, upon due Representation of these Things, cannot, I humbly conceive, be fully known before a Trial is made.

Dr. Wheelock collected large Sums in England[2] for his School— some thousands of Pounds by his own Confession. Can it be supposed that well disposed People would be less liberal to this Scheme, when under the Direction of so respectable a Body as the Society, & attended with so many promising Circumstances? Especially if proper Measures be taken to lay them before the Public, & collect Money. I humbly conceive that some vigorous Effort of this Sort is necessary to draw the Attention of the People. A single Mission in the old, beaten Way makes no Noise. Few regard it. But an extensive plan, with the Society at its Head, supported by Sir William Johnson's Influence here, & attended with the greatest Probability of Success, would not fail, I imagine, to command Notice, & awake the slumbering Charity of many Christians. Many just Objections be against Dr. Wheelock's Scheme. It is too contracted, injudiciously formed, & inadequate to the Design of Christianizing the Indians, to say no worse. Yet it serves the Ends of the Dissenters well enough, to make a Bustle; & will gain Credit, if no better Scheme is set on Foot.

I request that you, Good Sir, would be pleased to consult the Society & let me know their Sentiments of this Affair. My Intention is to represent the State, Number, Situation & some other Circumstances of the several Tribes of Indians bordering on this

[1] The Rev. Samuel Kirkland.

[2] One of his Indian pupils, Samson Occum, visited England and collected £10,000.

Government—to propose the Plan laid down by Sir William Johnson for the Conversion of the Indians, which appears the most rational & judicious I have yet seen, & obviate the Objections that have been propagated by the Dissenters of late with Regard to the first Emigrants to America, as if they had been all Dissenters who fled from Episcopal Persecution; which may also serve to obviate some Objections that have been raised to an American Episcopate—& to place in as strong a Light as I can the several Circumstances which now concur to insure Success to such an Attempt at Converting the Savages....

> With the sincerest Esteem, I am,
> Rev.ᵈ Sir
> The Society's
> And your most obedient
> and humble servt.
>
> CHARLES INGLIS.[1]

Mr Inglis' labours bore fruit a year later in a lengthy Memorial which he submitted to the Society. The Memorial consisted of an historical and topographical account of the Iroquois and specified the existing numbers and condition of the tribes. Then followed a series of arguments of a pronounced political nature setting forth the reasons why the Home Government should assist in the evangelization of the Iroquois, to which was appended a detailed plan specifying the number of missionaries and schoolmasters to be employed and the regulations under which they were to be governed. The Memorial concluded with a general review of the problem and emphasized those circumstances which pointed to the success of the scheme.[2] This document was taken to England by the Rev. Dr Myles Cooper and presented to Lord Hillsborough, the Secretary of State for the Colonies.[3]

About the same time Mr Munro wrote to the Society

---

[1] 'B' MSS. Vol. 2, No. 65.
[2] Letter, Inglis to S.P.G., *ibid.* No. 67.
[3] *S.P.G. Annual Report*, 1771, p. 21.

reporting a visit which he paid to the Mohawks in company with Sir William Johnson and some other gentlemen:

Reverend Sir,

...In June last I had a very Agreeable Journey up the Mohawk River, to Canajoharee the upper Indian Castle, which is Seventy Six miles from Albany, being Accompanied thither by Sir William Johnson, & Some of the principal Gentlemen of that Country. In this Castle, Sir William has lately built, at his own Expence, a very Neat & elegant Church for the use of the Indians; which being then finished, I had an Invitation from him to perform divine Service in it, & administer the holy Communion for the first time. Here, after reading the morning Prayer, I delivered Two Discourses; one to the White people, & another to the Indians by an Interpreter,—after which I administered the holy Sacrament to Nineteen Indian Communicants belonging to both Castles; and before my Departure gave them an Exhortation....

The Behaviour of these Indians on this occasion was remarkably good; The Solemnity & Seriousness of their Devotion was highly pleasing not only to me, but to all the Spectators. After divine Service they addressed me by their Interpreter, thanking me for my visit, expressing at the Same time their grateful acknowledgements to the Honourable Society for all favours, hoping their pious Care over them may be continued, & requesting above all things, that a missionary may be Sent without Loss of time, to reside in their Castle. Two Days following, on my Return to Albany, I waited on the Sachems of the lower Castle, & visited the Indian School, Which, I can assure the Society, is in a very promising way. The Schoolmaster is universally beloved by the Indians, & their Children are making considerable Proficiency under his Care, both in Reading & Writing. In Short Sir, It is hardly possible for me to express the Joy I felt on this Occasion; To See So fair a prospect; So many Indians behaving So decently, So inoffensively, & So civilized, must certainly Afford great pleasure to Every good man that has the Interest of Virtue & Religion at heart; To See So many Omens presaging Some future good, & Some greater Reformation; All which I must ascribe, under God, to the pious Care, Assiduity & Patronage of the Worthy Sir William Johnson & his family; who Spare no Costs nor pains in promoting the laudable Design of the Society. And here I am bound in gratitude to mention the infinite Obligations I am under to Col! Claus, Sir William's Son in Law;—A Gentleman

of a most Amiable Character, & highly respected in these parts;—
This Gentleman's Influence among the Indians is great; Well
acquainted with their Language & Customs; a true friend to
Religion, & to the Church of England; The Pains he takes in
translating my discourses to the Indians, which he does to their
great Satisfaction; The good Example he sets them in attending
divine Service & partaking the holy Communion, is truly praise-
worthy, & must forever endear him to me; In Short, to this
Gentleman, in Conjunction with Sir William's friendship &
Patronage, I owe all my usefulness among the Indians....

I am, Reverend Sir,

The Honourable Society's and

Your most Obedient,

Most humble Servant,

HARRY MUNRO.

Albany. Sep! 25!ʰ

1770.

To the Revᵈ Doctor Burton.[1]

A year later (October 1772) Sir William Johnson notified
the Society that he had obtained the services of the Rev.
Richard Mosley (formerly S.P.G. missionary in Litchfield
County, Connecticut) as missionary for Johnstown.[2] Thus
the parishes of Albany, Schenectady, Fort Hunter and Johnstown were now all supplied with ministers,[3] and thenceforward the missionaries at Albany and Schenectady were
able to devote their labours to their own congregations, the
work among the Iroquois being conducted from Fort Hunter
and Johnstown.

Meanwhile the Rev. John Stuart had returned from England after receiving ordination and had begun his ministry
at Fort Hunter in December 1770. In his first letter to the
Society (dated 30 January 1771) he reported that he had been
hospitably welcomed by the Mohawks and had visited Conajoharie on Christmas Day, when he preached and administered

---

[1] 'B' MSS. Vol. 3, No. 271. (The Rev. Daniel Burton, D.D., had
succeeded the Rev. Dr Bearcroft as Secretary of the S.P.G. in 1761.)
[2] 'B' MSS. Vol. 2, No. 93.
[3] I.e. the Revs. Munro, Andrews, Stuart and Mosley.

the Sacrament to twenty Indians. At Fort Hunter Mr Stuart held two services every Sunday, one for the Indian converts and a second for the European residents in the district who now formed a congregation (of various denominations) of some 200 persons.[1] Some months later Sir William Johnson repaired the chapel at Fort Hunter and provided it with "a new floor, pulpit, desk, Communion Table, windows, belfry and bell", which earned him profound gratitude from the missionary.[2]

In July 1772 Mr Stuart wrote the following account of his mission to the Society:

Fort Hunter, Tryon County. July 20th 1772.

Revd Sir,

I continue, as mentioned in my former Letters, to divide my Time & Labour between the indian & white Inhabitants of this Place.

The Indians, in general, behave decently, and attend the public Worship of God with great Reverence & Devotion,—and many of them discover Signs of Repentance & Amendment of Life; Altho' others still continue in their former State;—the immoderate Use of Spirituous Liquors is often attended with horrid Consequences, and, all the Steps I have yet taken have proved ineffectual to prevent them;—there appears in the Conduct of even the best of them something savage and cruel, especially when intoxicated. They are respectful and obedient to me, and give extraordinary Attention to my Advice.

Their Language being so barren & difficult to acquire I thought it expedient to procure a young Man of their own Nation, (who understands English) to reside with me as a private Tutor, & public Interpreter.—by his assistance I have given them a Sermon every Sunday, since March last—'tis uncertain how long he will continue with me, as I cannot afford him a sufficient Maintainance, to induce him to neglect Hunting, & reside constantly here. The smallness of the Society's Funds, & their extraordinary Expences have deterred me from making any Application for a small Allowance for him. I chose rather to appropriate Part of my own Salary to that Use.

[1] 'B' MSS. Vol. 2, No. 196.
[2] Letter, Rev. J. Stuart to S.P.G., *ibid*. No. 198.

I have frequently visited the Indians at Canajohare, and baptized their Children, preach'd to them, & administred the Holy Communion there. They frequently lament their Condition, in being deprived of a settled Minister to administer these Ordinances to them & perform the other Duties annexed to his office. In the Knowledge of Christianity, they are nearly the same as their Brethren here,—but their Practice is, in common, worse. I find it extremely difficult to act a conscientious Part among them, for, let their common Behaviour be what it will, they are desirous, in general, to partake of the Holy Communion. Now, to admit those who are notorious Drunkards & vicious in their Behaviour, brings a Scandal on Religion, and offends the sober Part of their Brethren:—And, to refuse them, reduces them to a kind of Dispair, and often urges them to commit worse Crimes than before; for they then are pointed at as Persons unfit for Society. My Method hitherto has been, to admit the sober, & to reject the notoriously vicious; altho I have been the Object of their Resentment for this Conduct, and have narrowly escaped the Effects of it.

My white Congregation increases,—divine Service is performed every Sunday Evening in English in the Mohawk Chapel,—the Audience is commonly about 100 Persons, of which 20 are Communicants, & the major Part of the Remainder professed Members of the Church of England. They have hitherto made me no allowance for this Labour, and, whether they will, or not, is doubtful; for tho they are numerous yet, generally, they are poor.

Upon the whole, I have the Pleasure to acquaint the Society that my Ministry in this Place, (through God's Blessing) appears to have been successful:—a more affecting Sense of Religion,—a more constant Attendance on public Worship,—and a visible Amendment in the Lives of many, are the happy Fruits which daily appear....

In the mean Time, Revd Sir,

I am, with the greatest Respect

your Friend & hum! Serv!

JOHN STUART.

N.B. The Number of Comm.^{ts}
on Whitsunday last was
Indian 14 } 1
white—13 }

---

[1] Letter, Rev. J. Stuart to S.P.G., 'B' MSS. Vol. 2, No. 199.

The Indian interpreter here mentioned by Mr Stuart as living with him was none other than the celebrated Joseph Brant (Thayendanegea), at that time a young man of twenty-nine.[1] The varying statements which have been given of this distinguished chieftain's origin may warrant a short account of his family and parentage.

From the researches of his biographer, certain evidences contained in the *Documents Relating to the Colonial History of New York* and the archives of the S.P.G., it appears that Joseph Brant was a grandson of the *sachem* Brant who visited England with "King" Hendrick and two other chieftains in 1710.[2] Joseph's father has been identified with "Nickus Brant" *alias* "Old Brant" (Aroghiadecka) who is mentioned several times in Sir William Johnson's dispatches and diaries and who was present at the signing of the Treaty of Fort Stanwix in 1768.[3] Nickus Brant married a daughter of "Old Abraham" (and therefore a niece of "King" Hendrick)[4] and had three sons, of whom Joseph was the youngest.[5] Joseph's sister, Mary ("Molly") Brant, became the acknowledged mistress of Sir William Johnson and through her the baronet's already great influence with the Mohawks attained an almost regal significance.

The first mention of Joseph Brant occurs when he was but thirteen years old as being with Sir William Johnson at the battle of Lake George. He also accompanied the expedition to Niagara in the following year.[6] At the conclusion of this campaign Sir William sent him to Dr Wheelock's school at Lebanon where he learnt to read and write in the English tongue. On the outbreak of Pontiac's rebellion Brant joined a loyal band of Mohawks who were engaged in co-operating with the Europeans against the rebellious Indians.[7] He had

[1] Cf. W. L. Stone's *Life of Joseph Brant* (1838), Vol. I, p. 27.

[2] Cf. Chap. II, p. 26, and the *sachems'* letter to the S.P.G., with Brant's signature (illustration facing p. 30).

[3] *New York Docs.* Vol. VIII, p. 113.

[4] Cf. a valuable Monograph by W. Max Reid (author of *The Mohawk Valley*).   [5] *Life of Brant*, Vol. I, pp. 19–20.

[6] *Ibid.*   [7] *Ibid.* pp. 22–5.

previously married the daughter of an Oneida *sachem*[1] and
when peace was declared he settled at Conajoharie, the
"Upper Castle" of the Mohawks. In 1772 his wife died and
shortly afterwards he applied to Mr Stuart to marry him to
her half-sister. This the missionary refused to countenance,
and the ceremony is said to have been performed by a German
minister.[2] By his first wife Brant had a son and a daughter,
but no children were born of the second marriage.

Meanwhile, affairs at Schenectady parish had improved
with the appointment of the Rev. William Andrews. A year
previously (1769) the congregation had (after numerous in-
terruptions) completed a new stone church dedicated to
St George.[3] Unfortunately, however, Mr Andrews suffered
from considerable ill-health and towards the end of 1773 he
felt it incumbent upon him to resign.[4] He was succeeded by
the Rev. John Doty, a young clergyman of twenty-eight who
was acting as missionary at St Peter's, Cortland Manor (near
Peak's Kill), New York Province.[5] A few months before this
the Rev. Richard Mosley had resigned from the cure of
Johnstown, largely on account of a protracted lawsuit which
had arisen between himself and the authorities over his claim
to celebrate marriages.[6] Thereafter (at the request of Sir
William Johnson) Mr Stuart, the missionary at Fort Hunter,
conducted occasional services at Johnstown until such time
as a new minister could be appointed.[7] The baronet had early
formed a high opinion of his capabilities and invited his

[1] According to W. Max Reid's Monograph, the mother of Joseph
Brant's wife is said to have been the daughter of "King" Hendrick
(*vide* Pedigree, Appendix B).

[2] *Life of Brant*, Vol. 1, p. 27. The officiating minister was
probably the Rev. J. J. Oël who remained among the Mohawks
until 1777.

[3] Edward F. Rines, *Old Historic Churches of America*, 1936,
Macmillan and Co., New York, pp. 140–1.

[4] Letter, Rev. W. Andrews to S.P.G., 'B' MSS. Vol. 3, No. 11.

[5] S.P.G. Journal, Vol. 20, p. 85. Mr Doty was a native of New
York and an M.A. of King's College.

[6] Letter, Rev. R. Mosley to S.P.G., 'B' MSS. Vol. 3, Nos. 297, 298.

[7] Letter, Rev. J. Stuart to S.P.G., 'B' MSS. Vol. 2, No. 201.

attendance at the conferences with the Six Nations at Johnson Hall.[1]

About this time Sir William Johnson was beginning to fail in health. In the autumn of 1773 he wrote to the Earl of Dartmouth that he was obliged to recruit his strength by a visit "to the Sea Side in order to make use of the Sea Water",[2] and in a further dispatch in the following April he recommended that in case of his death his nephew and son-in-law, Colonel Guy Johnson, might be nominated as his successor.[3] On Saturday, 9 July, Sir William held his last conference with the Iroquois, and on the Monday afternoon while the meeting had adjourned for the chiefs to deliberate, Sir William suddenly expired in a fit of apoplexy.[4] In compliance with the baronet's request Colonel Guy Johnson succeeded him as Superintendent of the Six Nations with Colonel Daniel Claus (Sir William's other son-in-law) as his deputy, while Sir William's son, Sir John Johnson, received his father's appointment as Major-General of the Militia.[5]

The death of Sir William Johnson occurred at the most critical period of the history of the American Colonies. Ever since the passing of the Stamp Act in 1764 the colonists had nursed a growing distrust of the Home Government which culminated nine years later in the "Boston Tea Party" (December 1773). This was followed in February 1774 by the impeachment of Chief Justice Oliver in the New York Assembly on the grounds that judges receiving salaries from the Crown were no longer entitled to public confidence—an action which was tantamount to denying the judicial (and in practice the executive) authority of the Imperial Government. In June the closing of the port of Boston by General Gage brought matters to a climax and resulted in the convening of the first Continental Congress at Philadelphia in September. This body, though not avowedly of a revolutionary character, drew up a "Declaration of Rights" which demanded the

[1] *New York Docs.* Vol. VIII, p. 282.
[2] *Ibid.* p. 395.   [3] *Ibid.* p. 419.
[4] *Ibid.* pp. 475 *et seq.*   [5] *Life of Brant*, Vol. I, p. 33.

PLATE XII

Sir William Johnson, Bart.
(From a contemporary engraving)

repeal of some thirteen Acts of Parliament passed since 1763, including the recent Quebec Act of 1774.[1] To such a sweeping demand there could be but one answer, for had it been complied with, the supreme authority of the British Parliament over the American Colonies would necessarily have terminated. For several generations such a contingency was wholly beyond the vision of our politicians, and in fact a century and a half were to elapse before the self-governing Dominions of the Empire were to obtain this result by the provisions of the Statute of Westminster.[2]

In the meantime the affairs of the Fort Hunter mission had been reported to the S.P.G. by Mr Stuart in the following letter:

Fort Hunter, Tryon County, Aug.[t] 9th 1774.

Rev.[d] Sir,

I take the liberty of acquainting the venerable Society of the present State of this Mission; which I should have done sooner, had I not defered it some Time, in Hopes that the Determination of some Things, long in Agitation, wou'd have enabled me to do it more fully.

I continue to perform Divine Service every Sunday forenoon in the Indian Chapel, in the Mohawk Language, to a regular & devout Congregation of Indians. And in the Afternoon, I preach to a large Assembly of white People, and catechize the young People of this Neighbourhood. The Church will contain upwards of 200, and is often nearly full,—they chiefly profess themselves to be Members of the Church of England, but few of them can be persuaded to become Communicants, neither are they disposed to make me any Allowance for my public or private Administrations. they have given ten Pounds currency to me, for three years and a half's Service.

I likewise have visited the Indians of Canajohare, as usual,— and preach'd & administred the Sacrament to them.—their Situation is really deplorable; For Drunkenness & Vice of every

---

[1] The Quebec Act legalized the retention of Roman Catholicism in Canada, which created great resentment among the Puritan colonists of New England. It also extended the western boundaries of Canada. This antagonized the people of Virginia, Pennsylvania, Massachusetts and Connecticut, who claimed part of this territory.

[2] 22 George V, Cap. IV (1931).

kind prevails amongst them to such a Degree, that several Times, I have not found a sufficient Number of them duly qualified, to whom I cou'd administer the Sacrament. However, they have Prayers read in their Church every Sunday, by an Indian of that Village, at which they generally attend.

Since the Departure of the Rev.ᵈ M.ʳ Mosley from Johnstown, I have (at the Desire of Sir W.ᵐ Johnson) frequently officiated there, —and have lately consented to preach regularly, once every Month, on Sunday afternoon to the People of Johnstown, until that Mission is supplied:—it being so nigh, that I can perform divine Service to the Indians at Fort Hunter, in the forenoon, and preach there in the Afternoon of the same Day. I am sorry to say, that M.ʳ Mosley's Behaviour there has contributed to strengthen the Prejudices of many against the Church.

The Church of England has lost a powerful & Zealous Protector by the Death of Sir William Johnson,—his Influence was always exerted in her Defence, when any Opportunity offered;—and indeed the Clergy of every Denomination have lost, in him, a generous Patron. His Death will be long regretted by all who knew him.

The Indians have long desired, that some pious Tracts, and particularly, that the New Testament might be translated into their Language;—S.ʳ William press'd me to prepare something of that Kind for the Press, and promised to pay the Expence of printing himself, in Consequence of which, I have, (with the Assistance of an Indian who understands English)[1] prepared a Translation of the Gospel of S.ᵗ Mark,—with a large & plain Exposition of the Church Catechism & a compendious History of the Bible, all in the Mohawk Tongue—and they are now nearly ready for the Press. But, as no mention is made of this in Sir William's Will, I cannot expect his Heirs will perform it. I wou'd be glad of the venerable Society's Commands, in this Matter,— whether the Manuscripts, when done shall be sent over to England?—or whether they wou'd chuse to be at the Expence of printing them in N. York, or Philadelphia?

Affairs in America are, at present, in a very critical Situation & particularly in Regard to the Indians.—the Indians to the Southward are actually in Arms, having murdered several Hundreds of white People,—the *five Nations* here profess themselves Friends to the English yet, But are thought, (by good Judges) to be wavering in their Judgment—and should the War become general, my Situation wou'd be by no means an eligible one. . . .[2]

---

[1] I.e. Joseph Brant.   [2] 'B' MSS. Vol. 2, No. 201.

The mention of an Indian rising at the end of this letter refers to what is known as "Cresap's War", so named after a certain Captain Michael Cresap whose wanton cruelty provoked it. In the spring of 1774 a party of land prospectors, led by Cresap, were robbed of their horses by some Indians while exploring near the Ohio. The white men determined to be avenged, and having murdered two Indians (without having conducted any investigations as to the identity of the thieves), they next slaughtered a number of other Indians after winning their confidence by a pretended friendship. These atrocities were soon followed by similar outrages in which two friendly *sachems*—a Delaware and a Shawanese—and some members of the family of John Logan (Tahgahjute),[1] the celebrated "Mingo [i.e. Iroquois] Chief" of the Cayugas, were murdered.[2] As a result of these repeated outrages Logan suddenly attacked an English settlement and numbers of the colonists perished. The Governor of Virginia, Lord Dunmore, thereupon raised a punitive expedition of over 2000 Provincials under the command of Colonel Andrew Lewis. On 10 October a fierce battle was fought near the junction of the Kanawha and Ohio Rivers, in which the tribesmen were heavily defeated and forced to make peace. It was at the peace conference that Logan made his famous speech which was ranked by Jefferson as being superior to any classical oration he had ever read:

I appeal to any White Man to say if he ever entered Logan's cabin hungry, and he gave him no meat; if he ever came cold and naked, and he clothed him not.... Such was my love for the Whites, that my countrymen pointed, as they passed, and said "Logan is the friend of the White Man". I had even thought to have lived with you, but for the injuries of one man. Colonel Cresap, the last Spring, in cold blood and unprovoked, murdered all my relations, not even sparing my women and children; there runs not a drop of my blood in the veins of any living creature.

[1] Said to have been named after James Logan, Wm. Penn's agent in America.

[2] Cf. *Life of Brant*, Vol. i, pp. 39–41, and *New York Docs.* Vol. viii, pp. 460, 461, dispatch of Sir W. Johnson, who alludes to Cresap's "cruelty and baseness".

This called on me for revenge. I have sought it; I have killed many; I have fully glutted my vengeance. For my country, I rejoice at the beams of peace; but do not harbour a thought that mine is the joy of fear. Logan never felt fear. He will not turn on his heel to save his life. Who is there to mourn for Logan? Not one.[1]

The close of this great chief's life was no less tragic. After the conclusion of the peace treaty he sank into a state of profound depression from which he sought relief in wild orgies of intoxication, and some years later he was killed by his own nephew whose animosity he had incurred.[2]

[1] Quoted in *Life of Brant*, Vol. 1, p. 46.
[2] Cf. F. B. Sawvel, *Logan the Mingo* (1921).

CHAPTER VII

THE REVOLUTIONARY WAR

(1775–1782)

On 19 April 1775 the shots fired at Lexington "which echoed round the world" were the prelude to eight years of fratricidal warfare unparalleled before or since in the annals of America. At the beginning of the conflict the balance of opinion lay fairly evenly divided. Actually the first Continental Congress of the previous year contained only a minority of avowed republicans, and many thousands of colonists, who later chose the cause of the "Patriots", were as yet unprepared to throw off British rule. To the republican leaders one important aspect of the situation was early apparent, namely the attitude which the Six Nations of the Iroquois would adopt in the coming struggle. In the past the influence of the Iroquois Confederation had exercised a profound effect on the struggle for dominion between French Canada and the Thirteen English Colonies, and the "Patriots" at once realized the necessity of neutralizing the powerful forces which could thus be marshalled against them. Early in April, some two weeks before the battle of Lexington, the Provincial Congress of Massachusetts wrote to the Rev. Samuel Kirkland (the Dissenting missionary to the Oneidas) desiring him to act as their intermediary by delivering an address to the Mohawk *sachems*. At the same time the Congress sent a further message to the Stockbridge or "River" Indians who maintained a close intimacy with the Oneidas.[1]

Meanwhile Sir John and Colonel Guy Johnson were using every endeavour to win over the Mohawks to the loyalist cause and by the middle of May (1775) the Republican Committee of Safety at Albany received information that Sir John

[1] *Life of Brant*, Vol. I, pp. 56–8.

had fortified Johnson Hall and had armed a number of Scottish Highlanders who lived under his protection at Johnstown.[1] From certain evidence which came to his notice it would seem that Colonel Guy Johnson had a lively apprehension that the republicans intended to abduct him and by this means prevent him from exerting his influence over the Iroquois.[2]

On 25 May republican deputations from Albany and Tryon[3] Counties induced the Mohawk *sachems* to meet them at Guy Park on the Mohawk River. At this meeting the deputies denied the reports concerning Colonel Guy Johnson's intended abduction and assured the *sachems* of their pacific intentions. To this gesture a cautious answer was returned by Little Abraham, who emphasized that his people had no wish to become involved in the White Man's quarrel and that they would at all times be pleased to hear the deputies' sentiments provided that these were made in the presence of the Indian Superintendent, Colonel Johnson.[4]

A few days later the Tryon County Committee wrote a strong letter to Colonel Johnson urging him to use his influence to restrain the Indians from interfering in the controversy between Great Britain and the Colonies. They received a non-committal reply in which Johnson expressed his surprise at the rumours that he intended "setting the Indians on the peaceable inhabitants of the country" and complained that he had been obstructed in his duties as Superintendent. That the Committee's fears were well founded was shown by Johnson's sudden removal to the westerly part of the Mohawk valley accompanied by a large body of Mohawks and his own personal dependants.[5] His cousin, Sir John Johnson, remained at Johnson Hall, which he intended should serve as a rallying point of the local loyalists should need arise.

---

[1] *Life of Brant*, Vol. i, p. 54.

[2] *New York Docs.* Vol. viii, p. 630.

[3] So named after General William Tryon (1725–88) who had been made Governor of New York in 1771.

[4] *Life of Brant*, Vol. i, pp. 70, 71.   [5] *Ibid.* pp. 75–7.

Towards the end of June the Tryon County Committee arranged a meeting with the Oneida and Tuscarora tribes through the offices of Mr Kirkland. At this conference the Indians gave a friendly welcome to the deputies and pledged themselves to remain neutral in the war. This event, which followed a few weeks after the landing of British reinforcements under Generals Sir William Howe, John Burgoyne and Sir Henry Clinton, and only ten days after the battle of Bunker Hill, gave considerable encouragement to the republican leaders.

In the meantime Colonel Guy Johnson had proceeded as far as Ontario where he convened a large Indian conference of the Mohawks, Cayugas and Senecas. He was accompanied by Joseph Brant (who had for some time been acting as his secretary) and Colonel John Butler and his son, Lieutenant Walter Butler.[1] At the close of the conference Johnson and his Mohawks moved to Oswego and thence sailed down the St Lawrence to Montreal where they received an interview from the Governor-General, Sir Guy Carleton,[2] and General Sir Frederick Haldimand.[3] At this conference Carleton and Haldimand induced the Mohawks to take up arms on the side of the Crown under the leadership of Johnson and Joseph Brant.[4]

---

[1] Colonel John Butler had long been an Indian interpreter and had attended the signing of the Treaty at Fort Stanwix in 1768. He later became Colonel Guy Johnson's deputy (cf. *New York Docs.* Vols. VI–VIII *passim*).

[2] Sir Guy Carleton, K.B. (1724–1808), first Lord Dorchester. In 1758 he was present at the capture of Louisburg and served under Wolfe at Quebec. In 1766 he was appointed Lieutenant-Governor of Quebec. He was largely responsible for the "Quebec Act". He succeeded General Gage as Governor and Commander-in-Chief of Canada in 1775 (cf. *Dict. Nat. Biog.*).

[3] Sir F. Haldimand, K.B. (1718–91), was a Swiss. He served in the Swiss and Dutch armies and in 1756 was appointed Lieutenant-Colonel in the 60th Royal Americans. He also served at Ticonderoga, Oswego and Montreal (1758–60) and commanded at New York on General Gage's recall. In 1778 he succeeded Carleton as Governor of Canada (cf. *Dict. Nat. Biog.*).

[4] *Life of Brant*, Vol. I, pp. 89, 90.

Meanwhile the second Continental Congress (at which George Washington had been elected Commander-in-Chief of the republican forces) had assembled at Philadelphia in May. Among other of its labours the Congress established an Indian Department divided into three divisions—Northern, Middle, and Southern—with Commissioners for each division, for the purpose of maintaining the neutrality of the tribes.[1] The jurisdiction of the Six Nations came under the Commissioners of the Northern division, headed by General Philip John Schuyler,[2] a great-nephew of Peter Schuyler, the first Mayor of Albany. On 15 August the Northern Commissioners held a protracted conference with the Iroquois at Albany which lasted until 2 September. The tribes represented were the Mohawks of the Lower Castle and some Onondagas, Cayugas and Senecas, the more prominent members of these tribes and the majority of the Mohawks having already accompanied Colonel Johnson and Brant to Montreal.

After much preliminary speech-making, two whole days were utilized by the Commissioners in a series of speeches voicing the demands of the Congress, which were interpreted to the Indians by Mr Kirkland. The Iroquois' answer was delivered by Little Abraham, who informed the Commissioners of the peaceful intentions of his people. He reminded the deputies that Colonel Johnson had advised them to remain neutral at his recent conference at Oswego[3] and asked that Sir John Johnson, the son of their great patron Sir

---

[1] *New York Docs.* Vol. VIII, p. 605.

[2] Philip J. Schuyler (1733–1804). Served with the provincial forces as a Captain in the Seven Years' War, and as a Major, and was present at Lake George, Ticonderoga and Fort Frontenac (1755–8). Represented Albany in the N.Y. Assembly from 1768 to 1775 and was a delegate to the second Continental Congress. Major-General in the Republican Army in 1775. Superseded and court-martialled in 1778 for the evacuation of Ticonderoga, but acquitted. Resigned from the Army in 1779 (cf. *Encyclopædia Britannica*).

[3] It seems doubtful if Johnson had in fact so advised them in view of his later attitude at Montreal, or else that he had deliberately dissembled his purpose.

William, might not be molested. He then made a similar request on behalf of the Mohawk missionary, the Rev. John Stuart, in these words:

> Our father the minister, was sent us by the King. He does not meddle in civil affairs, but instructs us in the way to Heaven. He absolutely refuses to attend to any political matters, and says they do not belong to him....The Mohawks are frequently alarmed with reports that their minister is to be torn away from them. It would occasion great disturbance were he to be taken away. The King sent him to them, and they would look upon it as taking away one of their body.[1]

On the following day the Commissioners made their answer in which they agreed *inter alia* to respect the person of Mr Stuart who, they declared, "was such a man as we love, and we are desirous of his remaining quiet and happy with you"[2]—a somewhat remarkable statement in view of the missionary's subsequent persecution at the hands of the "Patriots". After some further speeches the meeting closed. It was the last great Indian conference ever held at Albany.

During the next few months the activities of Sir John Johnson in the Mohawk valley had excited the suspicions of the Congress, and in January (1776) General Schuyler was sent with a military force to Johnson Hall to disarm the loyalists and commandeer their munitions. With a view to maintaining the goodwill of the Indians Schuyler proceeded to Schenectady where he was met by Little Abraham and a deputation of Mohawks. The *sachem* reminded Schuyler of the Iroquois' promise to remain neutral, and reiterated his previous request for the safety of Sir John Johnson, which they now heard was imperilled:

> It has [he said] been represented to you, Brothers, that it seems that Sir John is making military preparations, and that he is making a fort round his house; but, Brothers, as we live so near him, we should certainly know if any thing of that nature should be done, especially as we go there so frequently on account of our

[1] *New York Docs.* Vol. VIII, pp. 621–3.
[2] *Ibid.* p. 625.

father, the minister,[1] who sometimes performs divine service at
that place. We have never seen any hostile preparations made
there...and all things remain in the same situation it was in the
life of Sir William.[2]

It will be appreciated that Little Abraham's denials of Sir
John's military preparations were not consistent with the
facts. Schuyler himself was by no means misled by the
sachem's protestations but he nevertheless gave the Indians
his assurance of his goodwill towards them as also to Sir John
Johnson. On the following day Schuyler resumed his march
to Johnson Hall and was met by Sir John and several of his
retainers. The general thereupon offered terms to the baronet
whereby Sir John was to disband his Highlanders, surrender
his arms, munitions and military stores, and give his parole
not to leave Tryon County without the consent of the Congress. Having heard the terms the baronet asked for time
to consider them and returned to his mansion. After some
further negotiations in writing Sir John accepted a modified
form of the original terms[3] and handed over the arms and
munitions of himself and his Highland retainers.[4]

For the next three months affairs remained peaceful at
Johnstown, but in May General Schuyler received information which aroused his suspicions that Sir John was intriguing
with the English loyalists and the Indians. He therefore
ordered a regiment which was marching to Canada to visit
Johnstown and make the baronet a prisoner, but information
reaching Sir John in the nick of time he fled with a number
of his Highland retainers and local loyalists into the forests.
After three weeks of arduous travel they reached Montreal
where Sir John was warmly welcomed by the Governor. At
his own request Sir John received a colonel's commission
and at once raised two battalions of infantry, known as "The

[1] I.e. the Rev. John Stuart.
[2] *Life of Brant*, Vol. i, pp. 125–7. This is the last reference to
Little Abraham and his further history is unknown.
[3] These permitted him to go to any part of the Colony to the south
and eastward of Tryon County but not to any seaport town.
[4] *Life of Brant*, Vol. i, pp. 133 *et seq.*

Royal Greens", from those who had accompanied him from Johnstown and other loyalists who had fled to Canada. As a reprisal Sir John's vast estates in the Mohawk valley were confiscated by the New York Provincial Congress and were ultimately sold by the State.[1]

In the meantime Colonel Guy Johnson with his Mohawk followers and other Indian tribesmen had been fighting the Americans on the Canadian borders, and had taken prisoner Colonel Ethan Allen in a skirmish near Montreal on 25 September.[2] Colonel Allen had distinguished himself a few weeks after the Lexington fight by capturing Crown Point and Ticonderoga. At the latter fort he had issued his summons to surrender with the extraordinary phrase: "In the name of the Great Jehovah and the Continental Congress."

Meanwhile the Americans were using all their influence to recruit among the Canadians. To counter this Colonel Johnson asked Sir Guy Carleton for the command of a body of infantry wherewith to make a strong diversion against the enemy with a view to attracting the local Indians to co-operate. Carleton demurred, with the result that the loyal Indians became disheartened and dispersed to their homes. About this time a dispatch was received from the Secretary of State ordering an enquiry into the whole question of Indian co-operation, and Johnson thereupon decided to go to England and there make personal representations on these important matters, which had now been further complicated by the appointment of a certain Major Campbell as Indian Agent for Canada. On 11 November 1775 Johnson sailed from Quebec, taking with him Joseph Brant and a Mohawk warrior named Oteroughyanento as the representatives of the loyal Indians.[3]

[1] *Life of Brant*, Vol. I, pp. 143–6. Cf. also *New York Docs.* Vol. VIII, pp. 663, 682–3.

[2] *New York Docs.* Vol. VIII, pp. 636–7.

[3] "Journal of Colonel Guy Johnson", *New York Docs.* Vol. VIII, pp. 661–2. The presence of the Mohawk warrior with Brant is evidenced by Brant's speech to Lord George Germain which is headed: "The Speech of Thayendegeh, a Chief, accompanied by Oteroughyanento, a Warrior, both of the Six Nations. 14 March, 1776."

The arrival of Joseph Brant in London created something of a *furore*: he was courted by an admiring circle (which included James Boswell and Romney) and appeared several times at Court. It was during this visit that Romney painted his portrait which is reproduced as a frontispiece to this volume. On ordinary occasions Brant assumed European dress, but at ceremonial functions he appeared in the barbaric splendour of his native costume. This attracted considerable attention, especially his highly polished tomahawk which was engraved with the initial letter of his Christian name and his Mohawk designation: "J. Thayendanegea."[1] While in London the King conferred upon him the rank of Captain in His Majesty's Army—a singularly appropriate honour, the title of "Captain" being the highest military dignity used by the Indians themselves.[2]

Shortly before he returned to America Brant was received by Lord George Germain, who had recently been appointed a Commissioner for Trade and Plantations.[3] In the course of the interview Brant made a long speech in which he reaffirmed the Iroquois alliance with England and assured his hearer of their readiness to assist the King. He also stressed the want of English clergymen among the Six Nations and requested Germain to bring the matter to the King's special notice. In conclusion he expressed the hope that

the King and his great men will give us such answer as will make our hearts glad before we go, and strengthen our hands, so that we may joyn our Superintendent Col. Johnson in giving satisfaction to all our Nations on our return....[4]

[1] *Life of Brant*, Vol. I, p. 151.

[2] *Ibid.* p. 148.

[3] George, first Viscount Sackville (1716–85), known as Lord George Sackville from 1720 to 1770 and Lord George Germain from 1770 to 1782, having assumed that name under the will of Lady Elizabeth Germain. He afterwards became Secretary of State for the Colonies (*vide Dict. Nat. Biog.*).

[4] *New York Docs.* Vol. VIII, pp. 670–1. In connection with Brant's request for (Anglican) missionaries the following anecdote is mentioned by his biographer: Early in 1775, before it was known which side the Mohawks would join in the revolutionary war,

Brant returned from England in time to participate in the skirmish known as the Battle of the Cedars (some forty miles above Montreal) on 20 May where the American commander, Major Butterfield, was forced to surrender.[1]

It was now apparent to the Congress that Brant and his Mohawks constituted a decided menace to the popular cause and that every effort should be made to recruit from other Indian tribes as a counterstroke. To this end the Congress passed a resolution "that it was highly expedient to engage the Indians in the service of the United Colonies" and authorized Washington to employ the Indians of Penobscot (Maine Province), St John's (near Montreal) and Nova Scotia, who had in the meantime offered their support.[2] But in practice little use was made of this authority. General Schuyler, who was requested to recruit the northern Indians, was averse to the scheme; his own efforts and those of his fellow-commissioners of the Indian Department to win over the Six Nations having already failed, he probably considered that little material gain could be expected from the weaker Indian tribes.

The formal Declaration of Independence which was passed by the Congress on 4 July (1776) finally precluded any hope of a peaceful settlement of the struggle between Great Britain and her American Colonies. On 15 September the British army under Sir William Howe occupied New York, and the American forces were compelled to abandon the city, which remained in English hands for the remainder of the war. The evacuation of New York was followed by the British victory at White Plains on 18 October and the capture of Forts

---

Dr Wheelock, Brant's former (Dissenting) teacher and a republican in politics, was asked by the authorities to persuade Brant to influence his tribe in favour of the "Patriots". Brant replied to Dr Wheelock in a courteous letter in which he recalled the precepts of his teacher and in particular stressed one of his preceptor's favourite petitions: "that they might be able to live as *good subjects, and to fear God and honour the King*" (cf. *Life of Brant*, Vol. 1, p. 152).

[1] *Life of Brant*, Vol. 1, pp. 153–4.
[2] *Ibid.* p. 159.

Washington and Lee some weeks later. In the north Sir Guy Carleton defeated General Benedict Arnold in two naval engagements on Lake Champlain, and recaptured Crown Point. The "Patriot" army, which had now shrunk to a few thousand men, was experiencing the most humiliating period of its existence, and but for Washington's brilliant exploit at Trenton on 26 December it would inevitably have perished. This remarkable success at such a critical time had an immediate effect on the "Patriots'" *morale* and proved to be a deciding factor in the conflict.

Meanwhile Mr Stuart, the S.P.G. missionary to the Mohawks, was still remaining at his post at Fort Hunter. In the previous year he had married Jane Okill, and on 29 June 1776 his eldest son, George Okill Stuart, was born at the mission station.[1] In October 1775 Mr Stuart had reported to the Society that he had reappointed Paulus ("King" Hendrick's son) as reader at the "Upper Castle" of Conajoharie and that the Mohawks "had publicly declared that they would support and defend him [Stuart]"—an allusion to the request made by Little Abraham to the Indian Commissioners at the Conference in August.[2] Mr Stuart concluded his letter by regretting that he could not now complete his translation of the New Testament, as the Indian who was assisting him (Joseph Brant) was fighting in Canada with Colonel Guy Johnson.[3] This was the last letter which the Society received from Mr Stuart during the next six years on account of the extraordinary vicissitudes to which he and other S.P.G. missionaries were subjected. In most cases the Society's letters from America ceased during the war, and an entry in its Journal in 1777 records that: "In the present deplorable State of our Plantations, little or no Correspondence hath

---

[1] (Rev.) G. O. Stuart lived to become Archdeacon of Kingston and Dean of Ontario. His younger brother, James (afterwards Sir James Stuart, Bart.), who was born at Fort Hunter in 1780, became Chief Justice of Lower Canada in 1838 (cf. Monograph, *The Rev. John Stuart and his Family*, by the late Professor A. H. Young).

[2] *Vide* p. 142 *supra*.

[3] 'B' MSS. Vol. 3, No. 203.

PLATE XIII

The Rev. John Stuart, D.D.
(From a contemporary painting)

subsisted between the Society and its missionaries..."—an illuminating commentary on the complete disruption of relations between the two countries.

The next mention of Mr Stuart occurs in June 1777 following upon a treacherous attempt on the part of General Nicholas Herkimer, the President of the Tryon County (revolutionary) Committee of Safety, to murder Joseph Brant. The general and the Chief had been near neighbours before the outbreak of war and it is probable that Herkimer hoped he might yet be able to win over Brant to the popular cause. At Herkimer's request Brant met him at his headquarters at Unadilla, but unknown to the general the Chief was accompanied by 500 warriors. After a day of various discussions, the conference was adjourned till the next morning, and Herkimer then suggested to one of his men, Joseph Waggoner by name, that when Brant had arrived for the interview (which was to be held in a shed erected midway between the rival armies) Waggoner should shoot him down at a given signal.[1] Fortunately Brant seems to have been aware of some such design, and as he approached the general he said: "I have five hundred warriors with me armed and ready for battle. You are in my power; but as we have been friends and neighbours, I will not take advantage of you." He then signed to his men lying hidden in the bushes who rushed forward with a war-whoop and surrounded Herkimer and his officers. Brant then asked that Mr Stuart might be allowed to retire into Canada, to which Herkimer gave his assent, and thereupon the Chief led off his warriors into the forest and disappeared.

How long Mr Stuart remained at Fort Hunter is not

[1] *Life of Brant*, Vol. I, pp. 181 *et seq.* The evidence for this rests on Waggoner's written statement. That the meeting took place is corroborated by Colonel Daniel Claus in a dispatch to William Knox, Under-Secretary of State, which avers: "Joseph [Brant]... acquainted Col. Butler of his being threaten'd with a visit from the rebel General Herkimer of Tryon County, and actually was visited by him with 300 men with him and 500 at some distance..." (cf. *New York Docs.* Vol. VIII, p. 720).

definitely known. In October of the following year (1778) the Rev. Dr Charles Inglis (who had succeeded on the death of Dr Auchmuty to the incumbency of Trinity Church, New York, in March 1777) wrote a long letter to the Society in which he stated that Mr Stuart was a prisoner at Schenectady and had sent a message by a loyalist refugee to say that: "He remained at his charge at Fort Hunter, till all the Mohawks being loyal, were obliged to desert their Habitations & fly back to the Wilderness to avoid the Fury of the Rebels", and further that "the Indians have since taken a terrible Revenge by totally destroying the German Flatts [Tryon County] & several other Settlements".[1] The destruction of the German Flatts had occurred early in September when a body of Mohawks under Brant had made a sudden incursion on the settlement. The Flatts extended a distance of some ten miles along the most beautiful part of the Mohawk valley, the focal point of the settlement being a stone church built by Sir William Johnson, and "Fort Herkimer", the fortified mansion of General Herkimer's family. By Brant's orders the attack was made at daybreak and the whole settlement was set on fire. Only two lives were lost in the affray, a circumstance which reflects singular credit on the humanity of the Indian Chief.[2]

In the meantime the general persecution of the loyalist clergy (which was particularly violent against the missionaries of the S.P.G.) had fallen heavily upon the Rev. John Doty, the Society's missionary at Schenectady. Mr Doty had last written to the Secretary in June 1774 and over four years passed before his next letter was received. He was now (May 1778) in refuge at Montreal where he had been appointed a chaplain to the Royal Regiment of New York.

Montreal   May 20.th 1778

Rev.d Sir

Your very kind letter of October 28.th 1774 I received in the beginning of the following Winter; for which, on my own, and

---

[1] S.P.G. Journal, Vol. 21, p. 396.
[2] *Life of Brant*, Vol. 1, pp. 365–6.

the behalf of my flock, I beg leave to return the most grateful acknowledgments. As the season was then too far elapsed to admit of writing I deferred an answer until the spring, when I designed to have transmitted an exact Account of the Mission, and to have been constant and regular in my correspondence; but the general infatuation at that time rendering it imprudent to correspond even with a private friend I was obliged to wait for a more favourable Opportunity. After this our affairs proceeded from bad to worse, the friends of Government were persecuted in every quarter, and consequently the Church and its true members did not escape. I shall not trouble you with the illiberal treatment which myself, my congregation, and even the House of God have received from our factious neighbours—suffice it to inform you, that having been a sorrowful witness to the various sufferings of the one, above 15 months, interrupted in the divine service of the other and twice a prisoner myself, I thought it best with the advice and consent of my people to quit Schenectady, & retire with my family into the Province of Canada. This happened on the 23ᵈ of October last, shortly after the unfortunate surrender of Genˡ Burgoyne,[1] when the rebels, softened by their successes, permitted some few persons to go where they pleased.

At my first setting out I resolved to make the best of my way for England, where I hoped to remain in peace and quietness until the troubles in America were over, but my design was unexpectedly frustrated: before I could get here the ships were all sailed, and on my arrival I was nominated to be Chaplain in His Majesty's Royal Regiment of New York, of which Sir Jnᵒ Johnson is Lieuᵗ-Col Commandant; and soon after received His Excellency Genˡ Sir Guy Carleton's appointment to that Corps. By this means I am provided with present support, and my past sufferings and losses are rendered in some measure tolerable: for judge how great must have been the difficulties with which I struggled for two years and six months, when the price of every necessary was increased at least three fold on an average and the ability of my Congregation to support me less than ever. The greatest prudence could not prevent my becoming involved: and when I left Schenectady, the sale of my furniture and all my money, was insufficient to discharge my debts, and to defray the expence of my journey.

For these reasons I flatter myself that the Society (whose great generosity I have already experienced) will not be displeased at my conduct in leaving my flock, and taking upon me another

[1] This refers to Burgoyne's capitulation at Saratoga.

charge: especially since it was not my intention to desert them wholly, but only for a season; that, escaping the present storm, I might be of use to them in future. It would excite me to the most painful remorse was I in any degree to merit the displeasure of my Benefactors, who will, I hope, still consider me as their servant in Christ; and honour me with the continuance of their friendship and employment. And indeed the great Affection of my people (most of whom surrounded me at my departure, and with weeping eyes took their leave of me) is itself a great inducement to my return: an event for which I wait with the utmost anxiety, and in hope of which alone I remain at present in America. I say at present—for should I, after a while, be disappointed of my hope and have no clear prospect of a speedy reestablishment of peace and good Government, I shall still endeavour to cross the Atlantic.

Having said so much for myself, it is necessary that I now inform you more particularly of the state of my Charge. And here, that it hath been on the decline for three years past, I hardly need to acquaint you—however, I thank God for it! at least two thirds of them are yet remaining in the Parish; and these all of decent deportment, attached to their Church, and zealous for their King. In the course of my Ministration, I have baptised above one hundred infants; but the most of them were brought in from the circumjacent country, in which there are many poor families who belong to the Church of England, and amongst whom I have occasionally preached & baptised. But in the Town, when I left it, the number of souls under my care (exclusive of slaves) was 59....

Nor have I been less attentive to the poor negro slaves, of which there are many in the place; and they for the most part shamefully neglected. Soon after my settlement I opened a Catechetical Lecture for their benefit, and in a short time had about 20 pupils...nor have I ever had the least reason to reprove them....

...From this account you will readily discern the present weakness of the Congregation, which hath, in reality, but four & thirty supporters....The Town, from its situation and other local circumstances, promises to be a flourishing one; and should the present unhappy contest terminate to our wish, and the Society continue their accustomed benevolence (of which there is more need than ever), I doubt not but a few years would make the Church of England as respectable in Schenectady as in other places.

Though the length of my letter remonstrates against it I must add, that the situation of Mr Stuart at Fort Hunter was very disagreeable when I took my flight. He had been frequently threatened, and was obliged to be very retired. A great part of his flock having joined the Royal Army, are now in this Province under the direction of Col. Claus, at whose request I have taken upon me Mr Stuart's duty to them, and have already baptised 2 Mohawk infants, and married one couple. I beg leave to lay before you the inclosed [being a letter of appreciation of Mr Doty's services, dated 22 October 1778, a copy of which accompanied this] from my Wardens, who were obliged to write in a general and open manner to avoid any ill consequences from rebel inspectors.

And now, Revd Sir, with repeated acknowledgments for past favors, I beg leave, in the humblest manner, to subscribe myself the Society's, and your

Most obedient Servant in Christ

JOHN DOTY.

P.S. The Society's library I left in the hands of my Wardens.

To the Revd Doctor Hind.[1]

In addition to the missions of Fort Hunter and Schenectady the parish of Albany had also become vacant by the resignation (through illness) of the Rev. Harry Munro in the summer of 1775.[2] No other appointment was made, doubtless on account of the uncertainties of the times since the outbreak of war.

By the same packet which brought Mr Doty's letter, the Society received a lengthy communication from Colonel Daniel Claus, the Deputy Superintendent of the Indians, who had become a member of the S.P.G. some three years before:[3]

---

[1] 'C' MSS. (Canada). (The Rev. Richard Hind, D.D., had succeeded the Rev. Dr Burton as Secretary of the S.P.G. in 1773.)

[2] S.P.G. Journal, Vol. 20, p. 283.

[3] *Ibid.* Vol. 20, pp. 358-9. Sir John and Colonel Guy Johnson had also been elected on the same day, viz. 19 May 1775. The latter had attended a meeting while he was in England in 1776 at which he was empowered "by an Instrument in writing under the Society's Seal" to assure the Six Nations of the S.P.G.'s "benevolent dispositions towards them and their readiness to co-operate with Government in any measure that shall be adopted for the promoting among them the Christian Religion, as professed in the Church of England" (*ibid.* Vol. 21, p. 49).

Montreal 27ᵗʰ June 1778.

Sir

I take the Liberty of inclosing you a Letter from the Revᵈ Mʳ Doty of Schenectady whose Church among others in that Province was shut up by the Rebels, and he after Imprisonment and very great Abuse for his steady & loyal Behaviour, on General Burgoyne's failing to join Genˡ Sir Henry Clinton on Hudson's River, oblidged to quit the Province and seek Refuge in this Country; which Step the Faithful Mohawk Indians under Mʳ Stuard's [sic] Mission were also oblidged to take, being threatened by the Rebels, and plundered by Mʳ Kirkland's rebel Indians of Oneida for refusing to engage in their Cause; And the Mohawks being acquainted with Mʳ Doty were glad to have his Assistance, in baptizing their Children &ᶜᵃ in Mʳ Stuard's Stead, of which I suppose he has given you a Report.

On my Arrival here from Cork last June I was by order from His Majesty appointed Superintendᵗ of a Body of six Nation & other Indians intended for a secondary Expedition to cooperate with General Burgoyne by the Way of Fort Stanwix and the Mohawk River, in order to favor his Junction with Sʳ Hʸ Clinton at or about Albany. And altho these Indians were lucky enough as to defeat a Body of upwards of 800 Rebels advancing upon Us in Support of Fort Stanwix, yet some concurring unfavorable Events & Circumstances occasion'd that Expedition to miscarry whereby General Burgoyne's Operations were much injured.

Indeed the Generality of Indians on this Continent saw it their political Interest from the Beginning of this Rebellion to oppose the Rebels as much as in their Power, being sensible of the Americans having always had so great a Propensity of encroaching upon their Lands by foul Means & otherwise, and in particular became more & more troublesome to them in that Respect since the Conquest of Canada, and in short clearly foresaw that should they succeed in their rebellious Plan & become Masters of the Continent they would soon overrun their hunting Territory allotted them by His Majesty in 1768, and expel them. However this Endeavour of theirs was greatly checked by an ill judged Delicacy in the Rulers of this Country the two first Years, which had it not been the Case the Rebellion in my h̄b̄le Opinion must have been check'd in its Bud and Thousands of Lives thereby saved.

Now the Rebels having openly threatned the Indians to extirpate them whenever in their Power & take Possession of their Lands, they are detirmin'd to carry on the war against them to the last Extremity, And I apprehend if Matters were settled to Morrow on Governm.ts side they could not be brought so easily to make Peace with the Rebels after such Threats, being in general of an unforgiving, jealous & savage Temper. Yet notwithstanding this Conduct of the Indians in their own Cause as it were, the Rebels in Conformity to their genl Character do their utmost to persuade & influence the public ag.st Government of their being the Instigators & Employers of Savage Exploits & Cruelties; & which are published in their Papers with the most unjust & false Exaggerations, as I myself read in one of them touching our Affairs at Fort Stanwix, of which they published that enormous Untruth of Numbers having been murdered in cold Blood, when it can be made to appear with the greatest Truth that we merely acted defensively in preventing an Enemy to attack, dislodge & if in their power cut us to pieces; and not a Rebel was killed after being taken & brought to Camp, but as soon as possible purchased & released from the Indians & sent to this Place. The only Accident that happend in that Affair was that one Isaac Paris a Swiss, one of the Delegates of Tryon Co.y whose Life S.r Jn.o Johnson saved in the Action at the Risque of his Own, when carried off Pris.r at the latter part of the Action, The Garrison sallied out and the few Ind.ns w.th him were oblidged to fly for it, & either leave the Pris.r to the Rebels or destroy him, w.ch they did, & always do, when pursued by their Enemy. The Mohawk Chief Joseph Brant that was in London in 1776, has since his Return to his Country and Nation proved & distinguished himself the most Loyal and firmly attached Friend to His Majesty's Cause & Interest; he harangues his Warriors unweariedly to defend their Lands & Liberty against the Rebels, who in a great measure began this Rebellion to be sole Masters of this Continent and only for the Great King their father's interposing & protecting them they must have perhaps e'er now been deprived of every thing that was dear to them, wherefore they could not sufficiently exert themselves to espouse the King's Cause, that was so nearly connected with theirs. He was the most active Chieftain in the last Campaign under me, & by my Directions has all last Winter prepared them, & the other day attacked a rebel post called Cherry valley in Tryon County & cut off a party of upwards [of] 300 entirely. I am sure he must occasion some Diversion in favor of Sir Henry Clinton coming up Hudson's River as he keeps the whole Country alarm'd. And altho' he is a thorough Indian born, he allows of no Cruelties in his Exploits; his Proficiency in Christianity is amazing and incomparable, he has acquired the English Language so perfectly that he is the best Interpreter from that into yᵉ Iroquois Language, and has translated [a] great part of the New Testament.

In confutation of the Stigma the Rebels endeavour to throw upon the Officers employed by the Governmᵗ in the Indⁿ Service with regard to encouraging Cruelties: it can be proved by impartial living Evidence, that after General Burgoyne's Disaster, they have with Genˡ Gates's[1] Approbation thro the pressing Instance of his Officers, premeditatedly delivered over prisoners of Loyalists to the Oneida Indⁿˢ in the rebel Interest, bribing them with Sums of Money to torture & murder them, the former the Indians complied with, but had more Humanity than their Employers to perpetrate the latter. I fear I have tired you with this long Epistle, and beg Leave to conclude with most respectful Compliments & sincere wishes for your & the Honᵇˡᵉ Society's prosperity

Revᵈ Sir

Your most Obed. hble: servant

DAN. CLAUS

To

The Reverend Doctʳ Hind &ᶜ

P.S. We have just recieᵈ an Accoᵗ of the London Fleet, and General Haldimand on Board the Montreal being safe at Anchor abᵗ 60 Miles below Quebec, to the great Satisfaction of all his Majesty's loyal Subjects in this Provᶜᵉ Should you think it apropos to communicate part of this Letter to Mʳ Knox [the Under-Secretary of State] it might perhaps be satisfactory, having deferred writing to Governmᵗ untill I receive my orders by the Fleet.[2]

In this letter the mention of the expedition to Fort Stanwix refers to Brigadier St Leger's abortive attempt to capture the place in August 1777 while intending to join General Burgoyne's army. The fort (renamed Fort Schuyler by the Americans) was under the command of Colonel Peter Gansevoort with a garrison of between 700 and 800 men. St Leger's force consisted of some 1200 British regulars,

[1] Horatio Gates (1728–1806) served under Braddock at Fort Duquesne in 1755. Made Adjutant-General by Congress in 1775, he superseded Schuyler, and defeated Burgoyne at Saratoga in 1777.

[2] 'C' MSS. (Canada).

Hessian auxiliaries, Johnson's "Royal Greens" and a body of 800 Indians under Brant. Sir John Johnson and Colonels Claus and Butler accompanied the expedition.[1] The investment of the fort was begun on 2 August, and on the 5th a message was received from Brant's sister "Molly" (then residing at Conajoharie) that an enemy force was approaching the English camp. Sir John Johnson thereupon marched out to intercept this force with 400 Indians and a company of his own regiment, and on the following morning a brisk action took place in a ravine near the village of Oriskany, some six miles from Fort Stanwix. The Americans sustained a severe defeat and their commander, General Herkimer, received a shot through the leg which resulted in his death through inexpert amputation ten days later. The battle, though by no means decisive, prevented St Leger from effecting a junction with Burgoyne, and after a further three weeks' siege of Fort Stanwix without result, St Leger abandoned his project and retreated.[2]

The statements in Colonel Claus' letter regarding the "Patriots'" allegations against Joseph Brant, are of particular interest and importance as a vindication of the Chief's humanity, more especially in view of the aspersions made upon him after the battle of Wyoming (New York Province) in July 1778. The Americans having been defeated in this battle surrendered Fort Wyoming, and the unfortunate inhabitants of the settlement were either made captive by the Indians or fled unprotected into the forests. Many of these latter died of wounds and others were lost in the neighbouring swamp and were never heard of again. These unhappy incidents were exaggerated by hearsay into a story of horrible atrocities, which included the statement that seventy American soldiers were murdered in cold blood after having surrendered. This last allegation is shown by Brant's biographer to be entirely untrue, but those barbarities which in fact did happen

[1] *Life of Brant*, Vol. I, pp. 229, 230.
[2] Cf. Colonel Claus' dispatch to Under-Secretary Knox (*New York Docs.* Vol. VIII, pp. 718 *et seq.*).

were all attributed to Brant.[1] Actually the Chief was not present at Wyoming, being absent on another expedition at Schoharie (upwards of 200 miles away) when these occurrences took place.[2]

While the siege of Fort Stanwix was in progress General Burgoyne essayed an expedition of Hessians and Provincials against the village of Bennington, some forty miles south-east of Lake George at the foot of the Green Mountains, where large and important supplies had been collected for General Schuyler's army.[3] The originator of this scheme was Major Philip Skene, a veteran of Fontenoy, Culloden, Lake George and Martinique, who had since his retirement settled on a large tract of land at Skenesborough, Lake Champlain.[4] The idea of this expedition was perfectly sound but unfortunately Skene unwisely advised that a small force would be sufficient for the purpose. The result was a complete disaster, the commander, Colonel Baum, being mortally wounded and some 300 Hessian dragoons cut to pieces.[5] The following account of the action (written a year later) by Colonel John Peters to his relative, the Rev. Samuel Peters,[6] a loyalist S.P.G. missionary who had sought refuge in England, gives a short but vivid description of the writer's impressions of the battle:

I wish you had a Ministry who knew their own Minds for Six Months together or the Business of the Nation—the North wind contrary to Nature blows from both Poles at once, if it was proper for a Soldier to pray, I would pray Jupitur [*sic*] or some other Divinity to send us an Euroclydon—

Gen! Burgoyne was brave but misled by a Maj! Skeen [*sic*]—

[1] *Life of Brant*, Vol. I, pp. 334 *et seq.*

[2] Cf. dispatch of Colonel Guy Johnson to Lord George Germain, *New York Docs.* Vol. VIII, p. 752. The English commander at Wyoming was Colonel John Butler.

[3] Sir G. O. Trevelyan, *The American Revolution*, ed. 1912, Vol. IV, p. 129.   [4] Cf. *New York Docs.* Vol. VIII, p. 415 footnote.

[5] Trevelyan, *The American Revolution*, Vol. IV, p. 136.

[6] The Rev. S. Peters, LL.D., b. 1735, S.P.G. missionary at Hebron, Connecticut, 1758–75. Resided in England until 1805 and then returned to U.S.A. Elected Bishop-designate of Vermont but not consecrated. Died 1826 at New York.

the first Step of his madness appeared in Sending me through the
Alps of Bennington—the Second in leaving Fort Miller & Crossing
the River—the third in Surrendering when there was no Necessity
for it—are Gen¹ & Lord Howe [i.e. Sir William and Admiral
Lord Howe] innocent of this Catastrophe?

At Bennington we lost above —— near 300 of which were the
Queen's Loyal Rangers—my Son & I stood alone when all the
Rear of my Division which led the Army were fallen at our Feet—
I almost believe in John Calvin, whose Bullets go by Commission,
seeing I retreated with a few Hundred near 30 Miles through
many Ambuscades under a continual Fire & was never once
touched by a Ball—thousands of which were aimed at me by the
Rebels who knew me.

Many of your and my Friends who fell on that Day will meet
us in the best of all Worlds—

Life is but a jest—adieu—J.P.¹

The first part of this letter, which deals with Colonel Peters'
experiences from the beginning of the war, has much interesting information which may warrant its inclusion here:

The Revᵈ Dʳ Wheelock, president of Dartmouth College in
New Hampshire, in conjunction with Deacon Bayley, Mʳ Morey
& Mʳ Hurd, all justices of the Peace, put an End to the Church of
England in the Cañas [i.e. Canadas] so early as 1775—they seized
me, Capᵗ Peters, & all the judges of Cumberland & Gloucester,
the Revᵈ Mʳ Cosset² & Mʳ Cole³ & all the Church People for
200 Miles upon this River [Connecticut], & confined us in close
jails after beating & drawing us through water & mud. Here we
lay some time & were to continue in Prison untill we abjured the
King & sign'd the League & Covenant, similar to that in Noll's
Time,⁴ excepting they fought the King's Troops & we were to
fight the Ministerial Troops—many falling Sick, some died, one
of which was Capt. Peters's Son—we were removed from the jail
& confined in private Houses at our own Expense, Capt Peters &

¹ S.P.G. 'C' MSS. (America), Section III, No. 88. It is interesting
to note that Colonel Peters is not mentioned in Sir G. O. Trevelyan's
book, although he commanded the leading division of the expedition.

² The Rev. Ranna Cossit, S.P.G. missionary at Haverhill and Claremont, New Hampshire, from 1773. Imprisoned by the revolutionists 1775–81. Transferred to Nova Scotia, 1785. Died 1815.

³ Samuel Cole, S.P.G. schoolmaster at Claremont from 1770.

⁴ I.e. Oliver Cromwell.

myself were guarded by 12 rebel Soldiers while sick in Bed & we paid dearly for this Honor. & others fared in like manner—I soon recovered from my indisposition & took the first opportunity & fled to Canada, leaving Cosset, Cole, Peters, Willis, Porter, Sumner, Taplin &c &c in close Confinement where they had Misery, Insults & Sickness enough. My Flight was in 1776 since which, my Family arrived at Montreal, & inform me that many Prisoners died. That Capt Peters had been tryed by a Court Martial & ordered to be shot for refusing to lead his Company against the King's Troops, he was afterward reprieved, but still in jail, & that he was ruined both in Health & Property; that Cosset & Cole were alive when they came away, but were under Confinement, & had undergone more Insults than any of the Loyalists, because they had been Servants of the Society which under Pretence, (as the Rebels say) of propagating Religion, had propagated Loyalty in Opposition to the Liberties of America—if the Rebels had Said, that the Society for [the] Propagation of the Gospel were & had been the only Supporters of all the Religion & Loyalty that is or ever was in New England, they would have for once spoke the Truth—But this Suits not with their Plan.

The letter concludes with a postscript from which it may be assumed that Colonel Peters intended to pay off old scores on Dr Wheelock and his satellite, Deacon Bayley:

N.B. next week I am with some whites & Indians to pay my Respects to Dʳ Wheelock & *Deacon* Bayley—I have 80 Savages by me all painted, they Powwow & gnash their Teeth with Fierceness —If I succeed, expect, (by poor Cosset if he yet lives) a Tobacco Pouch made of Bayley or Wheelock's Scalp, & a Bowl made of their Skulls for the Calves' head Club[1] by the 30 of next January.

[1] According to the *Encyclopædia Britannica* the Calves' Head Club was formed soon after the death of Charles I in derision of his memory. It met annually on 30 January, the anniversary of the King's execution, when the dishes served were a cod's head representing King Charles, a pike representing tyranny, a boar's head representing the King preying on his subjects, and calves' heads representing the King and his adherents. After the Restoration the club met in secret, but in 1734 a riot broke out after the meeting and the club was dissolved. It would seem from Colonel Peters' postscript that the club had been resuscitated—possibly by radical sympathizers with the American republicans. The writer's mental picture of the club members drinking from the skulls of the republican Dr Wheelock and Mr Bayley is an amusing example of eighteenth-century satire.

In the following October (1778) Mr Doty informed the Society that soon after his last letter (20 May) his regiment was ordered to Quebec where it remained until September and proceeded thence to Sorel, a garrisoned township on the St Lawrence some fifty miles below Montreal, where he intended to stay during the winter with his family. Mr Doty further mentioned that he had recently seen "some of his [missionary] Friends who had been banished from the State of New York for refusing to swear Allegiance thereto". He learnt from them "that his poor little Flock [at Schenectady] had been almost entirely dispersed; and that the very few remaining were in the most deplorable Circumstances".[1]

A few weeks later occurred the memorable invasion of Cherry Valley by Captain Walter Butler, and Brant. Butler had been arrested in July 1777 while on a secret visit to the German Flatts for the purpose of winning over to the King's cause a number of the disaffected residents. At General Benedict Arnold's orders, Butler was court-martialled and sentenced to death as a spy, but he was subsequently re-prieved, and imprisoned at Albany.[2] In the following spring he managed to escape, and having rejoined his father, Colonel Butler, he persuaded his parent to allow him to organize an expedition into Tryon County in revenge for his own imprisonment. With his father's permission Walter Butler ordered Brant to join with him, and marched to the valley with a mixed force of Rangers and Indians. As at Wyoming many atrocities were committed, some thirty of the in-habitants, including women and children, being murdered. As had happened before Brant was unjustly accused of being the author of this barbarity, but in fact he did all in his power to prevent it. Actually he had not wished to join the expedi-tion both from his dislike of the Butlers and from the fact that he was ordered to serve under the younger Butler, whose military rank was only equal to his own.[3] But the fact that

[1] S.P.G. Journal, Vol. 21, pp. 497–8.

[2] *Life of Brant*, Vol. 1, pp. 256–7.

[3] *Ibid.* p. 379. Cf. also Professor G. M. Wrong, *Canada and the American Revolution*, p. 331.

Brant was the acknowledged leader of the Indians has not unnaturally credited him with being the instigator and perpetrator of these barbarities which have been frequently laid to his charge by undiscriminating or biased historians.

As a result of these incursions the American Congress decided to send a punitive expedition against the Iroquois, and in the summer of the following year (1779) General John Sullivan was ordered to conduct the operations with General James Clinton as his second in command. The campaign envisaged a comprehensive attack by two divisions, one from Pennsylvania up the valley of the Susquehanna to the intersection of the Tioga River, and the other from the north down the Susquehanna. The two forces were then to unite and to proceed into the Seneca and Cayuga country.[1] The expedition proved a success. On 29 August Sullivan inflicted a crushing defeat on the Indians at Newtown, and within a few weeks he had burned over forty Indian villages, destroyed their crops and plantations and scattered the Indians far and wide. Thenceforward the strength of the Six Nations was broken, many of the survivors fleeing into Canada. Brant with a chosen body of Mohawk warriors effected an escape to Niagara and continued to be a scourge to the Americans on several occasions until the end of the war.[2]

Meanwhile the Rev. John Doty was still at Montreal. On 1 September he wrote to the Society in the following terms:

Rev.ᵈ Sir,   Montreal September 1ˢᵗ 1779.

Contrary to my expectations I still remain in Canada, from whence I promised myself the happiness of returning to Schenectady before this time. But all in due season—That Gracious Providence which has hitherto smiled upon our arms will, I persuade myself, sooner or later restore peace to us; and again bless me with the enjoyment of my Country and my friends.

Besides my Regimental Duty, I continue according to my

[1] *Life of Brant*, Vol. II, p. 4.
[2] Notably an attack with Sir John Johnson on Johnstown, and an invasion of Conajoharie, both of which occurred in 1780.

ability, to serve the Mohawk Congregation as mentioned in my letter of May 1778. They have a Tract of woodland allowed them for the present, at about six or seven miles distance from this place, where they have built a few temporary huts for their families; and in particular a small log house for the sole purposes of a Church and a Council room. In this place I have, since my last, read prayers, on three different Sundays, to the whole assembled Village, which behaved with apparent seriousness and devotion: and, on my admonishing them to remember their baptismal vows, and acquainting them with my readiness to do anything in my power for them while in their present circumstances, one of their Chiefs answered for the whole, "That they would never forget their baptismal obligations nor the religion they had been educated in; and that it revived their hearts to find once more a Christian Minister amongst them, and to meet together as formerly, for the Worship of Almighty God". Since December 1778 I have baptised for them 9 Infants, and one Girl about 12 Years old: and it gives me great pleasure to assure the Society that as far as I am able to hear and observe, the Mohawks of Fort Hunter are more civilized in their manners than any other Indians.

I am sorry to say that the means of religious instruction in this Province are but few, the want of books proper for that purpose being very great: Bibles, Common Prayer Books, and small pious tracts, are all very scarce, especially with the soldiers, and poor refugees; and would be of very singular service if distributed among them. I am frequently applied to by them for books of this kind, and not having any to spare myself, because I left all my books behind me, it grieves me sorely to disappoint them. If the Society have any such to spare, and will be so kind as to order them for me to the Care of Col. Claus at Montreal, they shall be carefully distributed....

I most humbly represent my poor endeavours and myself to the venerable Society and am

Revd Sir

your obed^t serv^t

JOHN DOTY.[1]

To Doc^r Hind
Secretary to the Society for the
Propagation of the Gospel...St Anne's Westminster.

[1] 'C' MSS. (Canada).

Mr Doty's next letter was written a year later. In this communication he informed the Society that the Rev. John Stuart was still a prisoner at Schenectady, but that he had hopes of escaping to Quebec.[1] It was not, however, until another year had passed that Mr Stuart himself wrote to the Society an account of his activities since the early part of the war:

Montreal October 13th 1781.

Sir,

No doubt but the venerable Society is surprised that they have not heard from me during the four years past; Yet I flatter myself the following Narrative of my Situation will sufficiently apologise for my Silence.

At the Commencement of the unhappy Contest betwixt Great Britain & her Colonies, I acquainted the Society of the firm Reliance I had on ye Fidelity and Loyalty of my Congregation; which has justified my Opinion:—For the faithful Mohawks, rather than swerve from their allegiance, chose rather to abandon their Dwellings & Property; and accordingly went in a Body to Genl Burgoyne, & afterwards were obliged to take Shelter in Canada. While they remained at Fort Hunter I continued to officiate as usual, performing the public Service intire, even after the Declaration of Independence, notwithstanding by so doing I incurred the Penalty of High-Treason, by the new Laws.

As soon as my Protectors were fled, I was made a Prisoner, within the Space of four Days, or be put into close Confinement; and this only upon Suspicion that I was a loyal Subject of the King of Great Britain. Upon this, I was admitted to Parole, and confined to the Limits of the Town of Schenectady; in which Situation I have Remain'd for upwards of three years. My House has been frequently broken open by Mobs,—my Property plundered, and indeed every Kind of Indignity offered to my Person by the lowest of the Populace;—At length my Farm and the Produce of it was formally taken from me in May last, as forfeited to the State, and as the last Resource I proposed to open a Latin School for the Support of my Family; But this Privilege was denied, on Pretence that as a Prisoner of War, I was not intitled to exercise any lucrative Occupation in the State. I then applied for permission to remove to Canada, which after much Difficulty & Expence I obtained upon the following Conditions,—

[1] S.P.G. Journal, Vol. 22, pp. 209–10.

to give Bail in the Sum of £400 to send a rebel Colonel in my Room, or else return to Albany, and surrender myself Prisoner, whenever required. In Consequence of which, I set out on my Journey from Schenectady on the 19.th of September last with my wife & three small Children; and after suffering much Fatigue & Difficulty we arrived safe at S.t Johns in Canada on the 9.th Instant. The Mohawks are extremely happy at my Arrival, & flatter themselves that I will reside among them; But, having left the most Part of my private Property, by the depretiation of the Paper Currency & other Accidents peculiar to the Times,—And having a Family to maintain in this very expensive Place, I shall be under the Necessity of accepting of a Chaplaincy, which S.r John Johnson (with his wonted Kindness) is pleased to offer me in his Second Battalion.

I cannot omit to mention that my Church was plundered by the Rebels, & the Pulpit Cloth taken away from the Pulpit;—it was afterwards imployed as a Tavern, the Barrel of Rum placed in the Reading Desk.—the succeeding Season it was used for a Stable;— And now serves as a Fort to protect a Set of as great Villains as ever disgraced Humanity.

I left the Books belonging to the Mission with a Friend in Schenectady, as also the Church Plate, not thinking it safe to risque it with my own Baggage, not being even under the Protection of a Flag.

My Papers being mislaid, I cannot send the Notitia parochialis at present altho the Number of Baptisms has been comparatively small, none applying to me except a few distressed Loyalists. I have not preached a Sermon since the Declaration of Independence....

As soon as I can settle my Family in a convenient Situation I expect to visit the Mohawks (distant 7 Miles from hence) and shall continue to officiate occasionally for them, bestowing as much Attention on them as possible. I shall endeavour to write again to the Society this Fall, and shall from Time to Time give an account of my Proceedings. In the mean Time I am,

With great Respect,

Sir,

your very hum! Servant

JOHN STUART.[1]

[1] 'B' MSS. Vol. 2, No. 204.

A few days before Colonel Claus had written to the Society from Montreal where he had been serving under General Haldimand after the failure of Brigadier St Leger's attack on Fort Stanwix in 1777.[1] The letter was taken by Mr Doty who had decided to go to England.

Montreal 10.th October 1781.
Sir,

Permit me to recommend to you the Bearer, the Reverend M.r John Doty for an Introduction to Your Venerable Board. He has had the Care of a Congregation in the Town of Schenectady in the Province of New York as the Missionary from the Society; But the prevailing Spirit of Persecution and Oppression from the Commencement of the American Rebellion, which raged against the Ministers and Members of the Church of England, obliged him and his Family to quit his Mission in 1777: and seek an Asylum in this Province, where he has ever since remained. And as the greatest part of the Loyal Mohawk Indians and their Families were obliged to leave their quiet & peacefull Habitations ab.t the same Time; and nearly upon the same Motive, and settle in the Neighbouring Woods of this Place, & having had some Acquaintance with M.r Doty they requested me as their Agent to apply to him for taking Care of them in point of baptizing their Children, Marriages &c.a untill M.r Stuart their Missionary who was detained Prisoner among the Rebels might arrive, which charge M.r Doty cheerfully under took and has hitherto executed it to the Indians' perfect Satisfaction and Acknowledgment. And as M.r Stuart after a great deal of Chagreen [*sic*] and Trouble, has been released from his long Confinement on condition of sending a Rebel Prisoner after his Arrival here, in his place, otherwise to return again: is expected in a few days, he will then I suppose be able to resume his care of the Mohawks and the Departure of M.r Doty be not so much felt by them; Since their Residence here I have likewise engaged one Thomas a pious Mohawk from Fort Hunter, who used to act as Clerk for M.r Stuart and came off with his fugitive Tribe, to read prayers every Sunday & attend Funerals at their Village, and had them a log house built to meet in, which they strictly observe, and the House in Week days serves for a School for their children, which is carefully attended by one Paulus Sahonwadi[2] a Fort Hunter Indian who is very capable in

---

[1] Cf. *New York Docs.* Vol. viii, p. 815.
[2] This was "King" Hendrick's son.

that Employ; and as the Ind.ⁿ Schoolmasters never had any help to teach the Children by Primers or Spelling Books but were oblidged to make Use of Manuscript Scraps with the Alphabet &c.ᵃ wrote upon, which retarded their reading very much: I have lately composed a short Primer to facilitate their learning to read, by which Means their Children are coming on very fast now. And the Canajohare Mohawks residing at Niagara have applied to me to send them some likewise which I have done, And also last Autumn sent them a Number of the New published Prayer Books, of which I have sent by M.ʳ Doty a Specimen as well as a Primer for the venerable Society's Inspection, which you will please to present to them with my most profound respects.

> I have the Honor to be with great Esteem
>> Sir
>>> Your most obedient and most humble servant
>>>> DAN: CLAUS.[1]

To Dr. William Morice M.A.[2]

In the meantime events of the greatest importance had taken place elsewhere. General Burgoyne's capitulation at Saratoga in October 1777 had been followed in the spring of 1778 by an alliance between the Americans and France. In June of that year Sir Henry Clinton (who had succeeded Sir William Howe as Commander-in-Chief) evacuated Philadelphia, but in December Colonel Campbell with 3000 men of Clinton's army captured Savannah. This English success was followed by Clinton's capture of Charlestown, South Carolina, in May 1780 and it seemed that the Southern Colonies would be forced to submit. To this end Lord Cornwallis began his march through North Carolina and Virginia to join Clinton at Philadelphia. But the tide was now turning in favour of the Americans, and in October (1781) Cornwallis found himself surrounded at Yorktown, Virginia, by an allied army of French and Americans. After a siege of two weeks he was forced to surrender, and as a result of his capitulation

---

[1] 'C' MSS. (Canada).
[2] The Rev. William Morice, D.D., had succeeded the Rev. Dr Hind as Secretary of the S.P.G. in 1778.

the war virtually ceased. In the following May Clinton resigned the command and was succeeded by Sir Guy Carleton, who was invested with special powers to act as a commissioner for peace, and, after several months of protracted negotiations, England formally recognized the independence of the United States on 30 November 1782. Thus after 120 years of English rule the Union Jack[1] ceased to wave over New York and the American Colonies passed for ever from the British Empire.

[1] At this period the Union Jack consisted of the red cross of St George and the white saltire of St Andrew on their fields of white and blue. The red saltire of St Patrick was not added until the legislative union with Ireland in 1801.

CHAPTER VIII

"THE FAITHFUL MOHAWKS"

(1783–1807)

THE Peace of Versailles (signed on 3 September 1783), which gave effect to the articles agreed upon in the previous November, has been rightly subjected to grave criticism on its failure to provide safeguards for the unfortunate American loyalists and England's Indian allies. In the case of the loyalists it was agreed that Congress should "earnestly recommend" to the thirteen States the restitution of their confiscated estates and rights, that the laws directed against them should be revised, and that no future confiscations of their property should be made. Actually, this stipulated "recommendation" was of little significance as the legislatures of the various States vied with each other in passing laws against the loyalists who were thus deprived of any benefit from the Treaty. The question of adequate safeguards for the loyalists was, indeed, debated with great spirit in both Houses of Parliament, when the preliminary Articles of Peace were discussed, and Lord Loughborough voiced the opinion of many of his colleagues by stating "that in ancient or modern history there cannot be found an instance of so shameful a desertion of men who have sacrificed all to their duty and to their reliance upon our faith".[1] Unhappily the Government obtained a small majority in the division, and the bill authorizing the Treaty became law. The only consolation which the loyalists received was an Act passed in July 1783 which appointed "Commissioners for Enquiring into the Losses and Services of the American Loyalists". By virtue of this enactment a sum of over £3,000,000 was placed at the

[1] Quoted by Sir Charles Lucas, *A History of Canada, 1763–1812*.

disposal of the commissioners and some 4000 persons submitted their claims for compensation.[1]

While the Peace Treaty had at least made some attempt to
assist the loyalists, it disregarded the Red Indians altogether.[2]
By the terms of the Treaty, England "relinquished all claims
to the government, proprietary and territorial rights" of the
thirteen States and thus, in the words of the Mohawk *sachem*
Teyoninhokarawen,[3] "the ancient country of the Six Nations,
the residence of their ancestors from far beyond their earliest
traditions, was included within the boundary granted to the
Americans".[4] Whatever may have been the difficulties of the
English Government in their negotiations with the American
Commissioners, posterity cannot acquit it of a deplorable
ingratitude to those loyal aboriginals who sacrificed their
homes, their warriors and their country to the cause of the
English Crown.

When peace was declared the Mohawks were living in
temporary refuge on the American side of the Niagara River.
They were determined to remain under the British Flag and
to this end Joseph Brant approached Sir Frederick Haldimand, the Governor of Canada, to fulfil a promise made to
the Mohawks some years before by Sir Guy Carleton, that they
should be compensated by the Government for their losses
in the war. To his credit Haldimand immediately ratified his
predecessor's pledge by agreeing that a tract of land situated
on the Bay of Quinté, on the northern shore of Lake Ontario,
should be conveyed to them. In the following year Haldimand returned to England, but before leaving he was again
approached by Brant in connection with the Mohawk terri-

[1] These claims are preserved in the "Audit Office Papers" at the
P.R.O., and provide much valuable information.
[2] There is no mention even of the word "Indian" or "aboriginal"
in any of the ten articles.
[3] Generally known by his English appellation of "John Norton".
He was Brant's adopted nephew.
[4] *Vide* the *Memorial of the Six Nations* presented to Lord
Chancellor Camden by John Norton (quoted in *Life of Brant*,
Vol. II, p. 238).

PLATE XIV

Photo. Ashton, Brantford, Ontario

Statue of Joseph Brant (Thayendanegea) at Brantford

tory. By a mutual agreement with the Chief, Haldimand made a formal grant in the name of the Crown of some 1200 square miles on the Grand River, Ontario. In the course of time the town of Brantford was founded (so named after the chief), which became the headquarters of the Mohawks. A statue was erected at Brantford to the memory of Joseph Brant (Thayendanegea) in 1886.

While Brant was arranging for the settlement of the Mohawks with Governor Haldimand, Commissioners from the United States were engaged in making a treaty with the Six Nations at Fort Stanwix.

By the terms of the treaty the United States agreed to receive under their protection the Mohawks, Senecas, Onondagas and Cayugas who had fought against them in the war, on condition that the tribes should relinquish their claims to a large part of their former territory, and should deliver up all their prisoners, both European and Indian. For the fulfilment of the last provision it was agreed that six hostages should be handed over to the United States. On the other hand the Oneidas and Tuscaroras (who had remained neutral in the war) were permitted to remain in possession of their former territory.[1]

The treaty of Fort Stanwix was extremely repugnant to Brant, more especially as Captain Aaron Henry Hill (Kanonraron), a subordinate Mohawk *sachem* who afterwards married one of Brant's daughters, was selected as one of the hostages.[2]

In the meantime the Rev. John Doty, the S.P.G. missionary at Schenectady (who had returned to Canada in the spring of 1782), had again left for England in the autumn of that year.[3] He brought with him a letter from Colonel Claus concerning

[1] *Life of Brant*, Vol. II, pp. 243–4.

[2] *Ibid.* p. 245. This was one of the four daughters born to Brant by his third wife, Catherine, daughter of the chief *sachem* of the Turtle Clan (cf. Appendix B). Brant married her according to Indian custom, but in 1778 he remarried her under English law, the ceremony being performed by Colonel John Butler in his capacity as a J.P. of Tryon County (*ibid.* p. 55).

[3] *S.P.G. Annual Report*, 1783, p. 57.

a translation of the Prayer Book into the Iroquois language on which the colonel had been engaged.[1] With this communication Colonel Claus enclosed the following letter from the *sachem* Aaron Hill:

Niagara Sept! 1ˢᵗ 1782.

Brother,

I have received your letter, and the Books of Prayer, and Instruction of Children. The first time I received, July 28ᵗʰ 1782, Primers 75, and Prayer Books 15. and just now Aug! 21ˢᵗ —82, I received 25, all Prayer Books.

Brother,

We render you our highest thanks, and most heartily salute you, as many of us are Christians and Proselytes. It is entirely owing to you, that Christianity is upheld among us here. The good Spirit from above must have inspired you to compose the little Books of Instructions. We are now all supplied with new Books. Was it not for your being alive, we should be miserable; as we know of no person whatsoever in the Indian Service able to undertake the task. We thank you sincerely for your kind offer to supply us with more whenever wanted. We think what you have sent us now, sufficient, with what we had last Summer, most of which are good as yet.

I write you no news at this time, as the person that has the care of our affairs has wrote to the Commander in Chief what news he had by a Scout come in from the Highlands on Hudson's River, which gave an account of what passes at New York; some of which we had before, and seemingly is good.

I conclude with my hearty salutations to you, your Wife and Family, recommending your and their well-being to the Almighty, whom if it pleases, I hope to see you early next Spring.

AARON HILL—alias *Kanonraron*.[2]

Mr Doty also brought a letter from the Rev. John Stuart who was now working among those of the Mohawk refugees who had settled in the vicinity of Montreal:

Sir,

Having informed the venerable Society of my Arrival here in October last, and given a circumstantial Account of my Conduct

[1] S.P.G. Journal, Vol. 23, pp. 2–6.
[2] *Ibid.* pp. 6–8.

& Situation whilst among the Rebels: I have only to add, at present; that As soon as I procured a Settlement for my Family, I repaired to the mohawk Village, & was welcomed very affectionately by my indian Flock;—they voluntarily proposed to build a House for me, that I might reside amongst them, as formerly: But, notwithstanding this Token of their Affection was very pleasing to me, Yet, I did not find it convenient to accept their Proposal.

I thought proper to fix my Residence here, & attend them once a Month; and, in the intermediate Time, the indian Clerk reads Prayers, at which the whole Congregation attends with great Devotion.

Soon after my Arrival here I was appointed Chaplain to the 2ᵈ Battⁿ of the Royal Yorkers, and have met with every Encouragement & Indulgence from the Commander in Chief that I could reasonably expect.

I officiate regularly, once a Month, at the Garrison of Sᵗ John's, 30 Miles distant from hence.

And in November last, I opened an Academy, in this Town, for the Instruction of Youth; an Institution that was much wanted. Altho one Part of my Intention, I have not been able to put into Practice; that is, to catechize & instruct my Pupils in Public. For, there is no Church here that can be obtained for that Purpose.

I administered the Communion, on Christmas last, to 11 indian Communicants, & on Easter Sunday following to 13 Dᵒ

I have baptized 17 indian Children since my Arrival here. And 79 infants belonging to different Regiments, Loyalists, &c Also 5 Adults....

                    I am,
              Revᵈ Sir,
                 Your & the Society's
                 most Obedᵗ & very hum: Servᵗ
                       JOHN STUART.[1]

Montreal   7ᵗʰ Ocᵗ 1782.
Revᵈ Dᵗ Morice.

In the following July (1783) Mr Stuart informed the Society that the Mohawks near Montreal had removed to the

[1] 'B' MSS. Vol. 2, No. 205. (*Note.* Mr Stuart's subsequent letters are unfortunately no longer extant, but précis thereof are preserved in the Society's Journals.)

vicinity of Niagara where Sir John Johnson had convened a conference of the tribes. He also reported that:

the Plate belonging to the Mohawk Chapel is yet safe; as also the Furniture of the Reading-Desk and Communion-Table. The Pulpit-Covering was stolen, when the Church was plundered. Neither is the Society's Farm at Fort-Hunter considered by the State as forfeited. The Plate and Books belonging to the Mission he has thought proper to order to be sent to Montreal, by the first safe conveyance; and waits for the directions of the Society, as to the rents of the Farm.[1]

In May 1784 Mr Stuart reported the suggested movement of the Mohawks to the Grand River as arranged by Governor Haldimand and Brant, and informed the Society that he had engaged a young Loretto Indian named Lewis Vincent to act as schoolmaster to a number of the Mohawks who had decided to remain at Quinté Bay. He himself applied to be appointed to Cataraqui (now Kingston, Ontario), the headquarters of the Quinté Bay area, so that he could minister to the Mohawks who resided there.[2] His request was approved by the Society, but it was not until more than a year had passed that he was transferred to Cataraqui.

Meanwhile the great loyalist migration to Nova Scotia and Canada from the former American Colonies was in progress. During the years which elapsed between the declaration of peace and 1786 more than 40,000 persons crossed into the British Colonies of North America. Large numbers went to Nova Scotia where they founded Shelburne, and others journeyed to New Brunswick and even as far as Cape Breton. Many thousands more migrated to Upper Canada and settled in the neighbourhood of Kingston, Quinté Bay, and the old French settlements at Detroit where they and their descendants were honoured by the British Government with the hereditary title of " United Empire Loyalists ". This distinction (abbreviated to the letters U.E.L. written after the surname) is indeed a fitting memorial to the men and women who gave

[1] S.P.G. Journal, Vol. 23, pp. 169–70.
[2] *Ibid.* pp. 379–82.

up their country, their homes and their livelihood to begin life anew in an unknown wilderness where they suffered untold hardships and privations for several years after their migration.

Not long after the arrival of the loyalists on the Niagara River, Mr Stuart journeyed from Montreal to visit their settlements, as described in his next letter (dated 17 July 1784):

...on the 2ᵈ of June he set out, and visiting on his way all the new Settlements of Loyalists on the River and Lake, on the 18ᵗʰ arrived at Niagara. On the Sunday after he landed, he preached in the Garrison, and on the Afternoon of the same day, to satisfy the eager expectations of the Mohawks, he proceeded on horse-back to their Village, 9 miles distant, and officiated in their Church. After a short intermission, they returned to the Church, where he baptized 78 Infants and five Adults; the latter having been previously instructed by his Indian Clerk, who regularly reads prayers on a Sunday, and lives a very sober and exemplary life. The whole ceremony was concluded with a discourse on the nature and design of Baptism. It was very affecting to Mr Stuart to see those affectionate people, from whom he had been separated more than seven years, assembled in a decent commodious Church, erected principally by themselves, with the greatest seeming devotion and becoming gravity. Even the windows were crowded with those who could not find room within the walls. The concourse of Indians on this occasion was unusually great: owing to the circumstance of the Oneidas, Cayugas and Onondagas being settled in the vicinity. All these people speak different dialects of the same language. Before Mr Stuart left their Village, he afterwards baptized, at different times, 24 Children, and married 6 couple.

On his way home, being determined to visit every Settlement of Loyalists, he remained some time at Cataraqui, and baptized all the Children that were presented for that purpose, and buried one. He next proceeded to the Bay of Quentie, 42 miles distant from Cataraqui, and was kindly received by the Mohawks settled there; and who were busy in building houses, and laying the foundations of their new Village named Tyonderoga. The School-house was almost finished, and must ere now be ready for the reception of the Masters and the Scholars. The situation of this Settlement is really beautiful; and as there are at present as many Loyalists at

Cataraqui as will occupy the Coast as far as the Indian boundaries, it is probable, it will soon become a place of consequence.

These loyal Exiles express the most anxious desire to have Clergymen sent among them: and they look up to the Society for assistance in their present distress....[1]

A year later (July 1785) Mr Stuart removed from Montreal to Cataraqui and, in a letter of 1 October addressed to the Society, sent a detailed report of his activities:

On his arrival at Cataraqui, the Commanding Officer of the Garrison was so kind as to allow him a large room in the Garrison, for the purpose of a Church, in which Divine Service is performed every Sunday. The Inhabitants give regular attendance; and he has sanguine hopes, that in a short time a large Congregation will be collected. They seem pleased to have the first Clergyman; and promise when it is in their power, to make him some allowance. At present, however, nothing of this sort is to be looked for. Common-Prayer-Books are much wanted; and he has ventured to give them hopes of a small supply from the Society. He requests, that some common Bibles, Prayer-books, and small Religious Tracts may be sent as soon as conveniency will permit. Wilson's Instructions to the Indians, and some good treatise on Infant Baptism would, he thinks, be very seasonable.

He has visited his former Flock, the Mohawks, now settled at the Bay of Quenti; and performed Divine Service, and baptized some children there. At the same time he took occasion to assure them of the continuance of the Society's care for them; and as a proof of it, informed them of the appointment of Mr Vincent, as their Catechist & Schoolmaster. They expressed great joy at the news; and at the same time shewed him the timber they have prepared for erecting a small Church, which they expect to have compleated early next Spring. Hitherto Mr Vincent is very diligent; and Mr Stuart hopes, he shall never have reason to repent of his having recommended him.

Mr Stuart has not yet had an opportunity to communicate the Society's benevolent intentions towards the Mohawks,[2] settled at the Grand River above Niagara. That is the only Settlement of the Six Nations, where a Missionary could at present be sent. They earnestly wish to have a Minister to reside among them. On

---

[1] S.P.G. Journal, Vol. 23, pp. 409–11.
[2] I.e. to send them a missionary.

their first settling there, they expressly stipulated with General Haldimand, that Government should build them a Church, and furnish them with a Minister and Schoolmaster. They have a Schoolmaster already who is paid by Sir John Johnson.

On his way to the Mohawk Village, he caused the Inhabitants of the different Townships to collect their Children at convenient places; and he baptized those who were presented to him. And he was pleased to find, in the second Township (sixteen miles distant from Cataraqui) a number of Families of the Church of England, who assemble regularly on Sundays, and read the Liturgy and a Sermon. M.r Stuart furnished them with proper Books; and has promised to visit them as often as possible. They also are in great want of Prayer-books.

On his journey from Montreal, he stopped at New Oswegatchie, a considerable Settlement of Loyalists, to visit a M.r Bryan, a Clergyman of the Church of England, who settled there a twelve-month ago. It is now about four years since he fled from the Colonies to the Province of Quebec for protection, with the other Loyalists. He has preached in that neighbourhood during the year past, gratis, although in very low circumstances, with a Wife & four Children. The Inhabitants, amounting to 44 heads of families, have formally, at a public Town Meeting, chosen him for their Pastor, and have subscribed, according to their ability, for his support. But, as their present indigent circumstances allow them to pay him only in manual labour, by clearing and cultivating his Land, he requested M.r Stuart to mention his case to the Society; in the hope that he may be admitted into their Service, and have some small salary, to enable him to support the dignity of his character, and devote his whole time to the duties of his function....

Soon after M.r Stuart's arrival at Cataraqui, finding a School much wanted, he solicited the aid of Government, and offered to take the care of the School, until a proper person could be found. The Lieut. Governor professed great readiness to promote the undertaking, and promised boards, nails, &c. for the School-house. But as no salary was provided for the Master, the matter rests. M.r Stuart flattered himself, that either the Bounty for Montreal would be divided, or a provision from some other Fund assigned for that purpose; especially as Cataraqui will certainly be the Capital of all the new Settlements, and is very conveniently situated, in a wholesome climate, where, within a very few years, provisions must be exceedingly cheap. However, he is not discouraged at the failure of his first attempt; but shall continue to exert his best endeavours to establish a Seminary for the education of youth in Cataraqui; being persuaded, that the necessity and utility of such an institution will procure a fund for it's support, from some quarter or other....[1]

In the meantime the Rev. John Doty, while in England, had been appointed by the Society as missionary to the loyalists and garrison at Sorel.[2] He sailed from England in April 1784 and wrote his first letter to the Society in September. In this he reported that he found nearly 300 families of loyalists had recently removed from Sorel to Cataraqui to land allotted to them by the Government, and that some seventy families of loyalist Dissenters and Lutherans remained who all attended his services. For the first few weeks he performed services "in the Romish chapel" but as this was found "inconvenient to continue" he obtained the permission of the officer commanding the troops to "fit up a barrack" which accommodated some 200 people.[3] From now onwards Mr Doty remained as missionary at Sorel (known as "William Henry" for some years after 1787),[4] his former work among the Mohawks being now in the hands of Mr Stuart. In 1785 he purchased "one of the best houses" in the town which he "fitted as a Church...and opened for service on Christmas Day". Soon afterwards the Lieutenant-Governor, Brigadier-General Hope, gave a donation of five guineas, Captain Barnes, of the Artillery, a bell, and Captain Gother Mann, of the Engineers, "some boards and timber which enabled them to add a steeple to the Church, which was finished about midsummer".[5] In such manner the first English church in Old Canada was built.

Mr Doty remained at Sorel until 1803 when he resigned from the mission. He retired to Three Rivers (Quebec

[1] S.P.G. Journal, Vol. 23, pp. 190–5.
[2] S.P.G. Annual Report, 1783, p. 43.
[3] Ibid. p. 46.
[4] This was in honour of Prince William Henry, afterwards King William IV, who visited Quebec in that year in command of H.M.S. Pegasus (cf. Dict. Nat. Biog.).
[5] S.P.G. Annual Report, 1786, pp. 21–2.

Province), where he resided for the remainder of his long life, and died on 23 November 1841 at the great age of ninety-six.[1]

Some months after the departure of Governor Haldimand for England in 1784, Joseph Brant decided to follow him for the purpose of adjusting the claims of the loyal Mohawks for an indemnification of their losses with the English Government. The Chief sailed from Quebec towards the end of 1785, and his arrival in England was thus mentioned in a letter written from Salisbury on 1 December:

> Monday last, Colonel Joseph Brant, the celebrated King of the Mohawks, arrived in this city from America, and after dining with Colonel De Peister [a loyalist refugee] at the headquarters here, proceeded immediately to London. This extraordinary personage is said to have presided at the late Grand Congress of confederate chiefs of the Indian nations in America.... This country owes much to the services of Colonel Brant during the late war in America. He was educated at Philadelphia; is a very shrewd, intelligent person, possesses great courage and ability as a warrior, and is inviolably attached to the British nation.[2]

As on his previous visit to London ten years before, Brant was received enthusiastically by all and sundry. His friends included Sir Guy Carleton (presently to be created Lord Dorchester), who was about to succeed Haldimand as Governor-General of Canada, Generals the Hon. Sir Charles Stuart and Lord Percy (afterwards 2nd Duke of Northumberland), who had served with Brant in the Revolutionary War, the Earl of Warwick, Charles James Fox, and many other distinguished persons. The Prince of Wales[3] entertained him at dinner and sometimes took him to places "very queer for a Prince to go to" as the Chief used to relate to his friends. Fox gave him a silver snuff-box engraved with his initials, and the ubiquitous James Boswell became his intimate associate. Brant had several audiences with King George and the

[1] Cf. C. F. Pascoe, *Two Hundred Years of the S.P.G.* p. 870.
[2] MS. letter of Sir John Johnson quoted in *Life of Brant*, Vol. II, p. 249.
[3] Afterwards King George IV.

Royal Family, and although he refused to kiss the King's hand as being a brother ruler, he gallantly bestowed this courteous salutation upon good Queen Charlotte.[1]

Early in the new year Brant applied himself to the object of his mission to England, which had already been mooted by Sir John Johnson during his visit to London in the preceding summer. The Government had, however, allowed the matter to lapse, and, on 4 January, Brant wrote a letter to Lord Sydney, the Secretary of State for the Colonies, which is here reproduced as showing the excellent command of the English language which the Chief had attained:

My Lord,

The claims of the Mohawks for their losses having been delivered by Sir John Johnson, His Majesty's Superintendent General for Indian affairs, to General Haldimand, and by him laid before your Lordship, who cannot but be well informed that their sufferings, losses, and being drove from that country which their forefathers long enjoyed, and left them the peaceable possession of, is in consequence of their faithful attachment to the King, and the zeal they manifested in supporting the cause of His country against the rebellious subjects in America.

From the promises made by the Governor and Commander-in-chief of Canada, that their losses should be made good, and that soon, when I left them, I was desired to put His Majesty's ministers in mind of their long and sincere friendship for the English nation, in whose cause their ancestors and they have so often fought and so freely bled,—of their late happy settlements, before the rebellion, and their present situation,—and to request their claims might be attended to, and that orders may be given for what they are to receive to be paid as soon as possible, in order to enable them to go on with the settlement they are now making; in some measure stock their farms, and get such articles and materials as all settlements in new countries require, and which it is out of their power to do before they are paid for their losses.

On my mentioning these matters, since my arrival in England, I am informed orders are given that this shall be done; which will give great relief and satisfaction to those faithful Indians, who will

---

[1] *Life of Brant*, Vol. II, p. 251.

PLATE XV

NE YAKAWEA
YONDEREANAYENDAGHKWA
OGHSERAGWEGOUH,

NEONI YAKAWEA
NE ORIGHWADOGEAGHTY
YONDATNEKOSSERAGHS
OYA ONI
TEKARIGHWAGEHHADONT,
OYA ONI
ADEREANAYENT.
NE TEAS NIKARIWAKE
RADITSIHUHSTATSYGOWA
RONADERIGHWISSOH
GORAGHGOWA A-ONEA RODANHAOUH,
ONI
WATKANISSA-AGHTOH
ODDYAKE ADEREANAYENT,
NEONI TSINIYOGHT-HARE NE
KAGHYADOGHSERADOGEAGHTY,
Netasberg Akyudadede neoni A-bondatteriehoony.

Iebena wadironghkwet, neoni Tekawandenayeh Kanyen-
tehága Tikawadenaghkta, ne neoni Radirihubhtátly ne
Radirighwaekonghkówa ronadenhá-oni, Kanyenke waon-
dye-té-nolinakeroenyo Ongwe-oewa.

KENGAYE ASE YONDEREANAYENDAGHKWA
ONI TAIOGHSOIOZOH
St. MARK RAORIGHWADOGEAGHTY,
Tekawandeúnnyoh Kayeukthára Rakwaáné
T'HAYENDANEGEA,
Roeiatyáh.

LONDON:
KAHISTOÑALHO C. BUCKTON, GREAT PULTNEY STREET,
GOLDEN SQUARE. 1787.

Frontispiece and title-page of the Mohawk Prayer Book (1787 edition)
S.P.G. Archives

have spirit to go on, and their hearts be filled with gratitude for the King, their father's, great kindness, which I pray leave, in their behalf, to acknowledge, and to thank your Lordship for your friendship.

JOSEPH BRANT, Captain, or

Thayendanegea.[1]

London, 4th January, 1786.

To this letter Lord Sydney sent a satisfactory reply in which the alliance and assistance given to Great Britain by the Iroquois was warmly acknowledged, and an assurance given that their losses as already certified by Sir John Johnson should receive full compensation, and that a favourable consideration should be given to the claims of others "who had pursued the same system of conduct". The letter concluded with a statement that Sir Guy Carleton should take the necessary measures for giving effect to these designs as soon as he arrived at Quebec.[2]

During his residence in London Brant found time to supervise a new edition of the Prayer Book and Psalms in the Mohawk language, to which was added the Gospel of St Mark translated by himself. The edition was published for the S.P.G. under the immediate patronage of the King, who took a personal interest in the production. The book is printed in alternate pages of English and Mohawk; it contains several engravings of scriptural subjects, and a frontispiece[3] representing the interior of a chapel with groups of Indians receiving copies of the volume from the hands of the King and Queen, a bishop standing on either side of the throne.

The history of the Mohawk Prayer Book dates from 1713 when the Rev. William Andrews employed his interpreter,

---

[1] *Life of Brant*, Vol. II, pp. 252–3.
[2] *Ibid.* pp. 255–6.
[3] The frontispiece and the Mohawk version of the title-page are here reproduced from a copy of the book in the possession of the S.P.G.

Lawrence Claessen, in making translations.[1] The book was printed in the following year under this title:

The Morning and Evening Prayer, and God his message, the Church Catechism, Universal Supplication [i.e. Litany] Some Chapters of the Psalms of the Old and New Testament, Together with other things, in the *Mohawk Language*. Translated by *Lawrence Claesse* under the Direction of *William Andrews*, missionary to the *Indians* from the venerable Incorporated Society for the Propagation of God his Word throughout the World.

"Give as an Inheritance to thy Son the Indian, and of the World the utmost parts for his possession."[2]

The next edition was published over fifty years later at the suggestion of Sir William Johnson to the Rev. Henry Barclay. Arrangements had been made to print it in 1763 but Dr Barclay's illness and death put a stop to the work. Two years later the Rev. John Ogilvie (who, like Dr Barclay, had a knowledge of the Mohawk language) took over the supervision of the work which was again interrupted by the death of the printer, William Weyman, of New York. After some further delay Hugh Gaine (the publisher of the *New York Gazette*) completed the publication in 1769.

After the first migration of the Mohawks to Canada during the revolutionary war, very few copies remained and the Mohawks petitioned Governor Haldimand for a new edition to be printed. This was performed in 1780 under the supervision of Colonel Claus, whose expert knowledge of the language enabled him to correct the whole volume.[3] To assist

[1] Cf. Chap. III, p. 42 *supra*. Some of the translations were obtained from the Rev. Bernardus Freeman, Minister of the Dutch Reformed Church at Schenectady (*vide New York Docs*. Vol. VIII, p. 815).

[2] Transcribed from *New York Docs*. Vol. VIII, p. 816.

[3] In this connection it may be of interest to examine Colonel Claus' parentage, which is not definitely known. According to the *New York Colonial Documents* (Vol. VIII, p. 815) Claus (sometimes written *Claesse*) "was probably a native of the Mohawk valley where he acquired in early life a knowledge of the Iroquois language". He is first mentioned in the *Documents* in June 1755 when he attended a conference of Sir William Johnson and the Iroquois as interpreter, to which post he had been recently appointed (cf. Vol. VI, p. 694 and *passim*). It would seem highly probable that he

the printer the Mohawk *sachem* and schoolmaster, Paulus (Sahonwadie), attended at the correction of the proofs so as to ensure the pages being bound in their proper sequence.[1]

After a few months in England Brant returned to America and in December (1786) attended a great conference of the Six Nations and other confederate tribes at Huron village, near the mouth of the Detroit River. At this council an address was drawn up to the United States in which the signatories declared their desire for peace, provided that no future treaties should be made by the Americans with separate tribes, and also that no encroachments should be made upon the Indians' territory beyond the Ohio.[2]

Following the Indian address, negotiations were spasmodically continued until January 1789, when Major-General St Clair, the Governor of the United States North-West Territory, concluded two treaties with the Iroquois—excepting the Mohawks—and six other principal tribes. But despite these treaties a general unrest among the Indians found vent in a rising by the Shawanese, Wabash and Miami tribes, and in September 1791 St Clair was sent with a strong force to restore order. He was defeated with heavy loss, and during the ensuing twelve months the Indians committed terrible depredations. To their credit the English and Canadian Governments used their utmost efforts to act as mediators, and at a conference with the tribes held by Colonel Pickering and other United States Commissioners in 1793 some English officers were present by special invitation. Unhappily these negotiations proved abortive, the Indians still claiming the Ohio as their boundary, which the Americans arbitrarily

was a son of Lawrence Claessen (or Claesse), the former Government and S.P.G. Interpreter, from whom (if this supposition is correct) he would obviously have learnt the Iroquois language. There is no doubt from the alternative spelling of his name that Colonel Claus was of Dutch origin and therefore of the same nationality as Lawrence Claesse(n) (cf. Rev. W. Andrews' letter, Chap. III, p. 45 *supra*).

[1] The above information has been obtained from the Preface to the 1787 edition and from *New York Docs*. Vol. VIII, pp. 815–17.

[2] *Life of Brant*, Vol. II, p. 265.

refused. As a result fighting broke out afresh, the Americans being commanded by General Wayne, who had succeeded St Clair. After a further year's campaigning Wayne prevailed upon the Indians to conclude the treaty of Greenville (3 August 1795), which specified the territory reserved for them west of the Ohio.[1]

Throughout this destructive war Joseph Brant had kept in close touch with General John Simcoe (who had been appointed the first Lieutenant-Governor of Upper Canada on the division of the territory in 1791) in an endeavour to obtain English assistance for the Indians. According to his biographer, Brant himself fought in some of the actions, although the Mohawks were (at least nominally) at peace with the Americans. On the cessation of hostilities the Chief was highly dissatisfied with Wayne's treaty and in a speech many years afterwards he averred that "the Indians, convinced... that they were mistaken in their expectations of any assistance from Great Britain, did not longer oppose the Americans with their wonted unanimity. The consequence was that General Wayne... induced them to hold a treaty at his own head-quarters, in which he concluded a peace entirely on his own terms."[2] It may be added that with the signing of the treaty the amazing military career of Joseph Brant—which had extended over a period of forty years—was brought to a close.[3]

Meanwhile the Rev. John Stuart was fully occupied in his new headquarters at Cataraqui (Kingston). Soon after his arrival, the Government granted him 200 acres of land situated to the west of the township, and later this was extended to include some more valuable property.[4] Towards the end of 1785 the Mohawks of Quinté Bay were making preparations to build a church,[5] which was completed some

[1] *Life of Brant*, Vol. II, pp. 308 *et seq.*; cf. also Sir Charles Lucas, *A History of Canada, 1763–1812*, pp. 281–6.

[2] *Life of Brant*, Vol. II, p. 395.

[3] He had first been in action under Sir Wm Johnson at Lake George in 1755 (cf. Chap. VI, p. 132 *supra*).

[4] H. C. Stuart, *The Church of England in Canada, 1759–93*, p. 55.

[5] Letter, Stuart to S.P.G., Journal, Vol. 24, p. 191.

years later "without any assistance from the Public". In 1790 regular services were held there by a Mohawk named Thomas who had formerly been a clerk at the Fort Hunter Mission, and in 1798 Mr Stuart reported that this duty was performed by "a son of their principal Chief...who understands English and who values himself much on being a godson of the Bishop of Nova Scotia".[1] This was the Right Rev. Charles Inglis, formerly Rector of Trinity Church, New York, who had been consecrated in 1787 as the first Colonial Bishop of the Anglican Church. The Bishop's Mohawk godson was the nephew of the *sachem* "Little Abraham" at whose christening Dr Inglis had stood sponsor when he visited the Mohawk valley with Dr Myles Cooper nearly thirty years before.[2]

In 1798 the church at Quinté Bay was rebuilt and enlarged by Lord Dorchester's successor, General Prescott, who provided it with a steeple. It was furnished with a "neat altarpiece, containing the Creed, the Lord's Prayer, and the Ten Commandments, in the Mohawk language, surrounded by the Royal Arms of England, handsomely carved and gilt, as well as with a fine-toned bell", which were given by the English Government. Part of the set of Communion Plate, which had been given to the Mohawks by Queen Anne in 1712, was in use at the church,[3] the other half being retained by the Mohawks at the Grand River settlement.[4]

In the same year (1785) that the erection of the church at Quinté Bay was begun, a church was built by the Government near the present town of Brantford on the Grand River, at the request of the Mohawks to General Haldimand.[5] This

[1] Letter, Stuart to S.P.G., Journal, Vol. 27, p. 380.
[2] Cf. Chap. VI, p. 121 *supra*.   [3] S.P.G. Journal, Vol. 27, p. 379.
[4] During the revolution the plate had been buried by the Mohawks to save it from spoliation by the Americans, and after peace had been restored the plate was divided, three pieces being taken to Quinté Bay and four pieces to the Grand River (cf. Lucas, *A History of Canada, 1763–1812*, p. 235 footnote).
[5] Stuart, *The Church of England in Canada, 1759–93*, p. 11. Cf. also letter, Stuart to S.P.G., Journal, Vol 23, p. 191 (quoted on p. 177 *supra*).

building was the *second* Indian church built in Canada, the first having been erected by a section of the Mohawks (chiefly at their own expense, according to the Rev. John Stuart)[1] who had established themselves near Newark, the present town of Niagara.

The church at Brantford also received recognition from the English Government by the gift of a Royal Coat of Arms in 1786. It was dedicated to St Paul and was generally known as the "Old Mohawk Church". In 1904, exactly 200 years after the first S.P.G. missionary began his work among the Mohawks, the late King Edward VII gave it the title of "His Majesty's Chapel of the Mohawks" in order to revive the original name given to the Fort Hunter Chapel by Queen Anne.[2]

In the summer of 1788 Mr Stuart paid a long visit to the Grand River settlement, of which he gave the following description:

...he embarked with Captain Brant & 4 other Mohawks on the 27th of last May, and reached the head of Lake Ontario in 9 days (distant from Kingston about 200 miles) from whence they proceeded on horseback about 25 miles to the Village called New Oswego; where he was well received. That on the Sunday following he preached and administered the Sacrament to 16 (four of them new Communicants), baptized 65 persons, 7 of whom were Adults, & married 3 couple. That the Mohawk Village is pleasantly situated on a small but deep River—the Church about 60 feet in length & 45 in breadth,—built with squared logs and boarded on the outside and painted—with a handsome steeple & bell, a pulpit, reading-desk & Communion-table, with convenient pews. That the Church furniture lately given by Government not having arrived (though at the date of Mr Stuart's letter at Niagara) he took with him the plate & furniture which formerly belonged to their Church at Fort Hunter—a small organ was employed in the service. That he was

---

[1] Stuart, *The Church of England in Canada, 1759–93*, p. 11; the late Sir Charles Lucas states that the Brantford Church was the first Protestant church to be erected in Canada, but this would appear to be incorrect.

[2] Lucas, *A History of Canada, 1763–1812*, p. 235 footnote.

accompanied on his return as far as Niagara (about 80 miles) by Capt. Brant and 15 other Mohawks who earnestly requested that he would visit them as often as possible, which he promised to do.[1]

Dr Stuart[2] received much assistance from Brant, of whom he had a very high opinion. Writing of the Mohawks on the Grand River in 1798, Dr Stuart stated that the members of this section of the tribe were much more numerous than those living at Quinté Bay:

They are [he wrote] under the more immediate eye & protection of Government & are, in a great measure, directed by Captain Brant, a sensible & enterprising chief. And their local situation procures them a constant influx of inhabitants from the other branches of the Confederacy or Five Nations. Besides, a large tract of valuable land assigned to them at the last peace [i.e. after the war between the U.S. and the Indians] has been so judiciously managed by Captain Brant as to induce many from other tribes to incorporate with them.[3]

Dr Stuart, the lifelong friend of Joseph Brant and the faithful Mohawks, continued his labours among them with undiminished zeal. In 1789 Bishop Charles Inglis of Nova Scotia appointed him his Commissary in Upper Canada and by the year 1803 five other missionaries had been appointed to parishes under his supervision.[4] These included his eldest son, the Rev. George Okill Stuart, and the Rev. John Strachan, who became the first bishop of Toronto in 1839. Dr Stuart died at Kingston, Ontario, on 15 August 1811 at the age of seventy-one. His epitaph in St George's Cathedral in that

[1] S.P.G. Journal, Vol. 25, p. 121.

[2] He received the degree of D.D. *honoris causa* from the College (now University) of Philadelphia (cf. A. H. Young, *The Rev. John Stuart and his Family*, p. 9).

[3] S.P.G. Journal, Vol. 27, p. 381.

[4] They were: Rev. John Langhorne, S.P.G. missionary at Ernest Town and Fredericksburg in 1787; Rev. Robert Addison, M.A., S.P.G. missionary at Niagara in 1792; Rev. George Okill Stuart, S.P.G. missionary at Yorktown in 1801; Rev. James Rudd, B.A., S.P.G. missionary at Cornwall in 1801; Rev. John Strachan, S.P.G. missionary at Cornwall in 1803.

city appropriately describes him as "The Father of the Church of England in Upper Canada".[1]

At the beginning of the new century Joseph Brant was nearing his sixtieth year. Since the conclusion of the Indian war with the United States he had devoted himself solely to the advancement of his people, who held him in peculiar veneration. A few years before his death he built himself a substantial dwelling house on a tract of land presented to him by King George III at the head of Lake Ontario. Here he resided for the remaining years of his life, the honoured friend of both English and Americans and a true benefactor to the members of his tribe. He died on 24 November 1807 and was buried by the church which he and his followers had erected in the Mohawk village on the Grand River.[2]

Brant was succeeded as chief by his youngest son John (Ahyouwaeghs), a youth of thirteen. The choice was made by his mother, Catherine Brant, eldest daughter of the head *sachem* of the senior Mohawk clan of the "Turtle". According to Indian custom Catherine Brant became in her own right the head of the Iroquois confederacy on the death of her husband, and as such she alone held the power of appointing a successor to the chieftaincy. In the English war with the United States in 1812 John Brant, then eighteen, led the Mohawk warriors as the allies of Great Britain, and distinguished himself in several of the actions. In 1816 he was visited at his home by Lieutenant Francis Hall, who described him as "a fine young man of gentlemanlike appearance, who used the English language agreeably and correctly, dressing in the English fashion, excepting only the moccasins of his Indian habit".[3]

[1] Stuart, *The Church of England in Canada, 1759–93*, p. 50.

[2] *Life of Brant*, Vol. II, p. 499. The epitaph on Brant's grave is as follows: "This Tomb is Erected to the Memory of Thayendanegea, or Captain Joseph Brant, Principal Chief and Warrior of the Six Nations Indians, by His Fellow Subjects and Admirers of His Fidelity and Attachment to the British Crown. Born on the Banks of the Ohio River, 1742. Died at Wellington Square, W[est] C[anada], 1807."   [3] *Ibid.* pp. 500, 522.

In 1821 John Brant went to England to make representations to the Government concerning the Mohawks' title to their lands. Six years later he was given the rank of Captain in the British Army and appointed Superintendent of the Six Nations by the Earl of Dalhousie, the Commander-in-Chief in Canada.[1] This appointment is of special interest, being the first occasion on which a Red Indian chieftain had been invested with the powers of a European administrator.

Unhappily the great promise which John Brant had shown was not destined to be fulfilled as his career was cut short while he was still in early manhood. The terrible outbreak of cholera which devastated London in the summer of 1832 made its appearance in the same year in North America, and John Brant fell a victim to the dreadful scourge. His mother, the venerable princess of the Iroquois, died five years later on 24 November 1837, which date, by a strange coincidence, was exactly thirty years—to the very day—after the death of her famous husband Thayendanegea.[2]

[1] *Life of Brant*, Vol. ii, pp. 524, 532.   [2] *Ibid.* pp. 534, 537.

APPENDIX A

DEED FROM THE FIVE NATIONS TO THE KING OF THEIR BEAVER HUNTING GROUNDS

To all Christian & Indian people in this parte of the world and in Europe over the great salt waters to whom these presents shall come—Wee the Sachims Chief men, Capt[ns] and representatives of the Five nations or Cantons of Indians called the Maquase[1] Oneydes Onnandages and Sinnekes living in the Government of New Yorke in America, to the north west of Albany on this side the Lake Cadarachqui sendeth greeting—Bee it known unto you that our ancestors to our certain knowledge have had, time out of mind a fierce and bloody warr with seaven nations of Indians called the Aragaritkas[2] whose Chief cômand was called successively Chohahise—The land is scituate lyeing and being northwest and by west from Albany beginning on the south west[3] side of Cadarachqui lake and includes all that waste Tract of Land lyeing between the great lake off Ottowawa[4] and the lake called by the natives Sahiquage and by the Christians the lake of Swege[5] and runns till it butts upon the Twichtwichs and is bounded on the right hand by a place called Quadoge[6] conteigning in length about eight hundred miles and in bredth four hundred miles including the country where the bevers the deers, Elks and such beasts keep and the place called Tieugsachrondio, alias Fort de Tret or wawyachtenok and so runs round the lake of Swege till you come to a place called Oniadarondaquat which is about twenty miles from the Sinnekes Castles which said seaven nations our predecessors did four score years agoe totally conquer and subdue and drove them out of that country and had peaceable and quiet possession of the same to hunt beavers (which was the motive caused us to war for the same) for three score years it being the only chief place for hunting in this parte of the world that ever

[1] Mohawks.   [2] Hurons.
[3] *North* west (*vide* p. 192).   [4] Lake Huron.
[5] Lake Erie.
[6] At the head of Lake Michigan (*Mitchell's Map of North America*, 1755). Now Chicago, according to *Map of the British Dominions in North America*, 1763, prefixed to *Charlevoix's Voyages*, 8vo, Dublin, 1766.—ED.

wee heard of and after that wee had been sixty years sole masters
and owners of the said land enjoying peaceable hunting without
any internegotion, a remnant of one of the seaven nations called
Tionondade whom wee had expelled and drove away came and
settled there twenty years agoe disturbed our beaver hunting
against which nation wee have warred ever since and would have
subdued them long ere now had not they been assisted and
succoured by the French of Canada, and whereas the Governour
of Canada aforesaid hath lately sent a considerable force to a place
called Tjeughsaghronde the principall passe that commands said
land to build a Forte there without our leave and consent, by
which means they will possess themselves of that excellent country
where there is not only a very good soile but great plenty of all
maner of wild beasts in such quantities that there is no maner of
trouble in killing of them and also will be sole masters of the
Boar[1] hunting whereby wee shall be deprived of our livelyhood
and subsistance and brought to perpetual bondage and slavery,
and wee have subjected ourselves and lands on this side of Cadarachqui lake wholy to the Crown of England wee the said Sachims
chief men Capt^ns and representatives of the Five nations after
mature deliberation out of a deep sence of the many Royall
favours extended to us by the present great Monarch of England
King William the third, and in consideration also that wee have
lived peaceably and quietly with the people of Albany our fellow
subjects above eighty years when wee first made a firm league and
covenant chain with these Christians that first came to settle
Albany on this river which covenant chain hath been yearly
renewed and kept bright and clear by all the Governours successively and many neighbouring Governm^ts of English and nations
of Indians have since upon their request been admitted into the
same. Wee say upon these and many other good motives us
hereunto moveing have freely and voluntary surrendered delivered
up and for ever quit claimed, and by these presents doe for us our
heires and successors absolutely surrender, deliver up and for ever
quit claime unto our great Lord and Master the King of England
called by us Corachkoo and by the Christians William the third
and to his heires and successors Kings and Queens of England
for ever all the right title and interest and all the claime and
demand whatsoever which wee the said five nations of Indians
called the Maquase, Oneydes, Onnondages, Cayouges and Sinnekes now have or which wee ever had or that our heirs or

[1] *Sic.* ? Beaver.—ED.

successors at any time hereafter may or ought to have of in or
to all that vast Tract of land or Colony called Canagariarchio
beginning on the northwest side of Cadarachqui lake and includes
all that vast tract of land lyeing between the great lake of Ottawawa
and the lake called by the natives Cahiquage and by the Christians
the lake of Swege and runns till it butts upon the Twichtwichs
and is bounded on the westward by the Twichtwichs by a place
called Quadoge conteining in length about eight hundred miles
and in breadth four hundred miles including the Country where
Beavers and all sorts of wild game keeps and the place called
Tjeughsaghrondie alias Fort de tret or Wawyachtenock and so
runns round the lake of Swege till you come to a place called
Oniadarundaquat which is about twenty miles from the Sinnekes
castle including likewise the great falls oakinagaro, all which [was]
formerly posest by seaven nations of Indians called the Aragaritka
whom by a fair warr wee subdued and drove from thence four
score years agoe bringing many of them captives to our country
and soe became to be the true owners of the same by conquest
which said land is scituate lyeing and being as is above expressed
with the whole soyle the lakes the rivers and all things pertaining
to the said tract of land or colony with power to erect Forts and
castles there, soe that wee the said Five nations nor our heires nor
any other person or persons for us by any ways or meanes hereafter have claime challenge and demand of in or to the premises
or any parte thereof alwayes provided and it is hereby expected
that wee are to have free hunting for us and the heires and
descendants from us the Five nations for ever and that free of all
disturbances expecting to be protected therein by the Crown of
England but from all the action right title interest and demand of
in or to the premises of every of them shall and will be utterly
excluded and debarred for ever by these presents and wee the
said Sachims of the Five Nations of Indians called the Maquase,
Oneydes, Onnandages, Cayouges and Sinnekes and our heires
[surrender?] the said tract of land or Colony, lakes and rivers and
premises and every part and parcell thereof with their and every
of their appurtenances unto our souveraigne Lord the King
William the third & his heires and successors Kings of England
to his and their proper use and uses against us our heires and all
and every other person lawfully claiming by from or under us the
said Five nations shall and will warrant and for ever defend by
these presents—In Witness whereof wee the Sachims of the Five
nations above mentioned in behalf of ourselves and the Five
nations have signed and sealed this present Instrument and

delivered the same as an Act and deed to the Honble John Nanfan Esqr Lieut^t Govr to our Great King in this province whom wee call Corlaer in the presence of all the Magistrates officers and other inhabitants of Albany praying our Brother Corlaer to send it over to Carachkoo our dread souveraigne Lord and that he would be graciously pleased to accept of the same. Actum in Albany in the middle of the high street this nineteenth day of July in the thirteenth year of His Maj^{ty's} reign Annoque Domini 1701.

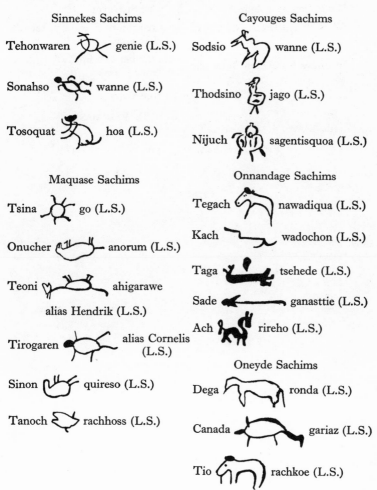

Sinnekes Sachims

Tehonwaren genie (L.S.)

Sonahso wanne (L.S.)

Tosoquat hoa (L.S.)

Maquase Sachims

Tsina go (L.S.)

Onucher anorum (L.S.)

Teoni ahigarawe alias Hendrik (L.S.)

Tirogaren alias Cornelis (L.S.)

Sinon quireso (L.S.)

Tanoch rachhoss (L.S.)

Cayouges Sachims

Sodsio wanne (L.S.)

Thodsino jago (L.S.)

Nijuch sagentisquoa (L.S.)

Onnandage Sachims

Tegach nawadiqua (L.S.)

Kach wadochon (L.S.)

Taga tsehede (L.S.)

Sade ganasttie (L.S.)

Ach rireho (L.S.)

Oneyde Sachims

Dega ronda (L.S.)

Canada gariaz (L.S.)

Tio rachkoe (L.S.)

Sealed and delivered in the presence of us

Pr Schuyler	Johannes Cuyler Alderman
J Jansen Bleeker Mayor	Dyrk Wessels justice
Johs Bleeker Recorder	James Weemes
John Abeel Alderman	Jonathan Broadhurst high Sheriff
Johannes Schuyler Aldern	M. Clarkson Secretary
David Schuyler Aldermn	S Clows Surveyor
Wessells ten Broek Alderman	R Livingston Secretary for the Indian affares
Johannes Roseboom Alderman	John Baptist van Eps ⎰ Interptrs Lawrence Claese ⎱

this is a true Copy

(Signed). JOHN NANFAN[1]

---

[1] From *New York Docs*. Vol. IV, pp. 908–11.

PEDIGREE OF "KING"

(Suppositiou

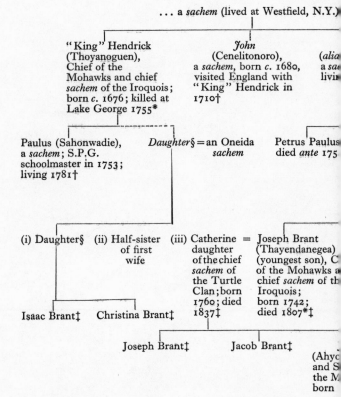

... a *sachem* (lived at Westfield, N.Y.)

"King" Hendrick
(Thoyanoguen),
Chief of the
Mohawks and chief
sachem of the Iroquois;
born *c.* 1676; killed at
Lake George 1755*

John
(Cenelitonoro),
a *sachem*, born *c.* 1680,
visited England with
"King" Hendrick in
1710†

(*alia*
a *sac*
livir

Paulus (Sahonwadie),
a *sachem*; S.P.G.
schoolmaster in 1753;
living 1781†

Daughter§ = an Oneida
sachem

Petrus Paulus
died *ante* 175

(i) Daughter§

(ii) Half-sister
of first
wife

(iii) Catherine =
daughter
of the chief
sachem of
the Turtle
Clan; born
1760; died
1837‡

Joseph Brant
(Thayendanegea)
(youngest son), C
of the Mohawks a
chief *sachem* of th
Iroquois;
born 1742;
died 1807*‡

Isaac Brant‡   Christina Brant‡

Joseph Brant‡   Jacob Brant‡

(Ahyo
and S
the M
born

* *New York Col. Docs.*   † S.P.G. Archives.

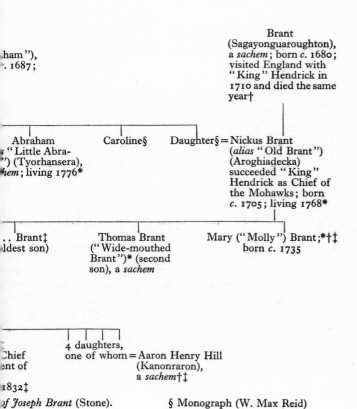

CK AND JOSEPH BRANT

given in italics)

| | Brant
(Sagayonguaroughton),
a *sachem*; born *c.* 1680;
visited England with
"King" Hendrick in
1710 and died the same
year† |

ham "),
. 1687;

Abraham	Caroline§	Daughter§ = Nickus Brant
"Little Abra- ") (Tyorhansera), *em*; living 1776*		(*alias* "Old Brant") (Aroghiadecka) succeeded "King" Hendrick as Chief of the Mohawks; born *c.* 1705; living 1768*

| .. Brant‡
ldest son) | Thomas Brant
("Wide-mouthed
Brant")* (second
son), a *sachem* | Mary ("Molly") Brant;*†‡
born *c.* 1735 |

4 daughters,
one of whom = Aaron Henry Hill
(Kanonraron),
a *sachem*†‡

Chief
ent of

1832‡

f Joseph Brant (Stone).   § Monograph (W. Max Reid)

J. W. L. 1937

BIBLIOGRAPY

MANUSCRIPT SOURCES

Archives of the S.P.G.
Audit Office Papers, Public Record Office, London.

PRINTED SOURCES

DAVID HUMPHREYS. *Historical Account of the Incorporated Society for the Propagation of the Gospel.* London, 1730.

CADWALLADER COLDEN. *History of the Five Nations.* (2 Vols.) London. 1755 edition.

J. BUCHANAN. *Sketches of the North American Indians.* London, 1824.

W. L. STONE. *Life of Joseph Brant, Thayendanegea.* (2 Vols.) New York, 1838.

H. R. SCHOOLCRAFT. *Notes on the Iroquois.* Albany, 1847.

J. R. BRODHEAD. *Documents Relating to the Colonial History of New York.* (Vols. I–VIII.) Albany, 1853–7.

—— *History of the State of New York.* (2 Vols.) New York, 1871.

F. PARKMAN. *Count Frontenac and New France under Louis XIV.* Boston. (Centenary Edition.)

—— *A Half-Century of Conflict.* (2 Vols.) Boston.

—— *Montcalm and Wolfe.* (2 Vols.) Boston.

—— *The Conspiracy of Pontiac.* (2 Vols.) Boston.

H. C. STUART. *The Church of England in Canada, 1759–93.* Montreal, 1893.

A. C. BUELL. *Sir William Johnson.* New York, 1903.

SIR G. O. TREVELYAN, BART. *The American Revolution.* (4 Vols.) London, 1905.

J. A. DOYLE. *The Colonies under the House of Hanover.* London, 1907.

SIR G. BOURINOT. *Canada.* London, 1908.

SIR C. P. LUCAS. *A History of Canada, 1763–1812.* London, 1909.

BECKLES WILLSON. *The Life and Letters of James Wolfe.* London, 1909.

A. G. DOUGHTY (Editor). *The Journal of Captain Knox.* (Champlain Society, Toronto.) (3 Vols.) 1916.

Cambridge History of the British Empire. Vol. I. Cambridge University Press, 1929.

F. W. SEYMOUR. *The Story of the Red Man.* London, 1929.

A. L. BURT. *The Old Province of Quebec.* Toronto and Minneapolis, 1933.

G. M. WRONG. *Canada and the American Revolution.* New York, 1935.

MONOGRAPHS

A. H. YOUNG. *The Rev. John Stuart and his Family (a Genealogical Study).* Kingston (Ontario), 1920.

—— *The Rev. John Ogilvie, D.D.* Kingston (undated).

Dictionary of National Biography. Oxford University Press, 1921–2.

INDEX

n = note

Abercromby, Major-General James, 88 *and n*, 90, 91, 94, 95

Abraham, The Heights of, 93, 96

Acadia (Nova Scotia), 25, 32, 42, 56, 61 *n*, 75, 76, 108

Addison, Joseph, 26

Addison, Rev. Robert, 187 *n*

Albany, N.Y., 4, 6, 7, 8, 10, 11 *and n*, 16–19, 21, 23, 24, 31, 32, 34, 35, 39, 41, 44, 47–9, 52–5, 57–9, 63, 65, 66, 67, 73, 74, 83, 84, 86 *and n*, 87, 91, 100, 102, 104, 105 *n*, 111, 113, 114, 116, 128, 129, 139, 142 *and n*, 143, 153, 154, 161, 165, 190, 191, 193

Albany County, 140

Albemarle, General George Keppel, 3rd Earl of, 108

Albemarle, William Anne Keppel, 2nd Earl of, 74 *n*

Algonquin tribes, 2, 3, 108

Alleghany River, 74, 75

Allen, Colonel Ethan, 145

American Loyalists, 120, 156, 160, 165, 169, 173, 175, 177
Commissioners for, 169, 170 *and n*

Amherst, Field-Marshal Jeffery Amherst, 1st Baron, 88 *and n*, 91, 92, 100 *and n*, 101 *and n*, 102–5, 111

Andrews, Rev. William (1), 33, 34, 38, 42, 43, 45, 46, 49, 50–2, 181, 182, 183 *n*
Letters from, 34–8, 38–40, 43–5, 47–9, 50

Andrews, Rev. William (2), 121, 129 *n*, 133

Andros, Governor Sir Edmund, 4 *and n*, 5 *n*

Anglican Clergy, Conference of, 16

Annapolis Royal, 25, 56, 58

Anne, Queen, 11 *and n*, 13 *n*, 14, 21, 23, 25, 26, 28, 30–4, 44, 81, 185, 186

Anse du Foulon (Wolfe's Cove), 93, 95

Anson, George Anson, Lord, Admiral of the Fleet, 58

Arnold, General Benedict, 148, 161

Auchmuty, Rev. Samuel, D.D., 114 *and n*, 150

Barclay, Rev. Henry, D.D., 53–61, 63, 64, 66, 69 *n*, 86 *n*, 93 *n*, 94 *n*, 105, 111 *and n*, 114, 182
Letters from, 56–7, 58–9, 59–60

Barclay, Rev. Thomas, 24, 34, 35, 48, 52, 53, 86 *n*

Barnes, Captain, 178

Barre, Governor de la, 4

Barton, Rev. Thomas, 109
Letter from, 109

Bartow, Rev. John, 16 *n*

Battles:
Bennington, 158, 159
Blenheim, 24 *n*
Bunker Hill, 141
Bushy Run, 110
Off Cape Finisterre, 58
Culloden, 158
Dettingen, 56, 96 *and n*
Dunbar, 97
Fontenoy, 158
Lake George, 80, 83, 132, 142 *n*, 158, 184 *n*
Lexington, 139, 145
Newtown, 162
Oriskany, 157
Oudenarde, 62
Quebec, 96, 97
St Foy, 100
The Cedars, 147
Trenton, 148
Whiteplains, 147
Wyoming, 157, 158 *and n*, 161

Baum, Colonel, 158

Bayley, Deacon, 159, 160 *and n*

Beach, Rev. John, 64 *and n*

Bearcroft, Rev. Philip, D.D., 65, 104, 129 *n*

Bellamont, Richard Coote, 1st Earl of, 8, 9, 11, 12
Blathwayt, William, 9, 10 n
Bleeker, Captain John, 40, 194
Bondet, Rev. Daniel, 16 n
Boscawen, Admiral the Hon. Edward, 88
Boston, Mass., 5 and n, 16, 69, 86
"Boston Tea Party", 134
Boswell, James, 146, 179
Bouquet, Brigadier-General Henry, 109 and n, 110
Braddock, Major-General Edward, 75-7, 79, 82 n, 85 and n, 87, 101 n, 156 n
Bradstreet, Colonel John, 90, 110
Brant, Catherine, 171 n, 188, 189, and Appendix B
Brant, John (Ahyouwaeghs), 188, 189, and Appendix B
Brant, Joseph (Thayendanegea), 26 n, 132, 133 and n, 141, 142, 145 and n, 146 and n, 147 and n, 148, 149 and n, 150, 155, 157, 158, 161, 162, 170 and n, 171 and n, 174, 179, 180, 181, 183, 184 and n, 186, 188 and n, 189, and Appendix B
   Letter from, 180-1
Brant, Mary ("Molly"), 132, 157, and Appendix B
Brantford, 31, 171, 185, 186 and n
Brown, James, 51 n
Browne, Rev. Thomas, 105 n, 111, 114, 117
Bryan, Rev. Mr, 177
Burgoyne, Lieutenant-General John, 141, 151 and n, 154, 156 and n, 157, 158, 164, 167
Burlington, N.J., 23
Burton, Colonel, 97
Burton, Rev. Daniel, D.D., 129 and n, 153 n
Butler, Colonel John, 141 and n, 149 n, 157, 158 n, 161, 171 n
Butler, Captain Walter, 53 and n, 141, 161
Butterfield, Major, 147

Calcutta, 87
"Black Hole of", 87
Callières, Governor de, 8

Calves' Head Club, 160 and n
Calvin, John, 159
Campbell, Major, 145
Canseau, N.S., 56, 58
Cape Breton Island, 58, 61 n, 62 n, 63, 94, 108, 174
Carleton, Governor Sir Guy, 1st Lord Dorchester, 141 and n, 145, 148, 151, 168, 170, 179, 181, 185
Carolina, North, 28 n, 39, 40, 167
   South, 46, 47
Cataraqui (Kingston, Ontario), 3, 67, 174-8, 184, 186, 187
Cayuga Country, 162
Cayugas, 1, 3, 7, 8, 71, 141, 142, 171, 175, 190-3
Chamberlayne, Edward, 13 n
Chamberlayne, John, 13 and n
   Letter from, 13-14
Chamberlayne, Sir Thomas, 13 n
Champlain, Lake, 3, 4, 32, 77, 80, 84, 100, 101, 148, 158
Champlain, Samuel de, 103
Chandler, Rev. Thomas Bradbury, D.D., 65 and n
Charles I, 160 n
Charles VI (Emperor), 56
Charlestown, S.C., 167
Charlotte, Queen (of George III), 180, 181
Chatham, William Pitt, 1st Earl of, 49, 87, 88, 91
Cherokees, 71
Cherry Valley, 155, 161
Chester, Pa., 16 n
Choiseul, Duc de, 107
Christ Church, Philadelphia, 51 n
Claessen, Lawrence (Interpreter), 34 and n, 41, 42, 45, 48, 51, 52, 182, 183 n, 194
Claremont, N.H., 159 n
Clarendon, Edward Hyde, Earl of, 11 n
Clarke, (Acting) Governor George, 55
Claus(e), Colonel Daniel, 76, 128, 134, 149 n, 153, 157 and n, 163, 166, 171, 172, 182 and n, 183 n
   Letters from, 154-6, 166-7
Claus(e), Mary (née Johnson), 76, 172

Clinton, Governor George, 17 *and n*, 57, 61, 62, 63, 64, 68, 71–3
Clinton, General Sir Henry, 141, 154, 155, 167, 168
Clinton, General James, 162
Clive, Robert Clive, 1st Lord, 3
Cole, Samuel, Sm., 159 *and n*, 160
Colonial Administrative Service, 18
Colonial Episcopate, 120 *and n*
Compton, Right Rev. the Hon. Henry, Bishop of London, 9, 10 *n*, 16 *n*, 23, 24
Conajoharie, 26, 67, 69, 80, 90, 116 *n*, 119, 120, 128, 129, 131, 133, 148, 157, 162 *n*, 167
Conestogas, 2
Connecticut, 6, 135 *n*
Connecticut River, 159
Continental Congress, 134, 139, 142 *and n*, 143–5, 147, 156 *n*, 162, 169
Cooper, Rev. Myles, D.D., 121, 124, 127, 185
Letter from, 122–4
Cork, 154
Cornbury, Edward Hyde, Lord, 11 *and n*, 14–16, 18, 23, 24
Cornwallis, General Charles Cornwallis, 1st Marquis, 167
Cossit, Rev. Ranna, 159 *and n*, 160
Courtland Manor, N.Y., 133
Cresap, Captain Michael, 137 *and n*
"Cresap's War", 137
Cromwell, Oliver, 97 *and n*, 159 *and n*
Crown Point, 76, 80, 82, 91, 92, 100, 101, 145, 148
Cumberland, William Augustus, Duke of, 56 *n*, 75, 87
Cumberland County, Pa., 109, 159

Dalhousie, George Ramsay, 9th Earl of, 189
Dartmouth, William Legge, 2nd Earl of, 117, 134
Declaration of Independence, 107, 147, 164, 165
De la Motte, Admiral, 76
Delawares, 89
Dellius, Rev. Godfrey, 17

Denonville, Marquis de, 4
Detroit, 109
Detroit River, 183
Devonshire, William Cavendish, 4th Duke of, 87
Dieskau, Baron, 76–80
Dinwiddie, Lieutenant-Governor Robert, 74
Dominica, 108
Dongan, Governor Thomas, 4 *and n*, 8, 16
Doty, Rev. John, 133, 150, 153, 154, 161, 162, 164, 166, 167, 171, 172, 178
Letters from, 150–3, 162–3
Dover, Delaware, 121
Draeyer, Admiral Andreas, 53
Draeyer, Anna Dorothea, 53
Dragon, H.M.S., 32 *and n*
Duck, Captain William, 53
Dunbar, Colonel Thomas, 83 *and n*
Dunmore, John Murray, 4th Earl of, 137
Duquesnal, Governor, 56
Dutch, The, 2, 23, 35, 37, 47, 55
Dutch Ministers, 23, 36
Dutch Reformed Church, 17, 182 *n*
Dutch Traders, 35, 43–5

Easton, Pa., 89
Edward VII, 186
Elizabeth, Queen, 13 *n*
Elizabeth Town, N.J., 64, 65 *n*
Erie, Lake, 1, 71, 74, 99, 190
Evans, Rev. Evan, D.D., 16 *n*

Fairfield, Conn., 64 *and n*
"Family Compact", The, 107
Farrell, Captain, 78, 79
Five (Six) Nations, 1–4, 7–9, 11–14, 17, 20, 25, 28 *and n*, 29, 33, 41, 42, 45, 55, 62, 67, 69, 75, 76, 82–4, 98, 99 *and n*, 115, 134, 136, 139, 142, 145 *n*, 146, 147, 153 *n*, 154, 162, 170, 171, 176, 183, 187, 188 *n*, 189, 190–2
Memorial of, 170 *n*
Fletcher, Governor Benjamin, 6, 8 *and n*, 17
Florida, 108, 110
Forbes, Brigadier-General John, 89, 90

Forts:
Anne, N.Y., 24 *and n*
Carlisle, 109
Cumberland, 76, 83 *n*
Duquesne (*see also* Fort Pitt), 75
  and n, 76, 88, 89, 90, 101 *n*,
  156 *n*, 157
Frederick (Albany), 65
Frontenac (Cataraqui), 3 *n*, 7,
  67 *n*, 90, 142 *n*
Green Bay, 109
Herkimer, 150
Hunter, N.Y. (the "Queen's
  Fort", the "King's Fort"),
  32, 34, 35, 39, 40, 45, 48, 49,
  51–5, 64, 66–8, 73, 74, 102,
  105 *n*, 111, 114–17, 121, 123,
  129, 130, 133, 135, 136, 148 *n*,
  149, 150, 152, 153, 163, 164,
  166, 174, 185, 186
Johnson, 115 *n*
Le Bœuf, 74
Lee, 148
Lévis, 103
Ligonier, 109
Miller, 159
Niagara, 71, 76, 80, 90, 92, 97–9,
  103, 167, 174, 176, 186, 187
  and n
Orange, N.Y., 53
Oswego, 71, 85, 91, 101, 102,
  104, 141 *and n*, 142
Pitt (Pittsburg), 92, 109 *and n*,
  110
Stanwix (Fort Schuyler), 156–8,
  166, 171
Stanwix, Treaty at, 115, 117,
  132, 141 *n*, 154, 155
Ticonderoga, 79, 84, 88, 90–2,
  141 *n*, 142 *n*, 145
Washington, 148
William Henry, 85
Wyoming, 157
Four Kings, H.M.S., 33
Fox, Charles James, 179
Franklin, Benjamin, 85, 115 *n*
Franklin, Governor Sir William,
  115 *and n*
Frederick the Great, 56
Freeman, Rev. Bernardus, 182 *n*
French, The, 3, 4, 6, 10, 12, 25, 47,
  48, 58, 61–3, 68, 70, 71, 74–9,

83, 88–90, 92, 93, 96, 97, 100,
  107, 108, 191
French Missionaries, 8, 9, 12, 47,
  48
French Traders, 44
Frontenac, Count, 3, 5–8, 103
Fry, Colonel Joshua, 75

Gage, General the Hon. Thomas,
  101 *and n*, 113, 134, 141 *n*
Gaine, Hugh, 182
Gansevoort, Colonel Peter, 156
Gates, General Horatio, 156 *and n*
George I, 13 *n*, 48
George II, 26, 56, 62 *n*, 87
George III, 142, 146, 152, 154,
  155, 159, 161, 164, 179–81,
  188
George IV, 179 *and n*
George, Lake, 85, 158
George, Prince of Denmark, 13 *n*
Germain, Lady Elizabeth, 146
Germain, Lord George (*see* Sack-
  ville)
German Flatts, 90, 150, 161
Gibraltar, 83 *n*
Gladwin, Major, 109
Gloucester County, N.J., 159
Grand River, 171, 174, 176, 185
  and n, 186–8
Grant, Mrs Anne, 81 *and n*
Grant, Mrs Julia, 26 *n*
Great Lakes, The, 108
Great Meadows (Fort at), 85 *n*
Green Mountains, 158
Grenada, 108, 110
Grenadines, 108
Griffiths, Rev. David, 123 *and n*
Grimes, John, 24 *n*
Guadaloupe, 108
Guy Park, 140

Haldimand, Governor, General Sir
  Frederick, 141 *and n*, 144, 156,
  166, 170, 171, 174, 177, 179,
  180, 182, 185
Half-King, The (Scarouady), 85
  and n
Halifax, George Montagu Dunk,
  2nd Earl of, 82 *and n*
Halifax, N.S., 82 *n*, 93
Hall, Edward, Sm., 121

Hall, Lieutenant Francis, 188
Hamilton College, 117
Hanover, 56
Hanover, N.H., 117
Hansen, Hendrick, 40
Havana, 108
Haverhill, N.H., 159 *n*
Haviland, Major-General William, 100, 103
Heathcote, Colonel Caleb, 24 *n*
Hebron, Conn., 158 *n*
Hendrick, "King" (Thoyanoguen), 26 *and n*, 31 *n*, 33, 34, 35 *n*, 52, 57, 63, 67 *n*, 68, 69 *n*, 77, 78, 80–2, 91, 115 *n*, 132, 133 *n*, 148, 166 *n*, 193, and Appendix B
Herkimer, General Nicholas, 149 *and n*, 150, 157
Hessians, 157, 158
Hiawatha, 1 *and n*
Highland Regiment, The, 90
Hill, Abraham, 9, 10 *n*
Hill, Brigadier-General John, 32
Hillsborough, Wills Hill, 2nd Viscount (later 1st Marquis of Downshire), 10 *n*, 127
Hind, Rev. Richard, D.D., 153 *and n*, 156, 163, 167 *n*
Holland, 23
Holland, Edward, 54
Hope, Brigadier-General, 178
Houdin, Rev. Michael, 93, 94 *and n*, 95 *and n*, 96 *and n*
   Letter from, 94–5
Howe, Brigadier-General George Augustus, 3rd Viscount, 88 *and n*
Howe, Admiral Richard, Earl, 88 *n*, 159
Howe, General William, Lord, 88 *n*, 141, 147, 159, 167
Huddy, Captain Charles, 50, 51
Hudson River, 15, 16, 17, 24 *n*, 154, 155, 172
Hudson's Bay, 42
Hunter, Governor Robert, 24, 32–4, 35 *n*, 42 *n*, 45, 47, 49, 50
Hurd, Mr, 159
Huron, Lake, 1, 99, 190
Huron Village, 183
Hurons, 2, 3, 8, 190

Illinois Country, 108
Illinois River, 75
Indian Affairs, Commissioners for, 10, 17, 18, 26 *n*, 34, 35, 40, 41, 52, 54 *and n*, 57, 63
Indian Department, 142, 147
Inglis, Right Rev. Charles, D.D., 1st Bishop of Nova Scotia, 120 *n*, 121 *and n*, 124, 127, 150, 185, 187
   Letters from, 122–4, 124–7
Ingoldsby, Lieutenant-Governor Richard, 6, 23, 24
Iroquois, 1–4, 6, 8, 11, 13, 17, 24–6, 28, 33, 42, 47, 49, 51, 56, 58, 61, 62, 71, 75, 80, 89, 92, 109, 116, 121, 139, 140, 142, 143, 162, 181, 182 *n*, 183
Iroquois Confederacy, 1
Isle-aux-Noix, 103
Isle Perrot, 103

Jamaica, L.I., 16 *n*
James II, 4, 5
Jefferson, Thomas, President, 137
Jenney, Rev. Robert, LL.D., 51 *and n*
Jesuit Missions, 20 *n*, 125
Jesuits, 3, 7, 9, 30, 42, 102, 103, 112, 113
Johnson, Christopher, 62
Johnson, Colonel Guy, 116, 134, 139, 140, 141 *and n*, 142 *and n*, 145 *and n*, 146, 148, 153 *n*, 158 *n*
Johnson, Sir John, Bart., 134, 139, 140, 142–5, 151, 153 *n*, 155, 157, 162 *n*, 165, 174, 177, 180, 181
Johnson, Rev. Samuel, D.D., 54, 64, 105, 121 *n*
Johnson, Sir William, Bart., 17, 62, 63, 66, 68, 70 *n*, 75–80, 82 *and n*, 83, 84, 92, 101, 109, 110, 114, 115 *and n*, 116 *and n*, 117, 120–30, 132–4, 136, 137 *n*, 142, 144, 150, 182 *and n*, 184 *n*
   Letters from, 84, 118–20
Johnson Hall, 116, 121, 122, 134, 140, 143, 144
Johnstown, 116, 121, 129, 133, 136, 140, 144, 162 *n*

Joncaire, Chabert de, 57, 58 *n*, 92
Jonquière, Marquis de la, 71 *and n*
Jumonville, Ensign, 75

Kalm, Peter, 107 *and n*
Kay, Teunis de, 5
King's College, N.Y. (Columbia University), 54, 121, 124
Kirkland, Rev. Samuel, 117 *and n*, 126 *n*, 139, 141, 142, 154
Knox, William, 149 *n*, 156, 157 *n*

La Chine, 4, 103
Lamson, Rev. Joseph, 64 *and n*
Lancaster, Pa., 109
Lancy, James de, 53 *n*
Lancy, Stephen de, 62 *n*
Lancy, Susannah de, 62 *n*
Langhorne, Rev. John, 187 *n*
La Présentation (Fort), 70, 71
Lawrence, Brigadier-General, 88
Lebanon, Conn., 117, 132
Leisler, Jacob, 5, 6
Lévis, The Chevalier de, 100, 101 *n*
Lewis, Colonel Andrew, 137
Leydecker, Gerrit, 5 *n*
Lichfield County, Conn., 129
Livingston, Robert, 7, 11, 13, 14, 34, 194
    Memorial of, 7 *n*
Livingston, Robert, Junior, 54
Logan, James, 137 *n*
Logan, John (Tahgahjute), 137 *and n*, 138
Loudon, John Campbell, 4th Earl of, 84 *and n*, 85, 87, 88, 94, 95
Loughborough, Alexander Wedderburn, 1st Lord, 169
Louisburg, 56, 58, 61, 63, 82 *n*, 88, 94, 141 *n*
Louisiana, 98, 108
Louis XIV, 3, 42
Lovelace, John Lovelace, 3rd Baron, 24
Lydekker, Rev. Gerrit (Gerard), 5 *n*
Lydius, Rev. John, 17, 18, 23, 24

Madras, 63
Mann, Captain Gother, 178
Maria Theresa, Empress, 56
Marlborough, John Churchill, 1st Duke of, 42

Martinique, Capture of, 108, 111, 158
Maryland, 44, 111
Masai, East Africa, 2
Masham, Abigail, 32
Massachusetts, 6, 58, 61, 80, 135 *n*
    Provincial Congress of, 139
Matthews, Captain, 34
McKinnis (Maginnis), Captain, 78, 79
McLeland, Colin, Sm., 121
Miami (tribe), 183
Michigan, Lake, 99, 190 *n*
Miln, Rev. John, 52, 53
Minorca, 87
Mississippi River, 75, 98, 108
Mohawk Prayer Book, 181–2
Mohawk River, 16, 26, 62 *n*, 116, 119, 128, 140, 154
Mohawks (Mohocks, Mohogs), 1–3, 6–8, 18, 21, 26, 31, 34, 35, 37, 39, 40, 42, 43, 45, 46, 50–2, 54, 55, 57–60, 63, 64, 66–9, 71, 78, 80, 82, 83, 85, 86, 90–2, 98, 100, 102, 105, 114, 116, 117, 120, 122–5, 128, 129, 132, 139, 141–3, 147, 148, 150, 154, 162–7, 170, 171, 173–6, 178, 179, 182–7, 190–3
Mohawk Valley, 62, 90, 140, 143, 145, 150
Monckton, Lieutenant-General Robert, 95
Monmouth County, N.J., 53
Monro, Lieutenant-Colonel, 85
Montcalm, Louis-Josef de Montcalm-Gozon, Marquis de, 85, 100
Montgolfier, Right Rev. Étienne, 112 *and n*
Montmorency, Falls of, 92, 93
Montreal, 4, 6, 8, 27, 32, 59, 91, 92, 100, 101 *and n*, 102–6, 108, 111–13, 141 *and n*, 142 *and n*, 144, 145, 147, 150, 156, 160, 161, 163, 166, 172–4, 176, 177
Moor's Indian Charity School (Dartmouth College), 117, 118, 159
Moore, Rev. Thoroughgood, 13 *and n*, 15, 16 *and n*, 18, 19, 21, 23, 36
    Letters from, 18–20, 21–3

Morey, Mr, 159

Morice, Rev. William, D.D., 167 and n, 173

Moskito Shore, Bay of Honduras, 89

Mosley, Rev. Richard, 129 and n, 133, 136

Munro, Rev. Harry, 114–16, 123, 127, 129 n, 153
  Letter from, 128–9

Murray, Governor, General the Hon. James, 95, 100, 103, 110

Nanfan, Lieutenant-Governor John, 8, 193, 194

Newark (Canada), 186

New Brunswick, 174

Newcastle, Thomas Pelham-Holles, 1st Duke of, 61 and n, 87

New England, 4 n, 6, 23, 25, 48, 58

Newfoundland, 42, 108

New Hampshire, 58, 61, 159

New Jersey, 16 n, 21, 85, 94
  East, 16
  West, 16

New Netherland, 2

New Netherland Company, 2 n

New Orleans, 108

New Oswegatchie, 177

New Oswego, 186

New Rochelle, 16 n

Newtown, Conn., 64 and n

New York Assembly, 55, 134, 142 n

New York City, 4–7, 11, 15–17, 21, 23, 24 and n, 32, 33, 35, 46, 48, 55, 59–61, 64, 65, 72 n, 84 n, 105, 114, 122, 124, 141 n, 147, 168, 172

New York Gazette, 182

New York Mercury, 80

New York Province, 4, 6, 9, 12, 14, 16, 42, 48, 56, 58, 61, 161, 166

New York Provincial Congress, 145

Niagara River, 170, 175

Nicholls, Rev. Henry, 16 n

Nicholson, Lieutenant-Governor Francis, 5, 16, 25, 27, 30–4, 45

Nicolls, Governor Richard, 3

Northumberland, General Hugh Percy, 2nd Duke of, 179

Norwalk, Conn., 64

Nova Scotia, 65 n, 147 174

Occum, Samson, 126 n

Oël, Rev. John Jacob, 63, 69 and n, 73, 91, 111 n, 133 n

Ogilvie, Rev. John, D.D., 64, 65, 69 and n, 72 and n, 74, 76, 82–4, 85 and n, 86, 87, 90–2, 96 n, 97, 100, 101 and n, 102–4, 106, 111–13, 114 and n, 182
  Letters from, 65–8, 69–70, 72–4, 82–4, 85–6, 86–7, 90–1, 97–100, 100–1, 102–3, 104–6, 111–13

Ohio Indians, 85 n, 115

Ohio River, 71, 74, 75, 79, 98, 108, 137, 183, 188 n

Ohio Valley, 89, 90, 109

Oliver, Chief Justice, 134

Oliver, John, Sm., 34, 38, 51

Oneida Lake, 98, 102

Oneidas, 1, 3, 8, 20, 49, 104, 118, 125, 139, 141, 154, 156, 171, 175, 190–3

Onondaga (village), 6, 8, 41, 115 n

Onondagas, 1, 3, 6, 33, 40, 43, 45, 49, 70, 142, 171, 175, 190–3

Ontario, Lake, 4, 70, 71, 84, 90, 100, 102 and n, 141, 170, 186, 188

Orangist Revolution, 4

Oswegatchie River, 70

Owen, Rev. R., 16 n

Palatine Refugees, 24 n

Paris, 71 n

Paris, Isaac, 155

Peace of Aix-la-Chapelle, 63, 70, 71 n
  of Paris, 108
  of Ryswick, 8
  of Versailles, 169, 170

Peister, Colonel de, 179

Penn, William, 137 n

Pennsylvania, 16, 44, 109, 135 n, 162

Penobscot (Maine), 147

Pepperell, Sir William, 58

Peters, Captain, 159 and n, 160

Peters, Colonel John, 158, 159 and n, 160
  Letter from, 158–60

Peters, Rev. Samuel, LL.D., 158 and n

Philadelphia, 16 *n*, 142, 179
Philadelphia College, 121
Philipsburg, N.Y., 114
Philipse, Colonel Frederick, 114
Philipse, Margaret, 72 *n*
Philipse, Philip, 72 *n*
Pickering, Colonel, 183
Piquet, Abbé, 70, 71
Pitt, William (*see* Chatham)
Pocock, Admiral Sir George, 108
Pollexfen, Sir Henry, 10 *n*
Pollexfen, John, 9, 10 *n*
Pontbriand, Right Rev. Henri Marie Dubreuil, 112 *n*
Pontiac, Chief of the Ottawas, 108, 110
Pontiac's Rebellion, 108–10, 132
Popple, Sir William, 14
Porter, Mr, 160
Post, Christian Frederic, 89 *and n*, 90
Pouchot, Captain, 92, 103
Prairie de la Madelaine, 6
Praying Indians, 10
Prescott, General Robert, 185
Presqu'isle, 74, 92
Prideaux, Brigadier-General John, 92
Prior, Matthew, 9, 10 *n*
Pritchard, Rev. Thomas, 16 *n*
Privy Council, 13
Prussia, 56

Quebec, 3, 7, 8, 27, 30, 32, 85, 88, 91–3, 94 *and n*, 95, 96 *n*, 100, 108, 110, 141 *n*, 145, 156, 161, 164, 177, 179, 181
Quebec Act, 135 *and n*, 141 *n*
Queen's Loyal Rangers, 159
Quinté, Bay of, 170, 174–6, 184, 185 *and n*, 187

Recollect Friars, 103, 112
Redknap, Colonel John, 33 *n*
Revolutionary War, 6 *n*, 31, 65 *n*, 114, 115 *n*, 120, 146 *n*, 166, 182, 185 *n*
Rhode Island, 16
Ridgefield, N.J., 64 *n*
River Indians (Stockbridge), 14, 139
Rodney, Admiral George Brydges, Lord, 108

Romer, Colonel, 33 *n*
Romney, George, 146
Ross, General, 24 *n*
Royal American Regiment, 86, 87, 91, 98, 109 *n*, 113, 141 *n*
"Royal Greens", 144, 150, 151, 157, 165
Rudd, Rev. James, 187 *n*
Rye, N.Y., 16 *n*

Sachems:
Abraham, 67 *and n*, 68, 69 *and n*, 77, 78 *n*, 80, 83, 115 *n*, 116 *n*, and Appendix B
Brant (Sagayonguaroughton), 26 *n*, 31 *n*, 32, 132 *and n*, and Appendix B
Cornelius, 55
Daniel, 55
Etcwa Caume, 26 *n*, 31 *n*
John (Cenelitonoro), 26 *n*, 31 *n*, and Appendix B
Kanonraron (Captain Aaron Henry Hill), 171, 172, and Appendix B. Letter from, 172
"Little" Abraham (Tyorhansera), 115 *and n*, 116 *n*, 121, 140, 142, 143, 144 *and n*, 148, 185, and Appendix B
Nickus Brant (father of Joseph) (Aroghiadecka), 132, and Appendix B
Oteroughyanento, 145 *and n*
Paulus (Sahonwadie), 69 *n*, 74, 80–83, 91, 148, 166 *and n*, 183, and Appendix B
Seth, 73
Teyoninhokarawen (John Norton), 170 *and n*
[*Sachem*] Petrus Paulus, 68, 69 *and n*, and Appendix B
Sachems, Letter from, to Queen Anne, 27–8
Letter from, to the S.P.G., 30–1
Sackville, George (Germain), 1st Viscount, 145 *n*, 146 *and n*, 158 *n*
St Charles River, 93, 97
St Clair, Major-General, 183, 184
St George's Cathedral, Ontario, 187

St John's (Canada), 165, 173
St Lawrence, River, 2, 3, 32, 70, 88, 91–3, 96 *n*, 100, 101, 103, 141, 161
St Leger, Brigadier-General, 156, 157, 166
Saint-Pierre, Major-General Jacques Legardeur de, 79 *and n*
St Pierre and Miquelon, Islands of, 108
Sakamakers (the Chief *Sachems*), 44
Saratoga, 58, 61, 62 *and n*
   Capitulation of, 151 *n*, 156 *n*, 167
Saunders, Admiral Sir Charles, K.B., 91, 92
Saxe, Marshal, 76
Schenectady, N.Y., 6, 7, 21, 24, 32, 34, 39, 43, 116, 121, 129, 133, 143, 150–4, 161, 164–6, 171, 182 *n*
Schoharie, 158
Schuyler, Abraham, 25
Schuyler, Captain John, 6 *and n*, 7, 25, 32, 194
Schuyler, Colonel Peter, 6 *n*, 7, 16, 23, 25, 27, 32, 35, 62, 142, 194
Schuyler, General Philip John, 6 *n*, 142 *and n*, 143, 144, 147, 156 *n*, 158
Schuyler, Philip Pieterse, 6 *n*
Scott, Captain John, 51, 52
Seabury, Right Reverend Samuel, D.D., 1st Bishop of Connecticut, 119 *and n*
Seneca Country, 162
Senecas, 1–4, 6–8, 25, 48, 58 *n*, 71, 141, 142, 171, 190–3
Sharpe, Rev. John, 16 *n*
Shawanees, 183
Shelburne, N.S., 174
Sherlock, Right Reverend Thomas, D.D., Bishop of London, 64
Shirley, Governor William, 61, 80, 84
Shrewsbury, Charles Talbot, Duke of, 25
Silesia, 56
Simcoe, General John, 184
Skene, Major Philip, 158
Skenesborough, 158
Sloughter, Governor William, 6
Smith, Rev. Charles, 13 *and n*, 15

Smith, Captain Hervey, 97 *n*
Society for the Propagation of the Gospel, 12, 13, 15–18, 21, 22, 28–30, 32, 34, 37, 42 *n*, 43, 45, 51–6, 58, 60, 61, 63–70, 72–5, 80, 82, 83, 85–7, 89–92, 94, 97, 100, 102–6, 109, 111, 112, 114, 115 *and n*, 117, 119–30, 132, 135, 136, 148–53 *and n*, 156, 158, 160, 162, 164–7, 171, 173, 174, 176, 178, 181 *and n*, 183 *n*, 184 *n*, 185 *n*, 186
Sorel (William Henry), 161, 178 *and n*
Southwell, Edward, 12
Stamford, Thomas Grey, Earl of, 9, 10 *n*
Stamp Act, The, 125 *n*, 134
Steele, Richard, 26
Stepney, George, 9, 10 *n*
Stobo, Major Robert, 93 *and n*
Stoddart, Captain, 78, 79
Strachan, Right Reverend John, 1st Bishop of Toronto, 187 *and n*
Stratford, Conn., 54
Stuart, Andrew (father of John), 121 *n*
Stuart, General the Hon. Sir Charles, 179
Stuart, Ven. George Okill, 148 *and n*, 187 *and n*
Stuart, Sir James, Bart., 148 *n*
Stuart, Mrs Jane (née Okill), 148
Stuart, Rev. John, D.D., 121 *and n*, 129 *and n*, 130, 132, 133, 135, 143, 144 *n*, 148–50, 152–4, 164, 166, 172, 173 *and n*, 175, 176, 178, 184–6, 187 *and n*, 188
   Letters from, 130–1, 135–6, 164–5, 172–3, 174, 175–6, 176-8, 186–7
Sullivan, General John, 117 *n*, 162
Sulpician Friars, 103, 113
Sumner, Mr, 160
Sunderland, Charles Spencer, 3rd Earl of, 8, 29
Superior, Lake, 99
Surajah Dowlah, 87
Susquehanna River, 162
Sydney, Thomas Townshend, 1st Viscount, 180, 181

Symes, Susannah, 72 *n*

Talbot, Rev. John, 11 *n*, 16 *n*, 23
Taplin, Mr, 160
Tenison, Most Reverend Thomas, Archbishop of Canterbury, 9, 12, 13, 28, 29, 32–4, 49
Thomas, a Mohawk, 166, 173, 175, 185
Thomson, Rev. William, 109, 110
Letter from, 109–10
Three Rivers, 108, 178
Tidcomb, Colonel, 78, 79
Tioga River, 162
Townshend, Field-Marshal George Townshend, 1st Marquis, 95
Townshend, Rev. Jacob, 105 *and n*
Tracy, Marquis de, 3
Trade and Plantations, Commissioners for, 9, 10 *n*, 11–15, 17 *n*, 82 *n*, 84
Treaty, at Greenville, 184
of Utrecht, 28 *n*, 42, 71 *and n*, 99 *and n*
Trinity Church, New York, 59, 93 *n*, 94, 114, 121, 150, 185
Tryon, General William, 140 *n*
Tryon County, 140, 144 *and n*, 149 *and n*, 150, 155, 161, 171 *n*
Tuscaroras, 28 *n*, 39–41, 49, 141, 171
Tyenderoga, 31, 175

Unadilla, 149
Union Jack, 168 *and n*
"United Empire Loyalists", 174
United States, 171, 183, 187, 188
Urquhart, Rev. William, 16 *n*

Vaudreuil, Marquis de, 76, 92, 103
Veitch, Colonel Samuel, 25, 27
Venango (Trading Post), 74
Verelst, Simon, 26
Vermont, 158 *n*
Versailles, 107
Vesey, Rev. William, 59
Vincent, Lewis (a Loretto Indian), 174, 176

Virginia, 24 *n*, 51, 71, 74–6, 84 *n*, 135 *n*, 167
Clergy of, 121
Virginia Regiment, 89, 105, 109, 137
Vrooman, Justice, 34

Wabash (tribe), 183
Waggoner, Joseph, 149 *and n*
Walker, Rear-Admiral Sir Hovenden, 32
War of the Austrian Succession, 56
War of the Spanish Succession, 18 *n*
Warren, Admiral Sir Peter, K.B., 58, 62 *and n*, 70 *and n*
Warrenburgh, 62
Warwick, Francis Greville, 1st Earl of, 179
Washington, General George, 74 *and n*, 75, 76, 85 *n*, 89, 142, 147, 148
Wayne, General, 184
Wellington Square, Western Canada, 188 *n*
Wessels, Dirck, 17, 194
West, Benjamin, 96 *n*
Westchester, N.Y., 16 *n*, 119 *n*
Weyman, William, 182
Wheelock, Rev. Eleazer, D.D., 117, 118, 119, 125, 126, 132, 147 *n*, 159, 160 *and n*
Whiting, Lieutenant-Colonel, 78
Whitmore, Brigadier-General, 88
William III, 5, 11 *and n*, 12, 191, 192
William IV, 178 *n*
Williams, Colonel, 78, 79
Williams, Surgeon, 78
Willis, Mr, 160
Wolfe, Lieutenant-General Edward (father of James), 96 *n*
Wolfe, Major-General James, 3, 56 *and n*, 88, 91–5, 96 *and n*, 97 *and n*, 141 *n*
Woodstock, Mass., 65 *n*

Yale College, 53, 64, 65 *n*, 67
Yamasees, 46
York County, Pa., 109
Yorktown, Va., Capitulation at, 167

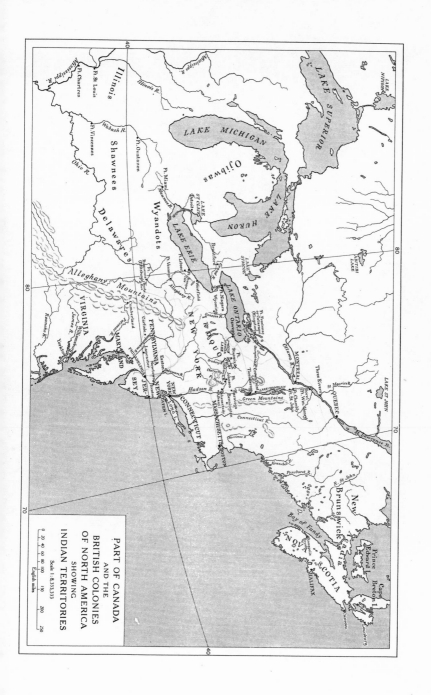

PART OF CANADA
AND THE
BRITISH COLONIES
OF NORTH AMERICA
SHOWING
INDIAN TERRITORIES

Scale 1:8,333,333

0 20 40 60 80 100   150   200   250
English miles